Praise for *The Shape of Dust*

'The light, restrained touch with which Lamisse writes makes this story so much more powerful. A socio-political critique with intellectual depth and a beautiful literary quality, I learned so much about strength, endurance and the unpredictable ways grief and helplessness and anger manifest in us.' **Randa Abdel-Fattah**

'Lamisse and Hazem Hamouda are generous authors, who take the reader on a compelling, raw and deeply intimate journey from the suburbs of Meanjin to the prison cells of Egypt and back again. This is an important and timely book. It is a tale of two countries and those who exist in both but belong to neither. At its core, *The Shape of Dust* is a love story. A tale of determination, devotion and duty told with courage and self-assuredness.' **Jan Fran**

'This is an extraordinarily brave, honest, and deeply intimate account of a family's struggle against a brutal bureaucracy. Lamisse somehow manages to be both personal and political, without ever becoming polemic. Their ordeal is painful, their love for one another uplifting. In the end it will make you angry at the injustices both grand and petty, that run from Cairo to Canberra.' **Peter Greste**

'Once I started reading, I couldn't stop. The patter and rhythm of modern Egypt was brought alive in a way I just haven't seen in a lot of texts. I was beyond moved by the strength, resilience and courage it took. Simply put, reading this book felt like a punch to the gut and I loved it.' **Hella Ibrahim**

AF865023

'Lamisse Hamouda's *The Shape of Dust* is a must read. Full-blooded and clear-eyed, this book is a deep dive into memories big and small, brutal and joyful, a ruthlessly reflective examination of the many things that bind us - and free us. As Lamisse herself describes, this is an effort to remember, an insistence on dignity, like food shared, like paper flowers made by the hands of prisoners.' **Omar Musa**

'A beautifully written, deeply personal and devastating account of arbitrary detention in Egypt and a family's inspirational fight for their father's freedom. This book is essential reading to understand the difficulties faced by Australians unjustly jailed abroad, the traumatic impact and burden on their families at home, and how to fight for – and win – freedom. It was a privilege to represent Hazem and his family, to work alongside Lamisse in that fight, and it was a privilege to read this book.' **Jennifer Robinson**

'Through this extraordinary real-life horror story, Hazem and Lamisse Hamouda have co-written a beautiful and emotional tale about the power of resilience, and the strength it takes to fight systemic violence... this book is a courageous and deeply moving documentation. It's a must-read for anyone invested in understanding and knowing the crippling realities of how traumas in our lives can bind us, divide us, or even heal us. And that, eventually, these things can bring us closer to ourselves and our own destiny.' **Fariha Róisín**

'Imbued with hard-earned wisdom, this gripping memoir is as courageous as it is generous. Hamouda insists on care and connection in the face of the most harrowing event of her life.' **Sara Saleh**

THE SHAPE OF DUST

A father wrongly imprisoned.
A daughter's quest to free him.

Lamisse Hamouda
with Hazem Hamouda

THE SHAPE OF DUST

Lamisse Hamouda
with Hazem Hamouda

PANTERA PRESS

PANTERA
PRESS

The information in this book is published in good faith and for general information purposes only. Although the authors and publisher believe at the time of going to press that the information is correct, they do not assume and hereby disclaim any liability to any party for any loss, damage or disruption caused by errors or omissions, whether they result from negligence, accident or any other cause.

First published in 2023 by Pantera Press Pty Limited
www.PanteraPress.com

Text copyright © Lamisse and Hazem Hamouda, 2023
Lamisse and Hazem Hamouda have asserted their moral rights to be identified as the authors of this work.

Design and typography copyright © Pantera Press Pty Limited, 2023
® Pantera Press, three-slashes colophon device, and *sparking imagination, conversation & change* are registered trademarks of Pantera Press Pty Limited. Lost the Plot is a trademark of Pantera Press Pty Limited.

This book is copyright, and all rights are reserved.
We welcome your support of the authors' rights, so please only buy authorised editions.

Without the publisher's prior written permission, and without limiting the rights reserved under copyright, none of this book may be scanned, reproduced, stored in, uploaded to or introduced into a retrieval or distribution system, including the internet, or transmitted, copied or made available in any form or by any means (including digital, electronic, mechanical, photocopying, sound or audio recording, and text-to-voice). This book is sold subject to the condition that it shall not, by way of trade or otherwise, be lent, re-sold, hired out, or otherwise circulated in any form of binding or cover other than that in which it is published and without a similar condition being imposed on the subsequent recipient.

Please send all permission queries to:
Pantera Press, P.O. Box 1989, Neutral Bay, NSW, Australia 2089 or info@PanteraPress.com

A Cataloguing-in-Publication entry for this book is available from the National Library of Australia.
ISBN 978-0-6487951-1-7 (Paperback)
ISBN 978-0-6487951-2-4 (eBook)

Cover Design: George Saad
Publisher: Lex Hirst
Editors: Anne Reilly and Lucy Bell
Project Editor: Kirsty van der Veer
Proofreader: LinLi Wan
Typesetting: Kirby Jones
Author Photo: Saja Hamouda
Printed and bound in Australia by McPherson's Printing Group

Pantera Press policy is to use papers that are natural, renewable and recyclable products made from wood grown in sustainable forests. The logging and manufacturing processes are expected to conform to the environmental regulations of the country of origin.

MIX
Paper | Supporting responsible forestry
FSC www.fsc.org FSC® C001695

The paper this book is printed on is certified against the Forest Stewardship Council® Standards. McPherson's Printing Group holds FSC® chain of custody certification SA-COC-005379. FSC® promotes environmentally responsible, socially beneficial and economically viable management of the world's forests.

'The heart of justice is truth-telling'
– bell hooks

In memory of a beloved mother and grandmother,
Zaineb Ellithy. 1932–2022

To the men of Tora Prison, and all those who've experienced the injustice of incarceration. We've seen you alive.

Contents

Introduction

When I started writing this book, I didn't know what story I was telling or for whom I was writing. Trauma loops around itself; it lassoes old traumas in with new ones and requires repetition for resolution. In those hazy early days, writing was simply a rope through the fog.

The first draft I wrote was 70 pages of utter madness; frantic, disjointed fragments held together by the thin thread of chronological time. Trauma fractures narrative; yet, having a narrative is part of creating our sense of self and our orientation in the world. Without narrative, we cannot orient ourselves. Memoir writing became my method of self-cartography: to map the world I inhabited and myself back into it.

As I wrote, I imagined I was speaking to my family and friends, telling them all the things I wanted them to know but couldn't say out loud. Having and holding an unspeakable experience alienates us. Vulnerability connects us. All I wanted was to feel connected again.

It's challenging to relay a life that lives across multiple, truncated identities: a Muslim who doesn't practise, an Arab who doesn't speak Arabic and an Australian who isn't 'Australian'. I had become so used to translating myself that I was unsure if I knew what it was simply to be witnessed. Yet, when gathered, these parts are whole, and this book is a place where I have been able to witness that, to hold it all with love and acceptance.

I spent an inordinate amount of time thinking about how best to work across multiple languages and worlds, all while remaining cognisant of my own internalised white gaze. Deciding that it would be strange if I were writing a book based in America and kept writing: 'she said in English', I decided against adding 'in Arabic' to the dialogue. Egyptians speak Arabic, and if we speak otherwise, I note that it is being said 'in English'. After all, it is primarily an Arabic-speaking world, though I represent it in English words and Latin letters. As for the transliterated Arabic, unless the translation has occurred in real time for me, you'll find it in the glossary. I found in-text translations distracting, taking me out of the world I was building in the book; this is not how conversation occurs in real life. Plus, I wanted the reader to have moments of being challenged by a language they don't speak, that they'd have to put in a little effort to overcome the alienation of not understanding. That being said, Dad opted for in-text translations. Dad felt that the side-by-side representation of both languages reflected the duality of voice in his world. That often, in his experience, he'd speak in Arabic, listen to Arabic, but still be thinking in English. Furthermore, the immediacy of an in-text translation better served the flow and urgency within Dad's sections. These are the ebbs and flows you'll find in this book; rather than create textual uniformity, we've sought to give space to the varying ways we chose to tell our respective stories.

While there are tangents into political reflections, I did not write an academic text, but what I hope is a political memoir (though, I think all memoir is political, regardless of whether the author declares it or not). I wrote to invite you into the interiority of an experience, of what it *feels* like. Like zooming in on a particle of dust, this singular experience is part of a blanket, a storm. I wrote with the feminist maxim at the forefront of my mind: *the personal is political.* While the shape is unique, the wider story is not.

Grappling with the wider political questions around this book, I recommitted to the deeply personal narrative as an insistence that I could only speak for myself, that I refused the saviour politics of 'a voice for the voiceless'. Rather, I write to add my voice to the lineage of speakers who've come before me, those speaking now – like Alaa Abdel Fattah, Sanaa Seif, Abdelrahman ElGendy, Mohamed Soltan and more – and those who'll speak after me. There is no silence around acts of injustice, only silencing.

Lastly, and most importantly, there is nothing without my father. I could not conscionably publish this book without his permission or participation. His voice is distinct and present throughout Part One. Though he stopped writing, he remains intermittently present through Part Two and Three via interviews. I'm grateful Dad trusted me with his words, with his story; that he allowed me to find a way to weave together our voices and map our experiences side by side. There was healing that came with working collaboratively, and intergenerationally, with my father. Through the medium of this book, we shared our grief and our trauma: we remembered together, we told our stories to each other and witnessed each other's pain, we debated and diverged in our interpretations of what we'd been through, accepting the differences between us. It was a reminder that there is never one story. With our act of remembering, and writing, we felt we made our contribution to keeping those we knew inside alive too: the men still there, and the men who died behind those walls.

While there is an argument to be made that we cement memory through writing, I counter-argue that it also externalises memory, thus releasing you of its burdens. This story doesn't only hold my pain; it holds my wisdom. By cementing this experience in writing, I no longer feel it needs to be cemented in my body. I don't need to hold onto it so tightly, to fear forgetting the promises we made to remember, to speak. I can trust that it is now held in this book.

Perhaps this is why we continue to tell our stories.

PART ONE

You do not have a legal right to consular assistance, and you should not assume that assistance will be provided.

– DFAT Brochure, Arrested or Jailed Overseas

Hazem

Thursday 25 January 2018

Cairo airport is almost empty – a strange sight in a usually crowded place full of tour groups and Egyptians visiting from abroad. There are none of the usual long lines for passport control, and I am alone as I walk to the entry booth. The Emirates flight from Brisbane was filled with passengers. *Where did they all go?*

A passport officer calls me forwards. With my Australian passport in hand, I step up.

She looks at me and asks, 'Enta Masri?'

I reply, 'Na'm, ana Masri, bas ayesh fe Ustraliya, ana gensity Ustraliyy.' Then I say the same sentence in English: 'I'm Egyptian, but live in Australia. I am an Australian citizen.'

She nods and types on her keyboard. After looking intently at her screen, she stops typing and picks up the phone. Face lowered, she dials and then whispers into the receiver. She doesn't want me to hear; I feel a little nervous.

She looks back at me as she puts my passport away, then asks me to wait: 'Istana hena showyah. Feeh tashaboh fe el'asmaa.' *Wait here, there is a match of your name to another name.*

The fact that there is confusion of my name with another name doesn't make me that worried as it's a common issue. I feel relatively confident that it will be cleared up quickly. I nod in understanding and seat myself on a chair nearby.

As the minutes pass, I get more nervous. For a small issue, it seems like it's taking too long. I start to feel unsure and uncomfortable. I reach for my phone to call my nephew, Yacoub, as he must be outside waiting for me. I explain what's happening, telling him that I've been delayed by a security check but I should be out soon.

Hanging up, I distract myself by snacking on one of those trail mixes from Woolworths – nuts, raisins and chocolate – that I had brought with me for the flight from Australia.

A man sits beside me. I look at him out of the side of my eye. He could be an undercover security guard. They're a common sight, so I don't allow myself to be bothered by his presence and offer him some of my trail mix since we're both sitting and waiting on this bench. He declines my offer.

After almost half an hour of waiting, two more undercover security men approach me. I know I haven't done anything wrong, but even so, their presence induces fear. When they ask me to come with them for a quick chat to clarify the apparent mix-up, I panic. Everyone in Egypt knows the risks of being taken by security services. To follow them screams danger, but I control the urge to run. I have to stay composed and calm. I have no choice; I must obey the authorities.

I walk with the two men until we reach a dimly lit office. The man sitting behind the desk flips through my Australian passport, then asks me to introduce myself and tell him why I am here. Thinking of my family, I tell him: 'Ana hena 'alashan ashoof ahly.' *I'm here to see my family.*

Then he asks me to give him my mobile phone.

This is no routine check or friendly chat. I refuse to hand it over. I remind him that I am an Australian citizen and I have the right to refuse, that before he can continue with any further questioning, I should be permitted to contact the Australian Embassy.

Until now, the two men who had escorted me to this office had been waiting outside, listening through the door. Upon hearing my objections, they both step into the room. Closing the door, they stand behind me. They're so close I can almost feel the heat coming off their bodies. By intimidating me, they remind me of what they could do: torture at the hands of authorities in Egypt is an open secret.

Rather than continue to object, I fold to the pressure. Hesitant, I pass my mobile phone to the man behind the desk. He snatches it from me, then pushes the phone back towards me and asks me to unlock it. I put in the passcode and he starts to look through my apps and messages. I'm furious at the violation of my privacy but I feel helpless to stop it. The two men still stand behind me.

A landline phone on the desk rings and the man answers. 'Mafeesh, haga 'ala al'mobile.' Since there is nothing incriminating on my phone, I hear him ask what else is required of him. To whatever the voice says on the other end, he nods as he grunts 'haadir', then hangs up. He tells me to wait outside, so I ask for my phone back. He aggressively rejects my request.

I step out of the office and sit down on a chair. The two security guards come out and stand near me. Soon, they are called back in. After a few minutes, one of them comes back and tells me to get up and follow him. I slowly stand. When I ask him what's going on, he ignores my question.

I refuse to move. Surely this cannot be legal. I shout at him, 'Ana eiz a'kalim al-qansool! Da mish qanooni! Ana mish hamshee ma'ak!' *I want to speak to the Embassy. This is not legal! I'm not coming with you!*

Before I know it, the second guard has exited the office and is standing behind me. I feel a hard, cold object press into my back. I stop shouting. Now I'm scared. This is serious.

These men have everything: my passport, my wallet, my luggage and my phone. No one knows that I'm about to be taken by them and I cannot contact anyone, not even Lamisse or Yacoub, to alert them as to what's happening. I am defenceless, disempowered to protect myself.

Suddenly, I'm pushed with force by the guard holding the gun. I move, stumbling at first. Both guards walk behind me, guiding me through a doorway and into a back corridor. I drag my feet. We go through door after door, and then an elevator takes us down to what looks like the airport basement.

We come to a stop outside yet another door. The guards open it and give me a shove. I stumble into a dimly lit room. In front of me is a steel door. Distracted, I don't notice the presence of another man in the room until he opens the door to reveal a cell.

The two men who dragged me here order me to go inside.

I refuse.

With a final hard push to my back, I fall into the cell and hear the door lock behind me.

Lamisse

Thursday 25 January 2018

Saja and Harun have been in town for a week now and they're ready to see more than Cairo. It's a long weekend, so we decide to join some friends heading to Dahab, a seaside town in the Sinai Peninsula popular with divers, hippies and budget tourists like us. Dad will arrive in Cairo this evening. He texted me a selfie wearing his Akubra hat during his stopover in Dubai, so I know he's on track. Given we're out of town, our cousin Yacoub will be picking up Dad from the airport.

After a 10-hour bus ride, we arrive in Sinai in the late afternoon and spend what's left of the day at a beach cafe. A few people brave the winter wind for a quick dip in the Red Sea. By the evening, we've checked into our hotel. Harun and I are sitting on the balcony connected to our double room; we chat while he games on his phone and I scroll through Instagram. Saja is hanging out in the courtyard with everyone else.

It's around eight in the evening when Yacoub calls with an update; I head inside to take the call. He says he's been waiting for three hours but Uncle Hazem has yet to emerge. He then adds that Dad isn't answering his phone, and he'll ask around and see if he can get any information. My stomach flutters in apprehension. Yacoub promises to call back with another update and our call ends.

Returning to my chair on the balcony, I don't quite know what to make of Yacoub's update.

'Dad's delayed,' I say matter-of-factly.

'Why?'

'Dunno ... Yacoub will call me back.'

Ten minutes later, my phone lights up: it's Yacoub again. I get up and go back inside. Free of my chatter, Harun puts his headphones into his ears. 'So,' Yacoub says, 'I asked my friend who works at the airport to see if he can find out where Uncle Hazem is.' He pauses. 'And he says that Uncle Hazem is with national security.'

I'm blank for a few seconds, then I'm flooded with excoriating terror, my stomach jolting me sickeningly out of the initial shock.

When I revisit this moment in my memory, all I have is the flash of an out-of-body image: me sitting on the edge of the hotel bed, keeping my conversation with Yacoub quiet so Harun cannot hear.

'What? Security? Why? That's so fucking weird! Why would he be with security?'

Adrenaline is pumping through my body. It pushes up against my skin, singeing my nerve endings and contracting my muscles. I want to sprint the 560 kilometres to the arrivals terminal at the airport.

Yacoub doesn't know why, but he says he'll keep waiting. He says maybe Dad won't be kept for long, maybe it's just routine, and there's nothing we can do except wait. He makes a point of mentioning that today is a difficult day. When I ask why, he reminds me of the reason it's a public holiday: it is the anniversary of the 2011 Revolution – how could I forget? That morning, we'd left an eerily quiet Cairo, wondering why there was an increased military presence around the city. Then Yacoub says it will be fine, that 'this is Egypt.' This alarms me further; never have I heard this phrase used in situations of good news.

I implore Yacoub to call me as soon as he has any news about Dad. 'Of course,' he promises. After he hangs up, I stay seated on the bed. I lower my head till it's between my knees and shut my eyes. I search my mind for a precedent of experience, a way to make sense of what I've been told. Everything in my body is telling me it's bad, but I try to rationalise the trepidation away: Is it routine? Am I overreacting? Maybe I shouldn't be so worried?

When I head back out to the balcony, Harun is still engrossed in his game, but now his headphones are resting on his shoulders. *Was he listening?*

Lowering myself onto the chair next to him, I take a deep breath.

'Sooooo …' I draw out the word, hesitating to say the thing out loud, before it rushes out: 'Dad'sbeendelayed becausehe'swithnationalsecurity.'

My brother's eyes don't shift from his screen. 'What does that mean?'

Taking another breath, I try to slow myself down. 'I don't know … But Yacoub is investigating it. He says he has a friend working in airport security.'

'All right. So, it's not bad?'

'I don't know … Like, I honestly have no idea what this means. That's all Yacoub told me.'

Shakiness starts to set in. The shock still peeling off me, I slowly realise that I do know something about Egypt's National Security Services. Tidbits of information surface, scratching down a chalkboard at the back of my head: extraordinary rendition, torture, disappearances. Until now, such terms had felt distant and intellectual, gleaned from my interest in human rights, from studying International Relations and listening to stories told between family and friends.

I need to steady myself.

Abruptly, I stand and announce: 'I'm going to get a drink.'

Harun groans. 'Ugh, fine.' He hates it. I want it. We're not going to argue over my drinking right now.

I go downstairs, find a beer and open it. Saja, my younger sister, is swaddled in a blanket to protect herself against the cold sharp wind, laughing loudly. Saja and the group of people we travelled to Sinai with are gathered around a white, plastic outdoor table. Music is blaring out of a portable speaker; beer and shot glasses litter the table. All, including Saja, are in their early twenties: three of them are exchange students from America and the other four are Egyptian. Saja is going through a stage of figuring herself out. After several years of wearing hijab, she recently took it off and is now pushing the boundaries that we were all raised with. I empathise with what she's going through. From questioning faith and seeking our edge, to knowing where our boundaries are, I see it all as a necessary part of a young person's process of self-exploration. A process that scares far too many Muslim parents, like our own. Yet, this stage requires the guiding rails of safety, love and support – not judgement, shaming or ostracisation. In encouraging Saja to visit me in Egypt, I had hoped the trip might support her on this journey. That this holiday could fill some of the gaps in the puzzle pieces of her identity, just like it had mine.

I catch Saja's gaze and nod at her. She nods back and grins. I can't tell her about Dad yet – I don't want to ruin the fun she's having – so I slip away from the group and rejoin Harun.

On the balcony, I take a sip of my beer. 'Do you reckon we should cut our trip short and go to Cairo tomorrow?' Harun is

19, he doesn't want to join the group downstairs; he prefers deep conversation to loud music, and the great outdoors over a stuffy club. Coming to Cairo, I knew his motivation for being here was to connect with Dad. We'd had many conversations about how I'd experienced Dad being a different person in Egypt. Lighter, more fun; it was a marvel to witness how his mother tongue brought him to life in a way that English never could. Harun wanted to connect with that person; he wanted to know more than the tired, stressed-out father he'd come to be familiar with, and I wanted him to know that version of Dad too. It felt like another important stage of development: the transition of allowing your image of your caregiver to expand from parent to person.

'Yeah, I don't know …' He turns off the game and puts his phone in his pocket. 'Nothing has really happened yet …'

'True … It could just be procedure or something …' We fall silent, looking out to the cloudless, star-speckled sky.

It's winter, the low season, and we're the only guests in this small compound. The hotel is surrounded by crisp, white-washed walls, and in the middle of the courtyard area below, there is a blue but empty pool. In the daylight, the mountains that define Sinai are visible from our balcony, as is the gentle Red Sea. As the sun sets, the horizon disappears into the night, making the separation between the sea and sky almost indiscernible. The sound of tipsy laughter ricochets through the open courtyard. Earlier, at sunset, we'd stood at the water's edge, watching the yellow lights flicker on the shores of Saudi Arabia. A surge of wonder had swept through me: *there is no beach in Australia where can you look across the sea and see another country.*

A slow four hours pass with no call or text from Yacoub. It's now almost midnight. Defeated by the wait, I crawl into bed. A few minutes later, I get a text.

I'm leaving the airport. Uncle Hazem will be with security over the night. I will call you in the morning.

I text back, thanking Yacoub and wishing him a good night's rest. Worn down by anxiety, I tell myself there's nothing more we can do and fall asleep.

Hazem

My watch says it's almost 10 pm. I'm utterly exhausted and bewildered, swirling in a haze of jet lag and confusion as I try to understand events so far. I cannot process any of it. Anxiety fills me; I feel lost, and at a loss.

The holding cell is small and brightly lit by fluorescent lights. There are no windows and it smells terrible. Seven bunkbeds fill the room. Not all of them are occupied, but the ones that are hold men from different parts of the world. To my scrambled brain, everyone looks strange and distant.

One man is from New Zealand: an old, scruffy white chap with a long beard and a sunken, sallow face. Cigarette in hand, he approaches me with a friendly demeanour and asks, 'Where are you from?' I promptly reply, 'I am from Australia', and we strike up a chat. His friendliness takes the edge off my nerves. While we talk, my eyes keep scanning the room. I notice two young African men; they look East African but I cannot tell where from exactly. They are both sleeping. There's a fourth man who looks Egyptian.

Hunger and thirst gnaw at me, and I look down at my watch. It's now going on 11 pm. I feel delirious with exhaustion, but I am unable to shut down my frantic mind. The Egyptian man wakes. He sees I'm new to the cell and approaches me. He asks me some questions, the usual curious questions, so I talk, trying to translate the conversation to the Kiwi man who stands with us. But the translating exhausts me further, and I start to feel that sickness in my belly that comes when you're desperate to sleep. I excuse myself and look for a bathroom. That's when I notice the toilet in the corner of the cell, stinking and filthy. Beside the toilet is a broken basin and dripping tap. No door. Just three walls around an exposed toilet. My anxiety jumps further. My mind is spiralling into incoherence; I don't know what I'm thinking or what I'm feeling. Everything in my brain becomes crackling white noise.

I go to the toilet quickly, then jump up onto a top bunk in the cell corner. No blankets, no sheets. Just a stained and smelly spring mattress. I look for a switch to turn off the lights. There isn't one; I'm informed by the Egyptian that the lights are on 24/7.

I put my arm over my eyes and try to sleep, but I can't relax. At about 1 am, two more men are pushed into the room. I can hear that one of them is from Jordan, the other from Kuwait. I give up on trying to sleep and approach the two men. I connect with the man from Kuwait, reminiscing about my childhood in Kuwait City as we trade stories about life in the Gulf in the late seventies and early eighties. It's a conversation that temporarily puts my fear at bay. By 3 am, everyone retreats to their bunks.

As I lie on my mattress, still unable to sleep, I pray.

It's almost 4 am: time for the dawn prayer. I get up, do my wu'du at the broken sink and perform the Fajr prayer. As I rise from the floor, something catches my eye. I glance up.

It's a camera. We're being watched.

I return to the bunk, hoping that this time I'll get some kind of sleep. Thankfully, I do fall asleep, but not for long. I'm soon woken by another man being pushed into the cell. His entry is followed by yelling and screaming. He is Nigerian. His face is filled with fear and confusion. He isolates himself to a bottom bunk, mumbling quietly and looking afraid.

I haven't had anything to eat or drink since the trail mix, so I take the risk of drinking from the tap in the toilet. My hunger has disappeared, buried under anxiety. Time seems to go by painfully slowly.

I lie back on the bunk, and this time, I think about my family. Sleep finally takes over me.

I am woken again by the other Egyptian man in the cell. He tells me, 'Yalla, na'sahlli i-goma'!' *Come on, let's pray the Friday prayer!* I get up and wash in preparation for the prayer. Just before I start my prayer, the man approaches me again and asks me to lead the Friday prayer and offer a sermon to the group in the cell. I decline as it's not obligatory to do so under the conditions of our adverse circumstances. He argues with me, trying to explain why we should continue with the usual format for Friday prayers.

The Jordanian man stands from his bunk and backs up my argument, saying we shouldn't have to do a full Friday prayer because of our circumstances. 'Plus,' he adds, 'we don't have enough numbers for a full congregation.' At that moment, the cell door opens and about ten Egyptian men enter the room. The Egyptian man imprisoned with me grins and triumphantly announces that we have the numbers for Jum'ah prayer. It seems a strange coincidence, but then, nothing is normal in this environment. I nod hesitantly in agreement to continue with a full prayer, and then ask the Egyptian man to make the Athaan. I offer a short sermon on the topic of gratitude, of how we must give our best efforts in life then leave the rest to God's Will.

The small congregation seem pleased with my sermon. After the prayer, we chat among ourselves. I find out that the group of men who had come into the room are all labourers who have been deported from Saudi Arabia after the termination of their contracts. When their contracts ended, they were first detained by the Saudis, then deported with nothing but the clothing they were wearing.

The door opens again. Two men walk in and ask me to walk out with them. I silently oblige and leave the cell without saying goodbye. I keep my head down as I follow them through more doors and corridors, all of it disorienting.

I'm led to a room with television screens, each showing the same image from a different angle: images of the cell I've just come from.

Three men are in the room, their guns visibly mounted by their sides. The room is filled with cigarette smoke. The men are young, with haughty demeanours. I notice my luggage open on the desk beside them. One of the young men asks me to go through the items in my suitcase and bag and identify them all.

I resist. 'Leh ana hena? Ana eiz a'kalim a'safeer!' *Why am I here? I want to talk to the Ambassador?*

'Ooskot!' the young man yells. 'Rod a'la soo'aly!' *Shut-up! You only answer my questions!*

The men look like rabid dogs ready to attack. I feel trapped, kidnapped. I still have no idea why I am going through all this. I can't run and I can't fight. Despair starts filling me and I feel physically sick.

I'm approached from behind by one of the young men, and I notice a brand new white shirt that my wife bought for me in his hand. He drops the shirt, and with his other hand, raises a blindfold.

It goes over my eyes.

Then my hands are placed into metal cuffs.

I scream, but no voice comes out. I start to shut down; I want to disappear. My legs are shaky, like they cannot hold my weight. I'm pushed from behind and told to walk. The men walk beside me, and I can smell the mix of their body odour and cigarettes. The walk seems long, but behind the blindfold, my sense of time is lost.

We slow down. One of them says, 'Feen el-box?' *Where is the prison truck?*

Lamisse

Friday 26 January 2018

I wake up early to my buzzing alarm. We've planned to go snorkelling today and want to get down to the Blue Hole before it becomes too busy with fellow tourists. Famous for being a deep natural sinkhole abundant with coral formations, the pathway to the Blue Hole is lined with plaques dedicated to all those drowned in its depths.

As I turn off my alarm, I see that I already have a text from Yacoub.

My friend says Uncle Hazem is still with security. I will go to the airport soon to find out. Apart from Harun and me, everyone is nursing a hangover. Saja confesses they've all had about two hours of sleep. They had taken a drunken dawn hike to watch the sunrise from atop a cliff edge.

'It was so beautiful.' Saja lets out an ethereal sigh, clasping her hands to her face, her eyes wide with earnestness. 'So, so beautiful.'

After breakfast and coffee, we head out through the heavy wooden gates of the hotel compound to find transport to the Blue Hole. A white Toyota ute pulls up. Our friend, and unofficial leader of the group, Suleiman, negotiates with the driver while the rest of us wait.

I take the opportunity to pull Saja and Harun aside and we huddle in a circle of three.

'So, Dad's still with security.'

'What?' Saja shoots me an accusing look. 'What do you mean *still with*?'

'He's been there since last night.'

'Since last night!' she explodes. 'Why didn't you tell me!'

My hands fly up, palms facing forwards in a gesture of self-defence. 'You were having fun and I didn't want to worry you! We hoped maybe it would be resolved by now, but it's not.'

Harun interrupts: 'So, what did Yacoub say?'

I reiterate what I know to them, filling in Saja on the details. I tell them that I'm worried enough to contact the Australian Embassy for advice.

Saja proposes we speak to Suleiman. 'It's their country. Maybe they understand things that we don't,' she says.

Their country.

The phrase echoes through me, reminding me that, despite whatever claims we make, we're outsiders. She's right, but I'm reluctant to agree. The longer I keep it quiet, the longer I can hold on to the hope that maybe this will solve itself, that it'll go away without a scene. I'm scared that if I tell people, especially a local like Suleiman, they'll react in a way that could confirm my worst nightmare.

With transport negotiations settled, we climb into the back of the ute. Speeding to the Blue Hole, our faces are sanded by the gritty, whipping wind. I'm sitting next to Suleiman, and I indicate I want to say something to him. Putting my hand to my face, I speak directly into his ear to explain what's happening. He responds with intensity, urging me to call the Australian Embassy as soon as we arrive at the dive site.

We climb out of the ute. Exposed, we're thrashed by the furious wind while the sea idles against a desert expanse fringed with pavilions that house cushions and low tables.

Suleiman comes up to me. 'Remember he's an Australian,' he says, concerned and in earnest. 'Don't let them treat him like an Egyptian.'

It sounds like a warning I should heed. 'Okay, I'll try,' I say.

He nods, then hurries back to the others, joining their loud, enthusiastic chatter.

After dumping our bags next to a table under the pavilion, the group stands and discusses the plan for the day. Harun couldn't be more excited while Saja is concerned about the water being too cold. Taking my cue from Saja, I excuse myself from the excursion by making a show of hating to swim in cold water. I'm not ready to let the whole group in on the situation, and I'm content with missing out. The last time I snorkelled in the Blue Hole, I had vertigo, despite being horizontal and buoyant in the salt water. The moment I looked away from the vivid, sloping coral wall and down into the dark centre, I would be overcome by that dizzy sensation of falling.

As everyone else runs off to go snorkelling, I call out for Saja and Harun to come back. They jog over.

'I spoke to Suleiman. I'm actually staying here to call the Embassy and figure out what I can do about Dad.'

'Oh, I believed that you were actually too cold,' says Harun.

*

Steaming black tea arrives in a pear-shaped glass cup. 'Shukran,' I murmur as the waiter places it on the table, along with a pot of crystallised sugar.

I've found the number for the Australian Embassy in Cairo. I stir in some sugar, take a sip of my tea and dial. There's a ring, then a voice recording clicks on to announce it's Australia Day. Since it's a public holiday, the Embassy is closed.

I go back to the webpage for the Australian Embassy in Cairo to see what other information I can find. There's a number for a 24-hour emergency consular services hotline. I open the Skype app on my phone to see if I still have credit. I do.

I dial.

A woman answers the phone. I tell her everything I know: Dad had a stopover in Dubai. When he was in Dubai, he texted me. When he arrived in Cairo, he texted me again to say he was on the tarmac. At some point, he was taken by the Egyptian Al-Amn Al-Watany, The National Security Services. As far as I know, he is being held at the airport, but I only know this because my cousin told me. My cousin knows this because he has a friend who works in airport security.

She informs me that, by law, we have to wait 48 hours. After this time, the Egyptian authorities are obliged to make a decision about what they will do with our dad and inform the Australian Embassy of this decision.

The most likely outcome, she says, is that my father will be deported.

'How do I find out if that's what they choose?' I ask.

'Your father will contact you from his transit country. If you hear from him, please tell us.'

The other two options are that he is released and allowed to continue his holiday, or he is arrested. Again, she reiterates for me to call the Embassy if either of these two outcomes occurs.

'So, forty-eight hours from the moment of his arrest?' I assume in this situation that 'arrest' means the moment he was taken by security. As such, I calculate that I should have an answer by Monday. I ask if this assumption is right.

'Yes,' she says. 'It means you should expect a decision from the Egyptian authorities by Monday. There isn't much you can do except wait for a decision.'

I thank her and end the call. Then I call Yacoub. He is quiet when I explain what I've been told.

I ask him if I should come back to Cairo and go to the airport with him. He tells me to stay in Dahab; it's the weekend now – and a long weekend at that – so no one will be working or taking work seriously. We might as well wait until Monday. In the meantime, he says he will check in again with this security friend. I wonder out loud if Dad is okay. He tries to reassure me: 'Don't worry, Uncle Hazem is strong. He will be fine.'

Despite the reassurance, I can't make any of this feel fine. I'm fluctuating between numbness and an overwhelming need to scream. I don't want to dump my fears all over Yacoub as he's doing the best he can. Plus, I'm certain he's feeling afraid too.

I thank Yacoub and he promises again to keep me updated. We end the call.

Alone, I take a sip of my quickly cooling tea. The wind is still relentless in its ferocity. I track back over my previous trips to Egypt and find myself in a memory from 2013.

It's my first attempt to live in Cairo. I'm 24 and I've decided to move into my grandfather's empty apartment.

I asked Yacoub and his brother, Amgad, to come with me to check our grandfather's flat. Dad had given me the keys to the flat before I left Melbourne. He asked me to look at it for him as he was worried it had fallen into disrepair. No one had lived there for almost seven years.

Yacoub, Amgad and I drove down to Heliopolis. The apartment was near the Presidential Palace. The air was thick with a whitish-grey smoke. People ran in all directions, their faces covered. Silent in the car, Yacoub drove slowly. When we pulled up to the entrance of the apartment block, Amgad turned to me. 'It's tear gas,' he said. 'Put your shirt over your nose and mouth and let's run into the building. Try not to breathe it in.'

Yacoub turned off the engine and pulled his shirt up over the lower half of his face. Amgad did the same, so I followed suit. After taking a deep breath, I opened the car door, scrunched up my eyes and ran for the stairs that hovered blurredly ahead. I pounded up the stairs to the first floor and skidded around the corner. Still holding my shirt over my face, I fumbled with the key and unlocked the door. Amgad and Yacoub stumbled into the dusty, run-down apartment with me. We shut the door, chests heaving. Amgad lowered his shirt and grinned mischievously. 'It's the anniversary of the revolution today!'

The 25th of January.

Returning to the present, I wonder if it was somehow risky for Dad to arrive in Cairo yesterday. A flash of fear rushes through me: I'd booked his flight and I'd chosen the date. Did I unwittingly play a part in Dad's arrest?

I watch the group drip their way up the sandy road towards me, sharing the path with ambling camels and speeding utes. They all drop heavily onto the cushions by the table and wrap themselves tightly in their towels. More hot tea is ordered.

Harun is exploding with excitement. 'Wow! That was amazing! But not enough time. Man, I felt like I had just started swimming and then we already had to go back. Twenty minutes is not long enough. There is so much to see!'

Saja's teeth are chattering.

'Get dressed,' I say firmly. 'Don't stay in your wet towel and bathers if you're shivering.'

She wraps her hand around a glass of freshly-delivered hot tea. 'Later. I'm gonna drink this first.' An edge of defiance laces her response.

With this strange, looming sense of imminent danger, I feel responsible for my younger siblings' safety. My fear is coming out as bossiness, the need for control. Clocking it, I tell myself I must watch out not to regress into their once tyrannical eldest sister: we're good now, we're equals.

As the group is distracted by the business of getting warm, Harun shuffles closer to me and whispers, 'So, what did the Embassy say?'

Saja comes over too. 'Yeah, did you speak to them?'

I speak in a low voice. 'Yep, I did. They said we have to wait forty-eight hours and then a decision is supposed to be made. There's nothing we can do until then so we might as well enjoy the rest of our day here. We don't need to be rushing back.'

'Two days seems like a long time to wait,' Saja says.

Harun and I agree.

Hazem

I'm pushed inside the truck and hear steel doors close behind me. I don't know what's happening, or where this truck is going.

It smells like urine. There isn't much ventilation and the air is heavy and stale. I remember the story of 37 men who were killed inside a prisoner transportation truck after a rogue guard threw in a tear gas canister to stop them from complaining about the suffocating lack of air. It's just me in here and I feel claustrophobic.

The engine roars. I fall onto the side of the truck and find a steel bench melded onto the wall. I manoeuvre myself into a sitting position while the truck lurches between gear shifts. We drive around for what feels like an hour, maybe more.

My ears prick up to the sounds of a steel gate opening. The truck rolls inside, the doors are flung open and someone begins screaming at me. They fling insults and profanities in between yelling at me to get out.

This is my worst nightmare: I'm in the hands of Egypt's National Security.

Though I immediately know I've arrived at one of their centres, I'm not sure if it's the headquarters or an off-site centre. Either way, these are the chambers of torture and disappeared men. I stumble out of the truck. I'm pushed to turn and ordered to walk. Blindly, I trudge forwards. A door opens and I enter a building.

My ears are greeted with distant screams and shouts: a blurred mix of interrogators and their victims. An acrid combination of blood, urine and faeces wafts into my nose. My clothes are taken off me and I find myself being strip searched, all while blindfolded. The handcuffs are only briefly removed as my shirt is taken off, and again as it's put back on.

All the while, a cacophony of yells surrounds me. A singular voice then pierces through the noise: 'Ooskot! Enta malaksh esm! Enta raqm tamanya wa 'ashreen!' *You don't have a name! You are number 28! So shut the fuck up!*

I can't even remember if I was talking or not, but I shut up.

It feels as though I can't get away from the sounds of the moaning, groaning and screaming. It seems to completely encompass me, and I can no longer tell if it's at a distance or happening right beside me.

Confusing commands are issued and I hesitate, unsure where I'm supposed to go or in what direction. Fatigue and confusion permeate my body as I fight the urge to crash onto the floor. Then a voice yells, 'Emshy alatool!' *Walk straight.*

The voice continues to issue commands: 'Shmaal! Yemeen!' *Left! Right!*

I trip and crash into the wall with my shoulder. A hand shoves my back. I'm pushed from behind.

'Emshy alatool!' the voice screams.

I keep swerving and swaying as I stagger forwards, propelled by my own momentum and the repeated pushes to my back.

I trip up some stairs, find my footing, and then try to focus on putting one foot in front of the other, going upwards. We ascend two, perhaps three, floors but I lose count.

Finally, I'm told to stop. There's a rattle of keys, a scrape of rusted steel tracks and voices are swearing. They tell the moans, groans and screams to shut up, shut up, shut up. A final aggressive push to my back sends me stumbling, and I fall onto bodies lying on the floor. My first thought is that these are dead bodies beneath me and I scramble frantically, trying to get back up even though I'm handcuffed, blindfolded and exhausted.

Then, hands move beneath me. Someone is pushing me upwards, trying to lift me off them.

The stench of blood, urine and sweat is overwhelming. A soft voice rises out of the darkness. 'Raqmak kam?' *What's your number?*

'Tamanya wa 'ashreen,' I reply. *Twenty-eight.*

'Ana raqm wahid, ana hena min talaat ush'hoor.' *I'm number one. I've been here three months now.*

He calls on the others to make space, and there's the sound of rolling, shuffling. I find myself on the floor, cramped between two bodies. The air is dense and stuffy, and there's a continual hum of groans and moans as the men adjust their fatigued, hurting bodies to accommodate me.

The soft voice tells me to rest, that I'm going to need it here.

The cell is quieter; the sounds of shuffling and groaning dim as everyone finds a new position, having now adjusted to my body. My mind is in utter turmoil; behind the blindfold, I'm assaulted by hallucinations, fuelled by my anxiety.

I don't know if I'm sleeping or dreaming or awake.

I don't how much time has passed.

My number is called.

I try to stand. My head spins, and I begin to collapse. Two rough hands grab my upper arms and pull me through the door. I'm led down stairs then through a corridor. I know we arrive at a room when a commanding voice tells the two hands that are on me to 'adhu!'. *Sit him down!*

I sit. A creepy silence hangs in the air, along with the piercing scent of cigarette smoke. Sounds issue from one of the national broadcasters. Is there a television in the room?

The commanding voice cuts through:

Esmak eh bil kamil?

What's your full name?

Enta u'doo ma'a il-Ikhwaan al-Muslimeen?

Are you a member of the Muslim Brotherhood Group?

Enta geet Masr leh?

Why did you come to Egypt?

Leh dakhil Masr begawaz Ustraliyy?

Why are you travelling on an Australian passport?

Ta'rif meen fe Masr?

Who do you know in Egypt?

Kalimni 'an ahlak.

Tell me about your family.

Leh hagerrt li-Ustraliya?

Why did you migrate to Australia?

Betishtaghal eh?

What do you do for a living?

Sakin feen?

Where do you live?

I answer the questions he fires at me. I hear some kind of device; perhaps it is something recording our conversation. Every now and again, in between the barrage of questions, the commanding voice pauses. Sometimes, they are long, lingering silences.

At one point, I ask him for a glass of water.

I tell the voice that I'm feeling sick. He commands one of the guards to get a glass of water for me. It takes a long time to arrive. He keeps questioning me and the questions become increasingly personal. It puts me on edge, and he keeps circling back to the same theme: he keeps asking me about the Muslim Brotherhood.

Finally, the guards are called to take me back to the holding cell. They drag me through the corridors and up the stairs. I'm beyond exhausted and completely delirious. My legs feel unable to coordinate with the commands issued by my churning mind. As I'm walking, I hear the sound of birds: it must be dawn.

I'm pushed back into the cell and I collapse onto the bodies; they groan and shuffle to make space for me again.

I fall to the floor and into unconsciousness.

I'm woken by Number One. He shakes my shoulder. 'Il-akl geh, lazim takul.' *The guards have brought some food. You need to eat.*

I don't want to eat food I can't see. I have no appetite and the food could be poisoned. I realise my hands are now cuffed in front of me but I can't remember when the position of my hands were changed. Feeling for the food, I can tell it's halawa and fouul. I know I should try to eat, but I can't bring myself to.

Though I'm not hungry, I'm incredibly thirsty. In thinking about water, I realise that I haven't been to the bathroom since Friday morning. Number One asks me who I am and where I'm from. I respond and then ask him the same questions. Everyone in the cell goes quiet.

Number One answers, then adds 'Fe camera foh, matshilsh il ghomayya wa illah hat rooh a'zl inferady.' *There is a camera in the top corner. Don't remove your blindfold or you will be taken to solitary confinement.*

At that moment, the steel gates grind open and a heavy slap lands on my face.

'Ooskot!' *SHUT THE FUCK UP!*

We all go silent. I don't speak again.

After some time, my number is called again. Soon, I'm back in a room with the smell of cigarette smoke hanging in the air. A new voice asks questions; it is harsher and older than the first voice. This voice assures me I am safe, that I'm entitled to my opinion and that this will all be over soon.

I'm confused; nothing about this feels safe.

He begins the questioning, again asking about my family, my career and my relatives in Egypt. I tell him the truth and explain that if I had something to hide, why would I come to Egypt? The questions shift to being more political and religious in nature, and he keeps asking the same question, repeated, among all the other questions: am I a member of the Muslim Brotherhood?

I keep saying no.

This continues for what feels like hours. My delirium is returning; the noise of the broadcasters in the background is distracting and too loud. Guards arrive and move my hands to be cuffed from behind. They adjust my blindfold and take me out of the room. Then I'm ordered to sit on the floor in the corridor.

I slide my back down the wall and sit with my knees drawn up. I can hear the steps of people coming and going past me, along with screams and shouts. I'm terrified, so I sit as still as possible, listening to the steps and the screams. The heavy shuffle of a guard's boots stop in front of me and a plate is placed on the floor. He commands me to eat. Then he uncuffs me, moving my hands from behind to the front of me. I don't touch the food; I just stay sitting there.

I'm taken to the interrogation room again. I'm asked the same questions again. I give the same answers again.

I'm sent back into the corridor and commanded to sit on the floor again. In the dark, behind a blindfold, I'm still clueless as to why this is happening to me.

I remain here for a while. Finally, a voice comes back and tells me to rise and walk. Hands turn me to the right direction and I'm ordered to walk straight. We pass through doors and a cool breeze sweeps over my face.

I'm outside!

I try to take a deep breath, but my chest is tight with panic. *Where are we going now?*

Lamisse

27 January 2018

We're leaving Dahab today. There are fewer military checkpoints on the bus ride back to Cairo, so we should get back to the city in about eight hours instead of ten.

A text from Yacoub says Dad is still being held at the airport.

Hazem

27–28 January 2018

From the cool breeze, I can tell that it is night-time. I'm not given much time to appreciate being outside as I'm hurried over to a truck. Steel stairs lead me back into the steel box, and this time, hands place me upon a steel bench. I remain blindfolded and handcuffed.

After a long drive, the truck comes to a stop. I'm rushed out of the truck and into a building. When we enter the building, we stop. The handcuffs are removed. Then, the blindfold is lifted. I think I've been in the dark for two days. I blink rapidly, trying to adjust to the uncomfortable brightness of the fluorescent lights. I swing my arms, enjoying the sensation of having them move freely. It's an amazing feeling and I linger in it for a brief moment as I take in my surroundings.

I realise that I'm in the National Security Prosecutor Building. The pleasant freedom of having my arms back is squashed by my shock. I'm led to the second floor, a guard on each side of me. Again, I'm told to sit on the floor and I seat myself in the cold corridor.

An hour passes.

Finally, I'm called into a large office. There are two men inside: one looks like a scribe, so I figure the other must be the prosecutor. He looks middle-aged, younger than I had expected. He asks my name and I answer.

Before he has a chance to ask follow-up questions, I state that I'm an Australian citizen and that I want a representative from the Embassy to be present. I add that I should have the right to call a lawyer, and to tell my family where I am. I feel my anger rising so I keep going: I tell him that this is kidnapping, that I've been blindfolded and handcuffed and interrogated without any reason.

He cuts me off and tells me, 'Da mish fe il-war'a, enta Masri witqabad alayk fe il-matar mushtabah innak au'duh ma' il-ikhwaan al-Muslimeen.' *This isn't in the paperwork. You're an Egyptian citizen and you've been arrested at the airport under suspicion of belonging to a forbidden political group, the Muslim Brotherhood.*

This is the first time I have been clearly told the reason I'm here. I'm shocked but determined to fight back. I deny the accusation and repeat my request for a representative from the Embassy to be present. The prosecutor tells the scribe to note the request. A wave of nausea rolls over me. I grit my teeth, waiting for the light-headedness to pass. I manage to stammer a request: 'Eiz haga besukar.' *I need something with sugar in it.* I know that this sensation is my blood pressure dropping. After all, I haven't eaten since the airport. My request is ignored.

Instead, I'm asked for my statement. I give it, reiterating that I reject the accusation while restating my innocence. I want to refuse to sign the paperwork. Yet, despite my outward anger, I'm swamped with helplessness. I know I can't do anything. I know I'm not being heard.

I sign the paperwork. In doing so, I submit to the fact that this is beyond me right now, but I am still hoping that this nightmare will somehow end quickly.

I'm escorted out of the building and back into the steel box of the prisoner transfer truck. My hands are cuffed again. Metal mesh covers the small opening. The door slams shut behind me and I hear a steel lever go over the door. Locked in, I'm not blindfolded, but it's nearly pitch-black in the truck. I tentatively feel my way through the space until I find the bench to sit down on.

An out-of-body sensation sweeps over me. I'm floating through space, floating inside my mind. Thoughts are mingled with memories. *Am I in a truck, or am I back home in Brisbane with my family?* Questions punctuate the images in my head: *Where am I? What's going on? What's going to happen to me? How did this happen? Does anyone know where I am? Will they find me? Are they worried?* I'm lost in this swirling cloud of confusion.

The truck starts up.

I start calling on Allah, quietly within my mind, to break through the hazy, distressing thoughts and questions. It's meditative to recite descriptors of Allah, reminding myself of his attributes, trying to remember that there is a higher power in the world beyond the prosecutor and the National Security services: God, the All-Seer, the All-Merciful, the All-Hearing, the All-Benevolent … 'Ya Allah,' I quietly plea, 'deliver us from injustice.'

As we rumble through the streets of Cairo at night, I can hear the honking of cars. The sounds evoke a sharp nostalgia that cuts through me. *That's right, I'm in Cairo.* It's so close I can hear it, but it's so far away. Three of my kids are here, my nephews and nieces, cousins, aunts and uncles. They're all here and I am … where? Where am I going? A breeze comes through the mesh-covered window, providing brief relief from the stagnant air of the truck.

Eventually, the truck rolls to a halt and the engine switches off. A few minutes later, I hear the lock lift and the door is flung open. There's a shout from a solider: 'Enta fi sig'n Tora.' *Hurry up! Let's go!*

I stand, then pause. I wait for the dizziness to pass, then I will myself forwards. I shuffle towards the door, towards the voice.

A hand grips my upper arm. I am guided down the stairs and out of the truck. I look up. A large steel door stands before me and, alongside it, guards armed with machine guns.

I am led towards the door by the solider beside me.

Not knowing where I am, I ask: 'Ana feen?' *Where am I?*

The solider responds: 'Enta fi sig'n Tora.'

You are in Tora Prison.

Lamisse

Sunday 28 January 2018

Saja and I are curled up in my bed together. Despite this, Saja is still wearing a long-sleeved top, sweater, coat and a woollen scarf. Like most apartments in Cairo, mine has no heating. Harun is also rugged up and in his own bed – a mattress on the floor – gaming on his phone. Even though my housemates are currently out of town, Saja and Harun are both staying in my room.

I've got my first day of class today. This is why I came to Cairo in the first place: to study at the American University of Cairo. Even though I've been waiting for this day for six months, I don't think I'll go. I don't want to be away from Saja and Harun. I don't want to meet new people. I just want to stay in bed, watch Netflix and wait for news about Dad.

In the evening, Yacoub calls and abruptly announces: 'I don't know where Uncle Hazem is.'

As Yacoub starts to explain, I catch the eyes of Saja and Harun looking expectantly at me.

'He doesn't know where Dad is.' I spit the information at them like a dart from the mouth. Saja wells up with tears and Harun looks away, distressed. I turn my attention back to Yacoub.

He continues: 'My friend in security said Uncle Hazem is not at the airport anymore. He doesn't know where he went. No one is saying where he is.'

It hasn't been 48 hours yet. I insist to Yacoub that the Embassy said we were supposed to wait, and that if the Egyptian authorities made any decisions about what they were doing with Dad, then they were supposed to inform us.

'Apparently, that's the law,' I add assertively.

Yacoub laughs. 'This is Egypt, ya Lamisse!'

I get defensive. 'I don't know!'

Hearing my distress, Yacoub shifts gears into a more reassuring tone. 'Look, I have a friend in the police. I will ask to see if he knows if Uncle Hazem is in one of the police stations here. And you ask the Embassy if they know where Uncle Hazem is when you call them tomorrow.'

Agreeing that this is the best course of action, we end the call.

Saja and I are sitting beside each other on the edge of the bed. Harun is standing near us.

I speak hesitantly, distraught with uncertainty and disbelief. 'So, Dad's not at the airport … But before we panic, let's see what the Embassy says tomorrow …'

'What do you think could have happened to Dad?' asks Saja.

A quiet knowing rattles inside me as my throat closes up and I choke out: 'I don't know.'

Hazem

I am taken through the steel gate. Behind it is an iron door. It opens and the soldier escorts me through. I find myself inside a prison courtyard.

It's night, and I can only see the shadows of the buildings, highlighted by lamps on poles. There are some men standing nearby, talking loudly. Some are in uniform, others are not – they're prison guards and officers. The soldier hands me over to them.

A man in plain clothing shouts at me to take off my clothes.

I look down at my handcuffs.

Another guard walks over and uncuffs me.

I strip down to my underwear, humiliation flooding through me. But I remain quiet and compliant. The urge to fight has simmered down. My desire to run away has all but left. The only thing I have left is frozen shock and submission; I just have to do what they say. My body moves, but my mind has left me.

My clothes are piled on the ground, along with my shoes, socks, watch and glasses. I'd been wearing the same clothes since I got on the plane at Brisbane airport. I can see they're stained and dirty. In the middle of this open courtyard, standing in my underwear as shadows flicker on the walls around me, I feel exposed, vulnerable and cold.

I'm painfully aware of the eyes on me, watching.

One of the guards throws me some white hessian pants and a shirt, then one of the prison officers barks at me, asking what my full name is. He commands that I be taken to El-Eraad.

'Mabna wahid, beh zinzana alif!' he orders. *Building Number 1, Section B, Cell A!*

I'm escorted out of the courtyard and through a series of steel doors and corridors. Prisoners talk in their cells behind the doors in the corridors.

One passageway is particularly sinister; my skin prickles in the air of heavy silence. Realising they're the solitary confinement cells, I shudder.

Finally, we stop and stand in front of a cell door. The guard unlocks it and pushes me inside. The lock clicking shut sounds like forever.

I stand, paralysed. I keep thinking I need to wake up, but I know I'm not sleeping.

Once again, that smell – now becoming increasingly familiar – hits me. The stench of urine. This time, it's mixed with the muskiness of damp. I look around the cell. There are people gathered on each side, a small space between them. I wonder why they're sitting in two groups. My state of shock and spinning thoughts are interrupted by a voice that emerges from the right side of the room.

'Assalamu'alaykum.'

A young man approaches me, takes my hand and guides me around the people lying on the floor as he tells me to watch my step. He stops, then asks two men to make space for me between them so that I can sit down.

'Eta' zibt?" he asks. *Did they hurt you?*

'Eh?'

'Darabuk?' he replies. *Did you get hit?*

'Lah, lah. Mahadish darabni.' *No, no. I didn't get hit.*

He explains that the stripping is often accompanied by a beating, and that sometimes prisoners need cleaning up.

He goes on to explain the cell to me: El-Eraad is a holding centre and I'm in a cell for prisoners waiting to be processed. Political prisoners occupy the right side of the room, away from the toilet. The people with criminal charges are on the left, closer to the smelly, makeshift bathroom. I count around 34 men in the cell, split almost equally between criminal and political prisoners.

I want to thank the young man, but I am lost for words. The chatter around me sounds like a low mumbling hum, the words indecipherable to me in my distress. I look around slowly, trying to take it all in, and then I ask, 'Ana at'shaan, fe mya hena?' *I'm thirsty, do you have any water here?*

I am given a bottle of water. I can barely swallow as my throat is dry and blocked. When the water slides down, I begin to feel a little more coherent. I can understand the words around me.

Esmak eh? *What's your name?*

Enta mineen? *Where are you from?*

Amalty eh? *What did you do?*

Gabuk hena leh? *Why did they bring you here?*

In their voices I can hear a range of emotions: doubt, suspicion, fear, concern ...

I answer with short, abrupt sentences. I'm suspicious and deeply uncomfortable. I still don't understand where I am. Plus, after everything that's happened, I'm afraid of cameras and informants.

Someone hands me some biscuits, and I gratefully take them to eat. A fluorescent light hangs over us. Like in the airport cell, time loses meaning under the single shining bulb that never goes out.

'Ana ta'baan, eiz a'nam,' I announce to the people around me. *I'm tired. I want to sleep.* They move to make space for me and I lie down on the exposed, cold, concrete floor. I shut my eyes, but my mind spins and spins and spins. I desperately wish I had an on/off button. So, I meditate in my mind, diverting my attention to making Du'a. I repeat words of prayer to calm my racing thoughts and it gives me a feeling of peace inside.

Someone approaches me. With a sigh, I mutter, 'Sibni l'wahdy.' *Leave me alone.* Their presence retreats. Despite lying there, I can't fall asleep. There's a strange body in front of me, and one behind me, and another man at my feet. I can't stretch out my legs; I'm stuck on my side, legs curled in a semi-fetal position on the concrete.

I shuffle, trying – and failing – to get comfortable.

Lamisse

Monday 29 January 2018

The woman at the Embassy in Cairo is surprised that Dad had been taken from the airport without them being informed. After our phone call, she sends me an email that schedules me for a meeting with the Ambassador on the following day and includes links and attachments. A hyperlink directs me to more information about 'Dual Nationality'. There is an attachment of the Consular Services Charter, and a brochure entitled 'Arrested or Jailed Overseas' issued by the Department of Foreign Affairs (DFAT). There's also a list of English-speaking lawyers in Egypt, and she recommends that I get local legal advice. The list carries a disclaimer: DFAT neither endorses these lawyers nor accepts any responsibility for the quality of the work they offer. Lastly, the woman asks me to keep the Embassy posted on any updates.

I'm confused by the repeated requests for me to keep them updated – why don't they update me?

After a quick glance through the brochure and link, it is immediately apparent that the assistance offered is limited and discretionary. I read back over the information with more focus: if a dual citizen is arrested in a country in which they have citizenship, regardless of what other citizenship they hold, such a person will be treated as a citizen of the country in which they were arrested. In short, it doesn't matter how long Dad has lived in Australia. He's been arrested in Egypt, so he'll be treated as an Egyptian.

In my head, I keep hearing Suleiman's warning: 'Remember he's an Australian. Don't let them treat him like an Egyptian.'

What's strange is that I'm functioning on the assumption that Dad's been arrested, but technically, he's simply vanished. If it were not for Yacoub and his contacts, I would have no idea that Dad had even been taken by the National Security Services. It is the taking by the National Security Services that led us to assume that he's been arrested. But why? Did he do something illegal? The document explicitly states that if you've done something illegal, been a nuisance to the Embassy or behaved recklessly or negligently, then assistance will be even more limited. What counts as reckless or negligent? Was it reckless of Dad to arrive in Egypt on the anniversary of the revolution? Negligent of me not to double-check the dates?

The document named 'English-Speaking Lawyers in Egypt' consists of five pages of names and contact details. What kind of lawyer do I need? A criminal lawyer? A human rights lawyer? I don't even know where Dad is, let alone what he's been charged with.

I go back to the 'Arrested or Imprisoned Overseas' document again. Poring over the passages, I read how the Embassy can only act within the frameworks of local and international law: it cannot interfere in the legal proceedings of another country. It states that Consular assistance cannot override local law, even when local laws appear harsh by Australian standards. As such, there may be limitations as to what can be done. Then I read the sentence: *and you should have realistic expectations about this.*

I yell at my laptop: 'But what on earth is a realistic expectation in this kind of situation?' I can't believe a person can disappear and all the Embassy does is send you a couple of brochures.

In 2016, just two years prior, an Italian PhD student was found dead in a ditch by a highway after having been missing for several weeks. Guilio Regini's body bore signs of torture characteristic of Egypt's National Security Services. While many Egyptian people are harmed or killed by a government violently engaged in counter-revolution repression, Regini's death sparked international outrage, as it appeared that the current regime in Egypt was unafraid to silence critics from beyond its citizenry too. What if this has happened to Dad?

I'm overwhelmed; the English-speaking lawyers on the list from the Embassy are abstractions I don't have the energy to decipher. I want a recommendation. I need to talk to someone who knows.

I call my friend Drew. We've been friends for years, having met as volunteers in Palestine. He's been living in Egypt for about five years now. He's American and his wife, Salma, is Egyptian. Salma has the heady combination of being both street-smart and book-smart; she's witty and politically astute. While I call Drew for the emotional support, I know that it's Salma who'll have the answers.

As soon as I tell Drew what's happening, he understands the urgency of the situation without me needing to go into detail. 'Hang on,' he says and informs Salma. Straightaway, she takes the phone off him: 'Lamisse, I'll connect you to a lawyer.'

My shoulders loosen and I exhale.

Salma tells me he's a human rights lawyer and he's trustworthy. Then she adds, 'But he doesn't speak English, so you'll need someone to go with you.'

'If you're working with this lawyer already, then it makes me feel like I can trust him too,' I say.

After I hang up, Salma texts me the lawyer's details. Then I call Amgad, my cousin and Yacoub's older brother. Amgad phones the lawyer. The lawyer tells him that we need to act quickly and find out where Dad's been taken. In transmitting the message from the lawyer, I can hear the unspoken addendum in Amgad's tone: *before anything bad happens.*

We agree to meet the following morning outside a courthouse near the airport. Amgad says if Dad was arrested, someone at this particular courthouse may know about it. We're also going to file some paperwork officially requesting information on Dad's whereabouts.

When I update Saja and Harun about this plan, they offer to come with me. I tell them no. I don't want them to. I don't want to feel responsible for them. I don't know what's ahead and I don't want to bear the burden of exposing them to potential harm. If they stay home, then I know they're safe. That way, I can focus on what I need to do.

Hazem

I must have fallen asleep because I wake up in the morning around eight. It's the most rest I've had since the airport.

When I open my eyes, I'm flooded with horror as I remember where I am. It's like I'm hallucinating this prison reality. I try hard to hold it together.

Three young men approach me. One is holding a piece of cardboard. On the cardboard is a pile of beans and some Egyptian flatbread. They all greet me, then I'm passed the cardboard plate of beans and bread. My hunger rears its head and I don't think twice about the food. I cram it down, eager to silence my stomach. It's my first real meal in four days.

One of the young men stays with me while I eat. He explains who they are and how they run the cell.

There is someone who brings in food from the guards outside. Others are responsible for washing clothes, allocating space for sleeping and booking time for the toilet, showers and prayers. He then tells me there are communication rules between inmates, particularly between the two sides: those facing criminal charges and those facing political accusations.

The explanations help me begin to connect to the fact that this is not a hallucination, and this allows me to start accepting my new reality.

I randomly remember some mindfulness training I'd taken in Australia and offer some suggestions to the young man. I appreciate the information he's given me, but now I want to talk about something that's not the cell. My choice of topic tickles his curiosity. A couple of the other young men overhear us and join our conversation. They're impressed by my ability to fluently speak Arabic and English, and they ask a lot of questions about life in Australia. They ask me pointed questions about work and my career. Then, they inevitably ask me why I'm here. I tell them what happened at the airport. They share their stories of how they were taken to Tora: university protests, Facebook comments. I feel a sense of mutual support and understanding between us.

One of the young men introduces me to an older man. I estimate him to be in his sixties. He introduces himself as Ibrahim. He tells me he was a school principal before his arrest, and that around half the men in the cell are from the Muslim Brotherhood. He introduces me to the men, and I'm surprised to hear that they're from all over Egypt. Some are from Upper Egypt – cities like Minya, Assyiut and Bani Soueif. Others are from cities in the Nile Delta: Mansoura, Mahalla, Domiyat, Tanta, Ismalilia, Zagazig. A couple are from the North Coast – cities like Alexandria and Marsa Matrouh. The rest are from Cairo. It's a lot of names, people and places, and it's overwhelming. My tired brain is zapped from the effort of these introductions.

There's an announcement for noon prayer. The men line up in front of the toilet to do Wu'du. I line up with them. When it's my turn, I step into the so-called bathroom.

It's a dark space, but a bright light comes from the top of the makeshift roof. A stinking piece of black plastic hangs at the entrance, mocking the concept of a door. The damp walls have some kind of moss or algae creeping up them. There's a tap on the lower part of the wall and a hole in the ground. There's no toilet paper. No mirror. No towels. Beside the hole is a couple of old water bottles. The water bottles are meant to be used as a shatafa.

I do what I have to do as quickly as possible. When I exit, one of the young men hands me his spare towel. I thank him. He tells me that I can have it. This towel is my first prison possession.

After we pray, we sit back down. Everything around me sounds deafeningly loud. It's too much. I stop trying to decipher the loud talking but it's all we have to do in the cell. The men's voices blend into some out-of-tune orchestral noise as I withdraw into myself. People leave me alone; it seems they can sense I need space right now.

Later that evening, another man hands me what becomes my second possession: a blanket. I'm slowly accumulating the things I need to find some comfort in this cell.

I'm relieved that I won't have to sleep directly on the concrete again.

It's a particularly cold winter night and there's no heating. We lay out all the blankets we have. We sleep huddled together to keep warm.

Lamisse

Tuesday 30 January 2018

The cab crawls its way over the bridge. Bumper-to-bumper traffic turns a ten-minute drive into forty.

I'm on my way to the Embassy. It's been two days and we still haven't received any information about where Dad could be.

The Conrad Hilton comes into view, and I ask the cabbie to pull up on the side of the motorway. Beside the Hilton is an office tower, and inside that tower is the Embassy. I pay, get out of the cab and walk up to the entrance. Opening the heavy glass door, I encounter a security setup. I plop my bag on the conveyor belt and walk through the body scanner. Then I pick up my bag and head to the elevators.

The Australian Embassy is tucked away on the 11th floor. It's a discreet office with locked glass doors. I pick up a phone stuck to the wall and give my name to a security guard visible on the other side of the glass doors. He buzzes me in, takes my passport and writes down my details.

The disorienting reality of why I'm here disrupts the mundaneness of the office. I take a seat and wait. Magazines on the coffee table offer up pictures of koalas and rainforests.

An older Egyptian woman comes out to greet me and then walks with me to the Ambassador's office. With an air of maternal care, she asks me how I'm doing and says she's sorry to hear about what's happened with my father. Later, I would find out she was also working at the Embassy during Peter Greste's case.

Part of me is confused by the juxtaposition of her genuine empathy within a sterile bureaucratic space and I want to push back against her concern, lest it land and make me cry. Managing to find some words, I say, 'Thank you. It is quite a difficult situation.'

We arrive at the office. Before I go in, she asks me to put my phone in a pigeonhole, then she opens the door to a large corner office with a panoramic view of the Nile. I take a seat on a plush leather couch. Regardless of how many times I've seen the Nile from different viewing points, I'm always a little in awe. I take a few seconds to soak in the sight of the ambling muddy water stubbornly pushing through the congested city.

The Ambassador comes in. He's friendly and professional. After some small talk, we get into a discussion about Dad, and he reiterates some points from the documents they've sent me. Then he says the Embassy will be following up on the case by making requests to Egyptian officials, but they can't push for information. All they can do is follow protocol and wait for answers from the authorities.

Excruciating anxiety returns and begins to cloud my brain. I find myself struggling to concentrate as the meeting goes along. Though I'm physically present in the room, it feels like there's another Lamisse speaking to the Ambassador. The real me is in the fetal position in the corner, watching this other Lamisse take charge.

At that moment, I experienced this disassociation from myself without a second thought. The memory comes up now as a half-developed photograph, as though I only had one eye open. The open eye saw the Ambassador in front of me, watched my hand gesticulating as I listened to my own voice, loud and emphatic. The shut eye was turned inwards, gazing at the curled-up Lamisse in the corner.

When the meeting wraps up, I'm exhausted and relieved. I shake the Ambassador's hand and thank him for his time. He reminds me that I should keep the Embassy updated, and assures me he'll let me know if the Embassy receives any information on Dad's whereabouts.

Out of the meeting, I hold on to one message: it's up to me to find the answers. If I find answers, then I can tell the Embassy and maybe then they'll be able to find more answers. But, it seems, the answers must first come from me. The weight of responsibility holds my chest hostage. I cannot allow myself to breathe until I find Dad.

The Egyptian woman returns to escort me out. She gives me a quick hug, pats me on my back and tells me it'll be okay. Her warmth briefly slips under my numbing shield and I want her to keep hugging me so I can cry on her shoulder. But I pull back, hastily thank her, and leave.

Out on the street, I wave down another cab and direct it to the courthouse. I'm meeting Amgad and the lawyer. The meeting with the Ambassador went for over an hour so I'm running late. It's a half-hour ride to the courthouse, through the clogged artery of 6th October, Egypt's longest bridge.

When we arrive in front of the neoclassical sandstone courthouse, I step out of the cab and look around. Empty chip packets, chocolate wrappers and cigarette stubs confetti the street. I spot a man waving at me. He's wearing a suit with a shirt and a sweater vest and holding a briefcase. This must be my lawyer, Saleh. When I walk over, he smiles widely and introduces himself. We quickly max out my mediocre Arabic with some small talk then quietly wait for my cousin. Amgad arrives soon after; he greets us then chats with Saleh. Amgad and I are the same age, separated only by three months. Through my visits to Cairo, we've reconnected as adults and built a close relationship; he's warm, funny, kind and sensitive. Yet, Amgad hasn't had an easy life. He's struggles with addiction and I worry about him. At the same time, I rely on him for support.

A tap on the shoulder pulls me out of my fretting. 'Let's go,' Amgad says.

We step into the courthouse. A large, grey photocopy machine sits in the middle of the foyer. People jostle and yell as they tussle to get photocopies of their documents made. A man at a makeshift stand sells tea, coffee and snacks to the waiting visitors. There are no signs, computers, desks, receptionists or automated systems that'll spit out a number for you. *How is one supposed to know where to go?*

It wasn't that the courthouse was uniquely terrible; it simply lacked the *pretence* of order. While it felt silly to be suddenly attached to a fantasy of law and order, I wanted the place to look like the Embassy: a cold, reassuring representation of the bureaucratic illusion of efficiency. It wasn't that I thought Australia was particularly ordered or just, as truth be told I didn't have much faith in the law, either here or at home. Picking past the veneer of order in Australia often involves some combination of inhabiting a marginalised identity, the disruptive experience of trauma or engaging in sustained, critical intellectual effort. For me, it began with the traumas of coming of age during the so-called War on Terror, and the institutional distrust this embedded into my psyche.

Despite this, I still wanted to believe in what we euphemistically call 'the system'. In the foyer, the fantasy of justice or fairness as an outcome of law and order revealed itself as a myth. Without the visual representation of order, I could not be lulled into belief that the institutions would be just. My desperate wish to believe that finding Dad could happen by 'following the law' fizzled out into panic.

Expertly weaving through the crowd, Saleh doggedly approaches the stairs. Amgad turns, urging me to hurry up. Dutifully, I speed up and follow them.

As we move up the stairs to the higher floors, it gets quieter. We walk down a long, stained hallway and arrive at a wooden door. Saleh knocks, then lets himself in. Holding the door ajar, he speaks to someone Amgad and I cannot see. He steps back and says we can come in.

In stark contrast to the chaotic foyer and dank corridors, the office is light-filled, clean and neat. Saleh greets a man standing behind a desk. The man is wearing a well-fitted suit; his slicked-back dark hair frames a pudgy baby face that would be pleasant to look at, if not for the hard eyes currently summing us up. He is imposingly large and tall – about 6'4", I estimate. My eyes slide towards the chunky gold watch on his wrist. Studying it, I notice the skin on his hands is as fair and smooth as the skin on his face. I recall the chipped, split nails and leathery fingers of the people working at the street market near my home. Suddenly, I feel immensely self-conscious of my cousin's ripped jeans, the lawyer's polyester suit and my own plain cotton shirt. *We don't look rich or important enough*, I think. *He's not going to take us seriously.*

This is Egypt: class matters.

He gestures for us to sit. I don't catch his name, but his watch reminds me of a J. Cole song so, in my head, I decide to call him Mr Nice Watch. Giving nicknames to authority figures becomes a pattern that helps me manage the intimidation I feel. To my surprise, Mr Nice Watch smiles at us. His eyes crinkle upwards at the corners. For a moment, he seems warm – almost genuine.

Mr Nice Watch, Amgad and Saleh launch into a conversation. I can tell they're making small talk so I sit quietly, but it annoys me. This is no time for niceties and pleasantries; get to the point! But tea is brought out to us and while they chat and laugh, I become restless and irritated. I think, *Hurry up! We're not here to make friends!* Again, I steer myself to remember that I'm the clueless one. I need to be patient and let Amgad and Saleh do their thing.

So, I shift my mind to another track: positive thoughts. *Maybe he's actually nice*, I tell myself. *Maybe this conversation is good. Maybe it'll lead us to Dad. Maybe he'll help us.* With these thoughts circulating, I start to hope.

I want to believe in these authorities *so* badly.

I want to believe that there's a process, regardless of whether I can see it or not. After all, we're already in it, right?

Whenever I hear my name or Dad's name mentioned, I smile and nod like I know what's going on. Surely I look silly when I do this, but I don't want to be rendered invisible by my muteness. I want them to remember that the person they're talking about is me, and the father they're discussing is mine.

The conversation drags on and I dissolve back into frustration; I'm bored and growing impatient. To distract myself, I dig my nails into my palm. I fight the urge to bang my fist on the desk and yell at Mr Nice Watch: *I demand answers! Where is my father?*

Finally, Amgad and Saleh stand up. Amgad motions at me to stand up too. I get up. It's over. We're leaving. Mr Nice Watch leans over the desk and extends his hand. While I want to believe the reassurances he offers me as he shakes my hand and smiles, a quote from my father pops into my head: 'Just because the lion bares its teeth, doesn't mean he is smiling.'

We leave the room and head back down the hallway to the stairs. I ask Amgad to translate the conversation and he answers with one devastating sentence: 'He says he doesn't know where Uncle Hazem is.'

'You talked that whole time and he doesn't even know where Dad is?' Dejection seeps into my tone.

Ignoring my visible disappointment, Amgad says firmly: 'It's complicated. He said we should check the police station and the airport. If we still can't find Uncle Hazem, we can come back to him in a few days.'

Gripped with all-consuming urgency, I reply, 'Let's go now then. Let's check the police station and airport today.'

But Amgad says we won't have time to do both. He suggests we try the nearby police station, which is a ten-minute walk away. Men arrested at the airport are often sent there, he adds.

It's now the afternoon; the winter sun streams across an empty, blue sky. We cross the busy main road, then wind through suburban streets lined with modest apartment blocks. I think through the tiny piece of information I've gleaned: retrace the possible steps security may have taken, then return to the courthouse. Start with the police station, then the airport.

Hazem

Sitting on a concrete floor is uncomfortable, let alone sleeping on one.

I miss my bed. I miss having a pillow. I even miss being able to sit on a chair.

This afternoon, I saw a man fill a plastic bag with warm water and use it as a heat pack. When I take my nap, I wonder if I can use this makeshift heat pack as a pillow by wrapping my towel around it.

I do it and it works.

The space I've been allocated as my own is a total of about sixty centimetres. These sixty centimetres are the entirety of my personal space.

The men I sleep between are Ahmed and Mustafa. They're both in their forties, married with children. Ahmed is a science teacher, and Mustafa used to work at the Ministry of Awqaf. Awqaf translates roughly to endowments, and the Awqaf is mostly responsible for overseeing the management of mosques. Both men are from Assyut, a city in the south of Egypt. Assyut is a famous Coptic city, and it's close to the village where my mother grew up. Ahmed and Mustafa had been collecting money to support the families of imprisoned men in the community – some of whom were men who belonged to the Muslim Brotherhood. This charitable act was technically illegal; collecting money for the families of imprisoned people is considered providing financial aid for a terrorist organisation. As such, they were arrested.

I enjoy their company. They are both quiet, sincere men and we talk often about our families together. Being separated from our loved ones is unbearable, but we can't help talking about it. Food and family are the most common topics between all the imprisoned men because we are all hungry and lonely.

We develop a kind of friendship between us three. Our little group is later joined by a man from El Qoseir, a small coastal city by the Red Sea. We call him by his town. He had been a maths teacher with a reputable social standing among the people of his city. El Qoseir was openly devastated at his imprisonment. While he mirrors our own devastation, we aren't as free with our emotions. His bright, black eyes often fill with tears and he almost always talks about his daughter, visibly distressed at being separated from his family. He was arrested because he was discovered to be financially helping some of his students … and the students he helped all had fathers who had been imprisoned or disappeared.

Being together in our suffering helps me feel less alone. I think that's why we share so much, why we came together as a group. We are family men; we've had average lives teaching, working and doing what we can to provide for our families and support people in our communities. Now, we are here, separated from all that has given us purpose, from all that has made our lives meaningful.

Later that evening, one of the young men urges me to write a letter.

'Akhooya gayy bokra, ana momken adeeh risala. Limiratak aw bentak.' *My brother is coming tomorrow; I can give it to him. He can message your wife, or your daughter.*

Turns out, prisoners who have been in this cell for more than a month are allowed visitors. My cellmate's brother is not only coming to visit, but he's bringing with him food and other supplies.

The young man hands me a pen and paper and I begin to write. I finish the letter. I go to write my wife's phone number on the top of the page.

My brain is empty. I can't remember her number.

For the rest of the evening, I try to remember. Numbers rise up in no particular order so I shut my eyes and concentrate, trying to see the numbers in my mind's eye as though they are on the phone screen.

It works. I scribble down Evelyn's number, relieved, and hand the letter to the young man.

Lamisse

The police station is surrounded by a wire fence. It's guarded by men in uniforms, their guns pointed at the entrance. We walk past the pointed guns and down a crumbling concrete path into a dark and sparsely furnished building. Blades of light slice through dust hanging in the air, illuminating smears on the unwashed windows.

We climb more stairs till we reach one of the upper floors. In my overwhelmed daze, I lose track of which floor we end up on. A bunch of men hang around the hallway. They're all plain-clothes cops.

Again, I'm trailing Saleh and Amgad, lost in my thoughts. Saleh approaches the men to ask for the head of the police station while Amgad hangs back with me. He translates the answer: 'The head of the station isn't available right now but he's going to return soon.'

We are taken to a room where we can wait. It's furnished with an aged brown leather sofa, several dark-stained wood desks and high-backed black office chairs. The blinds are drawn. Where the window is visible, so is a thick layer of grime across the glass. Cigarette smoke laces the stagnant air. I take a seat on the couch while Amgad and Saleh pull up chairs next to our escort of four cops. I stare at the floor, but I can feel eyes on me. To avoid any possibility of eye contact, I don't dare look up to interpret their gaze. I feel out of place and in danger.

Someone brings sweet black tea. Amgad and Saleh pull out their cigarettes and smoke in between sips, chatting with the cops. I don't reach for the tea; I need to become as small and invisible as possible and any movement will draw attention.

Two hours pass.

Fear dissolves into boredom and rumbling hunger. Relenting, I sip cold tea and wonder if Egyptians are good at small talk because so much of their lives is spent waiting for someone to arrive.

Another half hour passes, then the head of the police station strides in, his demeanour openly hostile. His shoulders are hunched, arms firm and straight at his sides. The taut stillness on his face holds the promise of snapping at any moment. He sits behind the desk stationed in the middle of the room. Amgad and Saleh get up, pull their chairs over to his desk, then sit back down. The head of police lights a cigarette and smokes it in quick, short puffs. My boredom flees; roaring fear returns.

I stay stiffly perched on the couch. Amgad and Saleh are just out of my earshot. Embracing the sense of helplessness that not speaking Arabic is giving me in these circumstances, I don't move. It makes no difference whether I can hear them or not.

In my mind, I run back over our day: we've visited a courthouse and a police station, but in physical terms, all I've done is sit, wait and walk. I've done very little, but the emotional toll from being trapped in my own splintering, anxious mind has made this day feel exhausting.

The men rise. They shake hands. I walk over to stand with Amgad and Saleh, then shake the hand of the head of police. The gesture is brief, his grip is limp and our eyes don't meet. The three of us leave the office and find our way back out into the bright, clear winter day. No one speaks.

We're close to passing the gun-wielding guards at the entrance when I can't hold it in anymore: 'So, what did he say?'

Amgad replies, 'Uncle Hazem isn't there. He is not at this police station, and he said he doesn't know where he is.'

My heart sinks. 'So, all that time and he also doesn't know anything …'

Amgad says we'll go to the airport tomorrow to see if Dad is still there or if someone knows where he went. I want to go now, but Amgad isn't keen. It's too late, he points out. It's approaching evening time. The day is over.

Despite the logic of his statement, I want to throw a tantrum, to throw myself onto the road, kicking and screaming, *'But I want to go to the airport now!'* Instead, I say my goodbyes to Saleh and Amgad.

I walk to the main road to find a cab. I've got nothing to tell Saja and Harun. I've got nothing to tell my distressed mother. It's the first time today I've thought of my poor mum, stuck in Brisbane and unable to do anything about her missing husband. She's relying on me to find him, yet I'm so useless. Without Amgad and Saleh, I couldn't have done any of this myself.

What must my dad be thinking? Does he believe we'll be able to find him? Is he even alive enough to be able to have such hope?

Lamisse

Wednesday 31 January 2018

The following morning, at around 11 am, I meet Amgad and Saleh outside the arrivals terminal. Usually, I love arriving at an airport: suspended spaces of promise; a people-watcher's heaven. Under the shadow of Dad's disappearance, all the appeal is lost. All that matters is that this was the last place my father was seen.

As we make our way through the airport, I wonder: *What happened here? What did they do to him? Where did he go?*

We walk outside and into a carpark, where Saleh guides us to an elevator that takes us to a basement. When the elevator doors spring open, I feel dizziness and nausea. Either there's bad energy in this place or it's my anxiety. Someone once advised me to not confuse anxiety for intuition; so, it's probably both.

We thread our way through darkened corridors and everything becomes a blur of shadows, hallways and doors as I trudge behind Saleh and Amgad. We arrive at a door.

I don't remember what this door looked like, but I remember something else: a steel door at the end of the corridor.

I wonder, *What's behind that?*

Saleh opens the door. Amgad follows him into the room, and I trail in last. There's a man with blue eyes seated behind a desk. The wall to his left is adorned with a gold calligraphic quote from the Quran in a black plastic frame. A vase of fake flowers is perched on a filing cabinet, the colours dull under a coating of dust. Above the flowers is a picture of a bird. The man behind the desk has the same trained impassivity as the head of the police, but without the thinly veiled threat of volatility; instead, he projects a quiet, self-assured power. I find this more frightening.

As the discussion proceeds, instead of staring at the ground, I decide to stare at this man. Should cracks appear in his seemingly impenetrable face – a flicker that might suggest a lie or a truth – I want to spot it. I gather up all my energy to concentrate on one question: *Where is my dad?* I hope that this demand is clear in my unwavering eyes. Whatever agency I can muster, I want to grasp it, no matter how delusional it may seem.

My eyes start to feel dry and cold, and I realise I haven't blinked in a while. I shut my eyes and open them again, then resume my staring. If I can't understand words, perhaps I can learn to understand the bodies and the faces that create them.

Amgad leans over and whispers in my ear. 'I think he knows. I think he's covering up.'

For the first time, I have confirmation of something I've suspected: that there is a withholding of information about Dad's whereabouts – deliberate obstruction even. While I believe the cop truly didn't know, my hunch is that Mr Nice Watch possibly did. And now, it seems that this man could know, but isn't telling.

Then again, if Dad has been unlawfully taken, why would they admit it? Though I know this state disappears people, the reality is that we're powerless to do anything about it. In view of our powerlessness, why wouldn't the state maintain denial and impunity?

The knowledge that my father has been disappeared lands heavily on me.

My god, this just became so real.

The conversation comes to a close. Amgad and Saleh stand, ready to leave, but I don't get out of my chair. I stay sitting, staring at the man.

Hysteria rises inside me, bubbling out.

'No. I'm not going. Tell him to tell me where my dad is.' I pause, struggling to contain myself. 'Tell him he has to tell us!'

From the corner of my eye, I can see that Saleh and Amgad are aghast that I've gone off script. My gaze is locked on this man. After ignoring my stare for the whole meeting, he finally turns and looks at me. I swear I can see pity and I'm not sure whether it's empathetic or patronising, though it would make more sense for it to be the latter. Tears start burning at the edges of my eyes, so I lurch to my feet and storm out of the room. No polite goodbyes, handshakes or sycophantic thank-yous.

I feel as though I'm about to start hyperventilating. I want to scream. Instead, I lean against the wall of the corridor and try to take deep breaths, desperately craving a cigarette.

The instant he emerges from the office, Saleh begins berating me. Amgad lets him finish his scolding, then translates it into one short, commanding sentence: 'You can't do that.'

Enraged by the reprimand, I also don't want to alienate the two people here to help me. My anger collapses into defeat. 'I'm sorry,' I say, forlorn. Saleh nods, satisfied with my apology.

We retrace our footsteps until we arrive at the airport carpark. As soon as we're outside, I light a cigarette and take a deep inhale.

'What now?' I ask Amgad as I exhale.

'We go back to the courthouse,' he says.

It's a short ride from the airport to the courthouse. When we arrive at Mr Nice Watch's office, he greets us with irritation. There's no tea, no small talk and no reassurances. Within a few minutes, he's sent us back out with a new instruction. Amgad and Saleh begin discussing between them. Both ignore my repeated question, 'What's going on?', so I shut up, stand aside and wait for them to finish.

With the tired attitude of an over-stretched parent, Amgad turns to me: 'We think he is also covering up. He clearly didn't think we'd be back so soon, which is why he was annoyed. So, we're going to file a request with the Prosecutor-General in Abbasiya.'

*

Abbasiya, the old administrative centre of Cairo, is filled with government buildings, offices and courthouses. Soon it will all be made defunct. The current president is building a new capital city: inspiringly called the New Administrative Capital, or NAC.

We leave the courthouse and head towards the micro-buses: an informal network of vans repurposed as public transport. We find the one heading to Abassiya. Saleh squeezes into the back seat, while Amgad sits beside me in the middle row.

Micro-buses don't have a schedule; they leave when they're full. So, while we sit and wait, I take this moment to check in with myself.

My first thought: Dad is dead; that's why they're covering up.

I fold forwards, cover my face with my hands and burst into loud sobs. Panicked, Amgad pats me urgently. 'Stop crying, Lamisse,' I hear him say. 'Please, stop crying. Not here. It's not appropriate. Please, Lamisse, you have to stop!'

But I keep crying. I'm scared. *What if Dad has been killed? Will I have to identify the body? Will he have torture wounds? Will I have to tell my mother that her husband, our father, is dead? What will happen to my family, to my siblings, if he is? Why is this happening to us?* I don't understand. This feels so big and petrifying. I don't even know what I'm doing; I'm just blindly following my cousin and lawyer around from building to building while they do all the talking.

The urgency in Amgad's voice intensifies and I gulp. Swallowing the shudders, I start to pull myself out of my distress, feeling guilty for stressing him out. What must this be like for him? He's tasked with guiding his naïve Australian cousin through the very bureaucracy that all Egyptians dread dealing with. He's already traumatised by the state; he doesn't need this trauma too.

A lady sitting in the back seat quietly passes me a tissue. 'Shukran,' I say, and wipe my nose.

The bus takes off.

I stare out the window, watching the browns and yellows of the city wash by. We pull up to another courthouse. A fresh skin of apathy has grown over me. I look up at the building, thinking, *What's the point?*

We enter yet another hazy maze of rotting bureaucracy. Grimy granite, paint peeling off the walls, dust hanging in the stale air, as the now familiar knives of light cut through the shadows. Behind the desks are stacks and stacks of paper. Staff pull out heavy books; with deft hand movements, they turn the fragile pages of dog-eared files. Their fingers run down penned margins, looking for names and locations of files. Entire lives are reduced to these sheets of decaying paper, yet somehow this decomposing beast of bureaucracy still functions. We wander from desk to desk – asking, waiting, receiving directions to a new section, a new desk, a new clammy file – and finding no answers.

Back at the entrance, we all light our cigarettes. Amgad breaks the heavy silence: 'Saleh says we need to come back another day. We're too late to sort anything out today.'

'Okay,' I say. 'Thank you for all the work you've done today.' I walk off, leaving the two of them talking and smoking outside the gates of the administrative building.

Bitterness climbs up my throat, tightening the hinges of my jaw. My mouth sets in a sullen, tense line. I find a cab and join the evening traffic crawl towards home.

Lamisse

Thursday 1 February 2018

It's been five days since Dad went missing.

We're going back to the Prosecutor-General's office in Abbasiya. We're going to file the formal request for information. Saja and Harun are coming too. Having now seen what this 'search' entails, I know the worst thing they'll experience is tedious waits.

Amgad and Saleh meet us outside the administrative building. As the five of us walk through the corridors with their peeling paint, our shoes create an echoing tap on the granite floors. 'Ba'd izznik,' we say softly each time we squeeze past other waiting people.

When we arrive at a wooden door, my heartbeat quickens. Saleh knocks, then enters the office, shutting the door behind him.

Outside, we wait, each in our own way. Saja's already large eyes seem to take up her entire heart-shaped face as she absorbs our surroundings and the passing procession of people. Harun, stoic and quiet, keeps his eyes downcast, taking only furtive glances at passers-by.

Saleh re-emerges.

Amgad informs us, 'Saleh gave in the paperwork. Now, we just have to wait for them to give us an answer.'

With that, we're back on the main street.

The slippery, fragile hope I held in these processes is gone. To cope, my cynicism creeps in as I struggle to reconcile the severity of the situation with the absurdity of this 'search': just knock on a bunch of doors, file some papers then go home to your cat.

Waiting to find out what's happened to Dad feels like waiting for a punch to land. I want someone to hit me, to just tell me the truth.

I ask Amgad if Dad could have been taken as part of an indiscriminate sweep of arrests, simply because he'd arrived in Cairo on the anniversary of the 2011 revolution. The thought has been in my mind since speaking with a friend who'd been involved in the revolution. He reminded me about the current regime's paranoia over possible future uprisings, and how they counter the perceived (and real) possibility of uprisings with disappearances and arbitrary arrests. Such tactics work to instil collective fear.

As I articulate this to Amgad, a part of me still believes it to be too far-fetched that some guy from Australia arriving to meet his kids in Cairo would be deemed suspicious.

'Sure, it's possible,' he casually answers.

Hazem

2 February 2018

It's my 54th birthday.

Last year, my family celebrated my birthday with a cake and cards. I reminisce on the sweetness of the memories, images of my mother, my wife and my kids floating in my mind's eye. I can hear their voices, feel their presence. They haven't left me; I carry them with me everywhere I go – even in here.

The cell door opens and one of the Shaweesh calls on all those inmates who haven't yet had their heads or beards shaved off, or had their mugshots taken.

When he calls my name, I leap up. In this moment, I can't care less about what lies ahead. It's an opportunity to leave the cell!

I walk out for the first time since arriving at Tora – we aren't allocated any outdoor time while we're being processed, though apparently that changes once we're moved on.

I pass through a corridor with three cells, all filled with people making a lot of noise. I reach a steel gate. To the right, I can see sunlight. There's a long corridor where prisoners are walking up and down. I leave the guard behind and join them in their pilgrimage up and down this narrow corridor, boxed in by wire and steel bars. To walk, oh to walk! It's such an exhilarating feeling to stretch my legs, to have more than sixty centimetres of space to move within. Above us, the sun shines weakly through the mesh, but it's still special to feel its rays. I look up and see the sky.

A man appears with his shaver. The prisoners begin lining up in preparation. The Shaweesh – who up until this point had let me go on with my walking – yells for me to join the line. I'm roughly shorn like a sheep. My hair and beard fall to the floor.

Despite the humiliation, I take in the scents of the outside world coming through the mesh; it's polluted fresh air, mingled as it always is in Cairo with smog and dust, but it's still fresher than the stale air in our cell. I'm marched on to another steel gate. Then, I'm ordered to carry a piece of cardboard with my prison number written on it. I hold it up and stand against a wall. My photo is taken.

With the click of the camera, it's official: I'm a political prisoner of Tora Prison. I make a note to refuse to memorise my prison number. Little did I know that I'd end up being here long enough that it would sear itself into my mind anyway.

After my photo is taken, my joy numbs into disbelief. My body feels frozen again. All the noise around me fades. To pull myself away from the inward spiral, I turn to the man beside me.

'Ezzayak?' *How are you?* I ask him with an air of joviality.

He looks at me blankly and doesn't respond. So, I turn to another man near me. He's an older man with a friendly face.

'Ezzayak, ba'alak ady'eh hena?' *Hi, how are you? How long have you been here?*

We have a short conversation that I don't remember, but at the time it is enough to bring me back to the present and out of my spiralling thoughts. But I never see that man again.

I'm called back to the cell. At knowing that I must return, my legs turn to lead. So, I procrastinate by chatting and milling about with some of the other prisoners who are still taking their daily walk. The Shaweesh yells at me. I turn and start walking down the corridor, dragging my feet, dreading being back in the cell with no escape and no outdoor time. Just 24/7 in that 5 x 8 metre space with forty other men, curling up into my allocated 60 centimetre space of concrete.

With impatience, the Shaweesh strides over to me and grabs my arm, pulling me and yelling at me to walk faster with him back to the cell. I have to comply, and my legs duly respond.

At least I got to see some sun for my birthday.

Lamisse

2 February 2018

It's six days since Dad went missing and none of us have mentioned that today is his birthday.

Meanwhile, Facebook reminds me of all the times I've made birthday posts for him.

I can hardly bear it.

Saja has gone out with some new friends. She's found an affinity to life in Cairo, adapting quickly, and willingly, to its rhythms and challenges. By contrast, Harun is now even warier of life in Cairo. Dad's disappearance has confirmed to him that Egypt is a dangerous, unappealing place, and he's more than ready to go back to Australia.

As it's just me and Harun at home today, I suggest a trip to Wadi Degla. The expanse of a desert ravine and relatively fresh air might help ease the tension that's weighing heavily on us both.

A welcoming archway frames the entrance to the wadi and a pathway leads us into a craggy valley of brown, yellow and orange rocks. A single tree, spiked and sparse, pushes up through the dry earth. The two of us take a long walk, discussing life and having a laugh. Then, inevitably, the conversation turns back to wondering what's happened to Dad.

'Why don't we find a hidden place and just scream?' I suddenly suggest to Harun.

'What do you mean?'

'Let's let it all out. There are hardly any people here; we can find a spot and just scream. We can get it out of us.'

My brother raises an eyebrow in interest. 'All right, let's do it.'

Moving at a faster pace, we scan the rocks on either side, looking for cracks we can climb through.

'There!' I point to a natural corridor that's formed between some rocks and break into a run. We scramble up, then carefully edge around the boulders of the fissure. We reach a clearing. There's graffiti and the burnt-out pit of a fire, but it seems like we're the only ones here at this moment.

I look at Harun. 'You ready?'

'You go first.'

I clench my fists and open my mouth wide.

'AAAAAAAAAAHHHHHHHGGGGGGGGGHHHHHHHHHHH!' I scream until I run out of breath.

'Whoa!' Harun looks surprised.

I laugh, then urge him to try it.

'AAAAAAAAAAAAAAGGGGGGGGHHHHHHHHHHHHHHHH!'

Over his scream, I layer my voice: 'FUUUUUUUCCCCCKKKKKKKKK!'

Taking another deep breath, Harun screams with me: 'FUUUUUUUUUUUCCCKKKKK!'

My next scream is too high-pitched and my voice breaks.

Harun winces. 'Ooh, that one hurt my ears.'

'Mine too,' I say, then hand him my phone. 'Take a picture.'

I scream, he takes a photo. He screams, I take a photo.

Sitting with my back against the rock wall, I text the photos to Mum: 'Harun and I letting our anger out.'

I glance up. Harun has climbed onto one of the boulders and is gazing into the depths of the rift.

'This is so messed up,' he says.

Hazem

I want to make more of an effort to familiarise myself with my situation. So far, I've been actively rejecting having to learn anything about the prison beyond what I'm told. But it's becoming more of a reality that I could be here for a while …

There's a couple of people who have been given space to sit by the cell door. They are the guys who let the food in. Every now and then, some people are called out of the cell to see the Mabahiz.

Tora Prison is officially managed by a prison warden, the Mā'moor. The Mā'moor commands the conscript soldiers in the prison – they're the Shaweesh. After the Mā'moor, there is the Mabahiz. The Mabahiz is linked to National Security Services and has a significant amount of authority and power within the prison. Meanwhile, the Mabahiz commands a group of prison guards called the Mokhber. In every cell, there are informants. They're prisoners who work as the eyes and ears of National Security Services, and they feed information to the Mabahiz. The National Security Services are deeply feared by all.

The prisoners explain to me that most political prisoners, if they're in the process of being investigated, are sent to Tora Tahqiq. Tahqiq simply means investigations – it's the equivalent of remand detention.

I figure that I'll probably be sent there if I don't get out soon. Every 15 days, I will be presented to a prosecutor, who will then decide whether I should stay here or not. His decisions are apparently based on evidence. I can't see how they would continue to keep me here. Surely, this has been a mistake. I'm supposed to have another hearing on 10 February. I rehearse what I'll say to the prosecution in my head.

The fact that no one knows I'm here haunts me. No one has shown up to the prison to visit me yet, not even a lawyer.

I hope my letter will reach my wife, Evelyn.

Lamisse

Saturday 3 February 2018

It's been seven days since Dad went missing.

When someone is missing, time becomes a slow blade drawn through your skin. It's a stretched-out wounding: you find yourself thinking you'd rather go through an amputation than have to deal with the pain of the steady, measured slice of unanswered time. I'm so desperate to know what's happened to Dad that I start to convince myself I'm ready for the news that he's dead. *Let us know*, I silently beg the universe. *Let us be shattered so we can deal and perhaps, eventually, heal.*

We've all got our maladaptive coping strategies and it's causing a lot of tension between the three of us: I want to hide, Harun wants to eat, Saja wants to run.

Harun and I argue over who's going to get breakfast. I want to stay in bed and Harun refuses to go shopping by himself. Saja breaks the stalemate by announcing that she'll go to the market for us instead.

She returns with fruit, cheese and bread, and pride.

'I feel so good being able to do this by myself! I think I could even live here.'

I appreciate the fact she's still finding love for Cairo, and I wish she could live here too. But I'm not so sure that's going to be possible for any of us anymore. Even if we do find Dad, how would we ever forget this?

Saja and Harun are leaving tomorrow. I don't want them to go; I don't want to be left alone, but I don't tell them this.

After breakfast, we listlessly mill about the apartment. Saja leaves to meet up with her new friends and once again, it's just Harun and me. I'm sad he's had such a terrible time and I want to carve out a pleasant memory for him, for us. When I suggest that we head down to the Nile to take a felucca ride, Harun is interested. I call Saja and we arrange to meet outside the Four Seasons Hotel by the Nile, then head down to the river to hire a sailboat.

On the way to the hotel, we pick up some McDonald's because Harun is hungry. In the cab, my phone vibrates: a text from Mum. It'd be around three in the morning in Brisbane. When I read that she's unable to sleep from the anxiety of not knowing where Dad is, I quickly respond. Then her texts start pouring in, a rapid fire of unanswerable questions. My panic rising, I reply as fast as I can, trying to calm Mum – and myself.

Harun elbows me. 'Lamisse! The cab driver is talking to you.'

The driver's asking where we want to stop. I look out the window and see the Four Seasons Hotel. 'Hena! Hena kwayis!'

In a flash, the driver swings the steering wheel and pulls up at the kerb. We're on a main road and cars are flying past us. Hastily, I thrust money at him and we jump out.

My phone is still buzzing. It's stressing me out. I have nothing to offer Mum. No reassurance or answers. I try to take a calming breath and return to the present: we're taking a felucca and I've got to remember where to go.

'Did you get the food?' Harun looks down at my hands and I follow his gaze. I'm holding a large Coke and my phone. I look at his hands. He's holding a Coke too. Neither of us are holding the brown paper bag with the big 'M' on it.

'Fuck. I left it in the cab.'

'But I'm so hungry.'

'I'm sorry, Harun.'

'Can Saja pick some more up for us?'

'It's too complicated for me to give Saja those instructions.'

He looks close to tears. 'You know, this hasn't been a good holiday.'

I don't have anything comforting to offer him either. My phone buzzes yet again, and I find myself blaming Mum. If she hadn't distracted me with her panic, then we'd have been able to capture a small moment of mindless pleasure, enjoying our Big Macs as the sun set over the Nile. Neither of us particularly love McDonald's, but it's nostalgic – a childish comfort food.

In glum silence, we wait for Saja to arrive. I text Mum to tell her that I'll speak to her in an hour if she's still awake. She gets the hint and backs off. Finally, my phone is still.

Saja is beaming when she arrives: she's gathered some survival Arabic and has just taken her first cab alone. Our cloudy mood doesn't stand a chance against her enthusiasm.

We pick our way down stone stairs to where some elderly men are hanging by the water's edge. One of them agrees to take us on his felucca. Once we're aboard, he adjusts the sails, then positions himself at the back of the boat, kneeling at the keel as he guides us out onto the river. The sun is starting to hang low, casting a warm glow across the water. The light reflects off the buildings that line the bank like crooked teeth. Onwards we sail, past old aristocratic properties and small mansions enfolded in greenery. For this moment, stress and fear are stripped from us and we are just three dumb diaspora kids appreciating a boat ride on the Nile.

Each of us is silent, lost in awe and self-reflection. I skim my hands across the top of the water. Countless times I've heard, 'Once you drink from the Nile, you always return.' Despite it all, I can't imagine not being able to come back to Egypt.

When we glide back to the jetty, it's almost night-time. The city takes on a different smell at night. By day, the air is heavy: dust is driven up by the cars, smog sticks in your nose and leaves a film of grime upon your skin. In the crisp, cool evening air, the heaviness begins to dissipate. By 3 am, the city is almost entirely still; people are asleep and the streets are unclogged. The air feels sharper and lighter, like the city can at last exhale, clearing its deteriorating lungs.

Once we reach the main road, I check my phone. There is a stack of text messages from Mum, along with several missed calls. My stomach lurches. Damn, is she still panicking?

The most recent message, hovering at the top of the list of green WhatsApp symbols says 'CALL ME' in capital letters. Before I call, I check the rest of Mum's messages and see that she's texted me an image.

I click to open it: it's a photo of a handwritten letter. The handwriting unmistakably belongs to Dad. My heart stops and thunders at once.

All my awareness channels into this image on my phone. I zoom in:

I'm in Tora.
… Help me.
Tell the Embassy …

Dad's pleading letter is filled with fear and confusion.

I look up at Saja and Harun. My eyes feel like they can't stretch any further; they're the widest and wildest they've ever felt. When I try to speak, my voice catches in my throat.

'It's Dad,' I choke. 'He's … he's in Tora. He's in prison!'

Saja starts crying and Harun stares back at me, stunned and silent.

I call Mum. She answers with a breathless, 'Hello?'

'Mum! Mum! Oh my god, Mum! What is this? What's going on? How did you get this?'

Her words come out in bursts: 'I got the message just now. I was praying and praying so much for your dad because it's the time for tahajjud. Then I got this message! Literally right after I was finished praying! It's from the brother of someone in the prison, someone in the prison with your dad. He's there. He's there in prison … God heard my prayers …'

Her voice fades into the distance as a scream rips out of me. It doesn't sound like my voice, but it is coming from deep inside my belly. My phone falls away from my ear and I grab onto the brick pylon by the stairs to steady myself. All I can do is scream and cry. Wadi Degla is nothing compared to the compartmentalised bucket of repressed fear and tension that is exploding open right now.

A part of my mind remains aware that my mother is still on the phone that is dangling in my hand. I put it back to my ear. I'm still hysterical but I can create some words: 'He's alive. Oh, thank god, Dad is alive.'

Mum sniffles and tries to offer some comforting words, but we're both too emotional to hold a conversation. After hanging up, I pull Saja and Harun towards me. We huddle around each other. Saja and I are crying. I can feel the tension in Harun's body, and it's like I am still holding onto the brick pylon. I don't know if he's talking to us or himself, but he keeps repeating the same words, 'I'm in shock. I'm just in shock.'

We grapple with a tide of conflicting emotions: relief to know Dad is alive and the horror that he's in prison. As we dwell on the latter, relief starts disintegrating into disbelief.

*

From: LAMISSE HAMOUDA
Sent: Sunday 4 February 2018 10:37 AM
To: AUSTRALIAN EMBASSY IN CAIRO
Subject: Update

Hi,

How are you?

Yesterday, we were contacted by a man whose brother passed on a letter from my father from prison. I can verify it is from my father because it is his handwriting. The letter states that he is in Tora, and that he was sentenced to 15 days' jail and will see the State Prosecutor on the 10th of Feb. His prison number is 61404679300. I have attached an excerpt from the letter.

We also filed the paperwork last week. I have attached the WhatsApp message my lawyer sent regarding the name of the document we filed (it's in Arabic).

Please let me know what our next step is. I have been told that it is possible for prisoners in Tora to receive visitors, and if so – I would like to visit my father.

> Also, my sister and brother leave tomorrow for Australia – I had spoken to the Ambassador about my concerns for their safety going through the airport …
>
> If you could give me a call today to discuss all this, that would be fantastic.
>
> Warm regards,
>
> Lamisse

There was a number scrawled on the top of the letter Dad had smuggled out. Two years later, while reconstructing a timeline of events for this book, I went through all my emails. When I re-read this email to the Embassy, I realised it wasn't Dad's prison number.

It was my mother's phone number.

Lamisse

Monday 5 February 2018

Saja and Harun are flying out this afternoon, but we have enough time to share breakfast together. I decide to mask my dread with generosity and head down to the markets: fresh bread, fruits, eggs, basterma and cheese. I prepare a breakfast banquet on my balcony.

They're both excited to be returning home to step into the next stages of their young adult lives: Saja's first full-time job as a graphic designer, Harun's first year of university.

Over breakfast, we discuss our other siblings: our youngest brother, Kareem, has just started high school. Our sister, Jasmine, is pregnant with her second child, and the youngest sister of the family, Amira, has begun her nursing degree. My hope is that they all stay on track with building their lives, and that Dad's imprisonment doesn't derail them.

Turning to the situation at hand, we discuss how we're going to tackle it: Saja says she'll financially support Mum during Dad's absence, and Harun offers to defer university to work full-time to contribute too. Neither of us wants Harun to defer, so we settle on a simple arrangement: I'll look after Dad, Saja works and cares for Mum and Harun will go ahead with his studies. We try to act upbeat, all of us grasping at the hope that we'll be able to handle this situation together.

When we pull up to the airport, I fight back tears. As their boarding time approaches, I am progressively petrified of being left alone in Cairo. Once they land in Brisbane, they're going to be part of a tribe of six supporting each other, while I'll be in Cairo on my own. I want to ask one of them to stay and help me navigate this situation with Dad, to confess that I'm nowhere near as brave as I'm making myself out to be.

But I don't.

A couple of years later, as I reviewed this section of the book with Saja, she was genuinely surprised by the above confession and says: 'I thought you were actually okay. If you'd asked, I would have stayed.'

When I reminded her about the job she had been about to start, her face soured. 'Yeah, I was excited, but fuck that place,' she retorted. A mere three months after starting her job, she was sexually assaulted at an overseas conference and quit. She opened a case against the perpetrator. Though the perpetrator was an Australian, that the alleged event happened in another country meant the case could not continue through the Australian legal system; this loophole meant the case had to be dropped. From Dad to Saja, my eyes were being opened to the fraught ways the law applied to citizens overseas. In 2018, we had no idea that in two years' time, we'd be witnessing the government fail thousands of Australians stuck abroad during the pandemic. Between an assault, losing her job and Dad's imprisonment, Saja subsequently fell into a deep depression. During this time, Harun stepped up to take over the role we'd allocated to Saja. He dropped his studies and took a job at a local Coles factory. As Saja and I dwelled on these memories, we agreed that it had truly been the year from hell. Yet, when I waved them off on their flight back to Australia, none of us dreamed that any of this other stuff was coming their way.

I walk back to the airport carpark to find a cab. Just a week ago, I was in the airport basement with Amgad and Saleh. I remember the security man with blue eyes. Amgad was right: he knew.

It's an hour-long drive back to my flat in Dokki. When I get home, I crawl into bed and pull the covers over my head.

Hazem

7 February 2018

I'm taken to see the Supreme State National Security Prosecutor. I'm not ready: they had said 10 February. It's a long day. In the space of a few minutes, I'm sentenced to another 15 days. It's a traumatic day, a day I still struggle to speak or write about.

I go back to the processing cell in the holding centre, ruined.

Lamisse

My housemates are back. One of them sends me an annoyed text, reminding me I've missed yet another week of cleaning the bathroom, that the dishes have piled up and he assumes that they're all mine.

He's probably not wrong to assume that.

February has progressed into a disassociated fog; I avoid anything that'll bring me into the present. For some, cleaning is cathartic. For me, cleaning is a meditative act: a moment of psychological stillness as the body interacts with its immediate environment. I can't face inner stillness – a stillness that might lead me to face the fresh wound inside me – so I am always thinking of the next thing to distract me: it manifests as a need to move, move, move. I've started attending classes again, trying to hold on to my path as a student. I don't want to be the daughter of a prisoner, I want to be a student with a bright future ahead of her.

Dishes can wait. I've got a life to save, a life to live, and a terror to hide and run from.

As such, I evolve into a terribly neglectful housemate.

Yet, our long-term share house functions in a state of permanent mild neglect. Two sideboards in the dining room hold an archive of all those who lived here before: abandoned books, university readings, knitting wool, fairy lights, broken lamps and various other knick-knacks. The couch set in the living room is lumpy and tattered, arranged in a clash of faded florals and stripes. The kitchen is composed of chipped counters and mismatched crockery. A door in the back corner of the kitchen leads to stairs that were once used as the servants' entrance, now it's for the garbage collectors. I make do with a pot with no handle, and saucepans that have long lost their non-stick capabilities. None of us responds to the regular yell of 'Roba bika!' and take the hard rubbish down to the collectors of recyclable unwanted goods.

I could clean. I could replace things.

Instead, I just work around the brokenness: adapting to the home rather than adapting the home to me.

If I'm not at university or with friends, I'm trying to learn as much as possible. I spend time researching and reading other cases of prominent current, and former, political prisoners: Alaa Abdel Fattah, Peter Greste, Mohamed Fahmy, Shawkan. I'm looking for anything that might indicate a legal precedent, outline a process, or predict an outcome. I read reports from organisations like Human Rights Watch and The Egyptian Initiative for Personal Rights. Then I skim through news articles looking for information that might demystify international human rights law, Egyptian law and Australian law. I paw through the Mada Masr English archive; it is the only independent, critical news outlet left in Egypt. I read until I cannot soak in any more information and panic blurs the words on the screen.

From my desk, I look out a window that faces a brick wall; the view feels entrapping, prison-like. I drag my desk into the middle of my room, arranging it to face the double doors that connect my bedroom to a wrap-around balcony. It is not a convenient place for a desk as it obstructs my walk to the wardrobe, but instead of looking at a brick wall, I get to look outside at the trees, the sky and the buildings: one is a salmon pink art-deco apartment block, faded and seemingly abandoned. After I finish researching, I go outside and sit on the balcony. Two dusty armchairs face each other, a rickety side table between them; on the table, a concave chalk rock overflowing with cigarette butts – this is where I allow myself to think. Looking out over the street from the fourth floor, this part of Dokki is lined with tall, leafy tress; a rarity in this concrete jungle. In spring, some of them will grow heavy with vibrant red flowers.

In the meantime, dishes stay unwashed as I sit, smoke and wonder what to do about Dad.

Hazem

Three senior prisoners from the political detainees, along with a couple of their helpers, are relocated to Building 3 in Tora Tahqiq. I'm told that Tora Tahqiq has four buildings. Building 3, I find out, is for people accused of belonging to the Muslim Brotherhood. Building 4 is for people accused of being against the government, irrespective of their political or religious affiliations. I wonder where they will send me.

Because there is a hierarchy within the cell, the removal of these men leaves a kind of leadership vacuum. Three young men from the political detainees group step up to take leadership positions left by the senior prisoners, but they're immediately challenged by two men from the criminal side.

Later that day, I'm woken from my nap by loud noises. I get up and find one of the young men has blood streaming from his nose, soaking his clothing. A deep cut above his left eye pours more blood down the side of his face.

I look around to see who has done this to him. One of the bald men from the criminal side is shouting, screaming profanities at everyone. All of us political prisoners on the right side of the room are still and quiet. I ask the bleeding man what happened. He explains that two of the men from the criminal side tried to relocate their Nimrah to the political corner to begin taking over the right side of the cell.

It's a strategic move: not only would they be further away from the toilet, it's also one of the corners we call the Merayah. These two corners are the best in the cell – away from the toilet, with a full view of the room – and they are both currently occupied by us. Yet, with the numbers no longer in our favour, the men from the criminals' side of the room want to take over.

A couple of us huddle together to discuss how we will handle the situation. I'm the oldest in the room, so I am given the authority of an elder. As such, I find myself nominated to intervene and reassert the informal code of conduct we established in the cell. I know it's a hierarchy that privileges the political prisoners, but so far it's an order that works, as it keeps the cell clean and organised. Plus, it's an arrangement I benefit from.

After the young man cleans himself up, we both go over to the two men who sought to take over our corner.

I admit I have a prejudice against the men on the criminal side. They seem so much more uncouth. Many of them are rough, loud and surly, especially when compared with the quiet, polite demeanours of the political prisoners. The criminals all smoke heavily; their speech is regularly laced with profanities and dirty talk. I loathe cigarettes, and often feel annoyed by the tobacco haze that fills the cell from their chain-smoking. They also expose a class divide among us; most of the political prisoners are from educated, middle-class families, while most of the men on the criminal side are from the working poor of Egypt. For example, I had found the young man who'd been hit to be polite and respectful. He'd taught Islamic Studies through an online university and was well-versed in Islamic law, classical Arabic and literature.

I know that the men on the criminal side of the room have led hard, hard lives. I feel empathetic towards them; living in poverty in Egypt can be a harsh, hungry, cruel and short life. At the same time, my capacity for empathy is limited by the fact that I'm trying to survive myself; my emotional and physical capacities are consumed by keeping myself sane and alive. I want a cell that is quiet, clean and free from violence – the prison, in and of itself, is already violent enough.

The two men are stubborn. Trying to reason with them feels pointless. The threat of violence is far too close to the surface of their faces. The bald man has razor cuts all over his clean-shaven head. Some cuts are visible on his body. He looks like a body builder who hasn't had a chance to work out in a while – soft, muscular and heavy. I wonder if it's illegal steroids that have given him this strange, bulky look. His teeth are a collection of black, broken gaps and stumps. The man with him is thin and wiry. While the bald man speaks with loud, obnoxious tones, the smaller man's eyes dart between us all, keenly watching. He speaks only to offer short interjections, objecting to our reasons as to why they shouldn't disrupt the established order. His eyes are deep-set, framed by dark circles. The colour of his irises is so dark they seem like shimmering ponds of oil.

Even though the two men eventually back off and return to their side, there's no final agreement that they won't try to take over again.

We discuss the dilemma with people on our side. It is revealed that the bald man was baltagy, a local thug and drug dealer. The thin and wiry man was charged with first-degree murder, and is waiting to be transferred to serve his sentence.

*

At around 2 am, I'm jolted awake by loud noises. A thundering argument is underway between the thin, wiry man and the large, bald man. The stream of profanities is so creative and awful that I'm briefly amazed that I've never heard half the phrases coming out of their mouths. But I can't understand why they seem to have turned on each other. I quickly realise that this argument has the potential to break out in a physical fight.

Everyone has woken and backed up against the walls, leaving space in the middle for the sparring men.

The silent code of prison fights is not to get involved. It's one lesson I haven't yet learned.

I get up and move towards the men, attempting to defuse the situation by standing between them.

The large, bald man sends me off with a quick, sharp push, telling me to mind my own business. I back off immediately and join the political detainees in one of the corners.

As soon as I've moved away, punches start being mercilessly thrown. The men stumble over our blankets and belongings on the floor. The bald man gets the wiry man in a headlock, repeatedly punching him in the face. He passes out, or seems to. Blood is pouring from his narrow face. The bald man lets go, letting him fall to the floor. As he moves away, the wiry man leaps up and grabs a plastic bag. He pulls out a razor blade from the bag and starts swinging it, rushing towards the bald man. The blade slashes him in the chest, then there is another slash, and another slash. Blood comes streaming out, thick and crimson. The bald man collapses to his knees, then falls face down onto the floor. The wiry man moves away from his body, screaming: 'Oltilak ana momken a'warak, oltilak balash ana. Bosily, ana akoon adel ma'ak.' *I told you I can hurt you! I told you not to mess with me! Look at me, I am going to be fair to you!* Then he reaches down to his plastic bag and pulls out a second razor blade. He throws it at the bald, now bleeding, man who struggles to get up, his breathing laboured and heavy.

He can't reach for the blade, so the wiry man yells at some of the criminal prisoners to find the blade and give it to him. But the razor is lost in the mess of blood and belongings. The bald man makes an effort to get up. He stands, swaying slightly. Then he slowly pulls his thumb across his neck – it's not a threat but a plea to get it over and done with. The wiry man leaps over and slashes him over and over and over again across the chest and stomach. The bald man falls heavily, like a wounded bull.

Two of the men from the criminal side scramble over to check on him, but he is unresponsive. One of them yells, 'Fe wahed bemoot!' *Someone is dying!*

The fight has gone on for almost an hour and it was not missed by the guards, who heard but had ignored it up until now. In response to the yell, they open the door and ask some of the men to carry the now unconscious man out of the cell.

A Mokhber then enters the cell and tells the wiry man – who has retreated to a corner and is sitting quietly – to hand over the razor blade. He refuses. Instead, he puts the bloodied blade in his mouth. He's dragged out of the cell by the Mokhber.

The door closes behind them and we hear it lock.

There is a brief pause, like a collective exhale among us. Then we quickly and quietly get to the business of cleaning: wiping up the blood, washing the things that got blood on them and reorganising our belongings.

By the time we finish, someone announces that it's time for Fajr prayer. It's almost dawn.

When we pray, I feel a sense of peace.

I can't help but feel relieved that those men are gone and the order of the cell will stay.

Lamisse

I meet Amgad in downtown Cairo so we can go see Saleh together. We walk through a corner of the inner city where car mechanics and their garages pool. Petrol, grease and chatter ooze around us as we make our way to Saleh's office.

We find the building and take a shaky elevator up to the ninth floor. The office is minimally furnished: a desk, two armchairs, a computer and an ashtray. The Nile is visible from the window, though slightly obscured by towering buildings and a big bridge.

We sit on armchairs in front of Saleh's desk. As Amgad and Saleh catch up, I stay quiet. They take out their cigarettes. I reach into my bag and take mine out too. At least in Saleh's office, I can freely chain-smoke while they chat. Much like our days searching for Dad, I resentfully resign myself to muteness and wait for Amgad to translate.

Writing this now, I wonder: Why didn't I just change to an English-speaking lawyer? Why not take a chance on someone off the DFAT English-speaking lawyers list? Why did I stay in a situation that made me feel powerless? The truth is I didn't trust myself; I didn't believe that I could figure it out on my own. I was wracked with guilt that I'd somehow brought this situation into being by moving to Egypt and offering my father an opportunity to visit, without a second thought to the political context I was now living in. If only I'd stayed in Brisbane, if only I wasn't in Cairo, then he wouldn't have come here and he wouldn't have been arrested. I was afraid of making a choice that would lead us into further trouble. Frozen by fear and feeling supremely vulnerable, I was losing confidence in everything I once thought I knew to be true about the world and how it was supposed to work.

Thus, in the face of uncertainty, I only knew how to hide: stay quiet, watch and wait. Gather information while I kept my head down and followed orders. Let myself be guided by other people – people who knew this landscape more than I did – until I understood.

Amgad finally brings me into the conversation: 'So, Saleh said now that Hazem has been found, it shouldn't take very long.'

'What do you mean by that?' I ask.

'Well, he's under investigation. They said he is supporting terrorism.'

'What?' I'm shocked. 'Terrorism?'

Amgad looks uncomfortable. 'Yes ... they said he is supporting terrorism and spreading false information.'

Saleh interrupts with a comment. Amgad translates: 'He says the Arabic word specifically means ... um, sympathising. He is sympathising with terrorism.'

*

When I looked back over my diary entries to assemble this chapter, I could see that I didn't absorb what he'd told me. Soon after that exchange, I wrote in my diary that I still didn't know, or understand, why Dad was in prison – even though I'd been told. Did I not understand what it meant? Or did my brain outright reject information that it didn't want to deal with?

This led me into doubting my own memory: did I even have this conversation with Amgad? Did I make up this conversation with my cousin in retrospect to give myself a narrative? But I'm sure it happened: I can picture the office and their faces. I can hear their voices and the cadence of Amgad's American-accented English. Still, a voice in my head whispers, *But there's so much you don't remember, how can you be sure you remember this?* Perhaps my diary entries and memories reflect a contradictory possibility: that I was told, that I was in shock, and that I was struggling to make sense of it all.

In other words, the fragmented memories are clear and true, even if the thread I wove between them was of my own making. This is traumatic memory: it is both clarity and distortion.

*

Amgad continues: 'He is being investigated, so this means he will go to court every fifteen days and they will review his case. They can do this ten times. And then they must make a decision. But sometimes, he can be let out at one of these hearings. So, maybe he will come out sooner.'

'So, that could be in like …' I pause to calculate in my head, 'One hundred and fifty days … What's that? Six months? But maybe he could get out before?'

'Yes, six months … and maybe before that.'

'Okay, and then what happens after he gets out?'

'We will see. Don't worry about that now. Saleh says you need to have the Embassy fighting for your dad.'

'Okay. How?'

'They need to call Sisi, or other important people, and demand their citizen back.'

'Can they do that?' I pause, reflecting on what I know so far about the Embassy and its alleged capacities. 'The Embassy said I should follow Egyptian law, that it's better to keep it quiet and go through the process here …'

Amgad frowns, then translates this to Saleh. Saleh responds with an urgent tone.

Amgad turns back to me. 'If you do that, it could be a long time. Egypt is slow. If you have the Embassy, it could be faster. Saleh said this is what happened with another Embassy. They said they would leave Cairo if they didn't get their citizen back after one of their people was arrested.'

'A person was arrested and an Embassy threatened to withdraw?' This surprises me. It sounds too anecdotal, an 'it happened to my friend's friend' kind of story. Did any government care about an individual citizen that much, let alone a man categorised as a migrant and a Muslim, and now a terrorist and a prisoner?

In Egypt, the War on Terror has been weaponised as the framework that permits the State to violently suppresses civil dissent; in Australia, terrorism has been weaponised by the State too: from fear-mongering for votes, clicks and views, to legislation that infringes rights to privacy, freedom, safety and citizenship, all in the name of security. Yet, a little research and you'll find this is nothing new in the colony.

I knew Dad had strong opinions about the 2011 revolution, the Muslim Brotherhood and the current leader, President el-Sisi. We'd had countless debates about it; he, a supporter of the former Muslim Brotherhood President Morsi (who resided in the same prison complex that Dad was now in), and me with my wish for a secular, non-military option. Dad believes that Islamic law could inform politics and legislation, as his faith is inextricably linked to his politics. How was it that such a belief, one that encompassed an interest in Islamic political and legal scholarship, and its potential role in contemporary life, could be considered a criminal offence? Morsi or ISIS: it didn't matter whether it was the violence of war or a tumultuous attempt at democracy, if it came attached to Islam, it was suspicious. As such, discussion is foreclosed upon, narrowed into two choices: disavowal, or depoliticise your beliefs. Discursive violence had material world impacts: where nuance gets erased, people get erased too.

Yet, neither Dad or I were naïve; Morsi's reign was fraught with missteps and challenges. Everything in Egypt – from social life to the economy, media to the law – had been shaped by decades of military dictatorship. While there was a democratic process to elect Morsi, it was neither smooth nor free of issues. Once in power, who was to say the temptation toward totalitarian control wouldn't have taken over during Morsi's presidency? All we can do is speculate where these untraversed paths could have gone. Yet, what we do know is that, under el-Sisi, elections are still rigged, the pound inflated to record highs, and there is violent civic repression alongside an expansion of prison infrastructure, as well as 'structural reforms' furthering wealth inequality and undermining the few, fragile social services and subsidies that remained.

Amgad is still talking.

'… then the Egyptians gave him back. Your Embassy needs to do this for Uncle Hazem. They must tell Egypt that he is Australian first, not Egyptian.'

There it is again, the slipperiness of nationality. I'm tired of debating what is and isn't Egyptian or Australian, what makes us one before the other. Why must a dual national – or a so-called 'mixed-race' – person be such a source of confusion and suspicion?

'I don't know ...' I say hesitantly. 'I don't know if they will do that, especially because he's been arrested here in Egypt. The Embassy recognises he's Australian, but they say he is Egyptian first because he was arrested here in Egypt. It's international law: that's apparently how it works with dual citizenship. And I don't think I can pressure them like that. In the meeting, they said we should follow the law in Egypt.'

Raising his eyebrow, Amgad shrugs. 'As you wish.'

Amgad isn't necessarily wrong to believe that Australia could offer a better recourse to a just outcome, but I feel I can't fully explain the challenge I face to him. I don't want to grovel for help, I don't want to have to 'prove' my Australianness to deserve help. They'd said it clearly: 'He's been arrested in Egypt, he's Egyptian. Follow Egyptian law.'

While I see the injustices in Egypt and know them to be true, I also don't believe that my other country can claim moral superiority. Yes, there are benefits to belonging to Australia, but it is also a country that harms, a place mired in fundamental injustices. I look at my country and see genocidal settler colonialism, land theft, offshore detention centres, the White Australia policy and a slaughtered pig's head inside a bag tagged with a swastika left outside of the Islamic College of Brisbane. I see Liberal Party race-baiting, *Tampa*, Cronulla riots and Pauline Hanson's suggestion of internment camps for people labelled 'security threats'. I see greed and denial: a refusal to acknowledge ongoing colonisation lest extracted, stolen wealth be turned into reparations. As the daughter of a settler and a migrant, I often wonder: How am I to give back for all I've inherited as a settler? And where would I go if I heeded the message to go back to where I came from?

I tried to answer the latter by coming to Egypt, but now I better understand why Dad left. Seeking a principled stance isn't about rehashing my identity issues or Instagram activism; it was about learning how to better understand where I stand within it all, to engage with the unequal distributions of power and resources, and with that understanding, to expand into holding multiple, conflicting truths: yes, we're experiencing the terrifying disempowerment that prison puts upon a person *and* we hold privileges that can change our circumstances through avenues that most people inside Egypt's prisons can't access. I can't ignore those avenues.

Face it, Lamisse, I think, *your being Australian is going to be your biggest leverage to ending this situation.*

But how?

Hazem

I've been here nearly three weeks now.

My next hearing is coming up in a few days. Again, I'm rehearsing everything in my head, hoping that this time I'll get a chance to plead my case. I keep going over what happened, reviewing how I got here while trying to make sense of it all to know what I can say to the judge.

I'm still hoping my message to the family got through. Obaida, the young man who smuggled out the letter for me, is going to have a visit from his brother today. I've given him another letter to take to my family. There's a big risk in smuggling out letters. The punishment for being caught is seven days in solitary confinement – a dark, damp cubicle where you don't get anything but the clothes you're wearing. There are no visits, no books, no one to talk to and no outdoor time. I shudder to think that it can get worse than this.

The days are blurring into one long, strange day.

Every day at 7 am, the guard opens the cell door and delivers our food. It's always the same: fouul and halawa.

We gather in groups of 5–8 people and eat from the same large foam plate. I've been rationing my medication for my blood pressure and cholesterol – it's the only medication I was allowed to take with me into prison. The two pairs of underwear I was given are already wearing thin; the soap we use for our washing – called subona meri – is harsh as it's made solely from sodium hydroxide with a little bit of fat. I can't shower every day because we share one shower between forty men. The water is left running from the shower head all day and night so as to wash our bodily waste down the hole called the toilet. To shower, we have to stand over the hole, a foot on each side. The constantly running water also helps with managing the smell, which would otherwise fill the cell. I've also only got one pair of pants and one jacket. Since I have no spare clothes and it's winter, I can't wash them often. I sleep in them and spend my days in them. I always feel dirty, even after a shower.

We do our best to stay clean. We rotate our blankets throughout the day to make space for congregational prayers, sweeping the floor when we do. Because a lot of us do our five daily prayers, we are also doing the ritual wash daily and it really helps with our personal hygiene in the absence of regular showers.

No one has lice, but most of us have scabies.

I caught scabies almost straightaway, and it seems to have not left me. I'm itchy across my hands, thighs and around my genitals. At night, it flares up and it is almost unbearable with the intensity of the relentless prickling and itching. Everyone tells me to do whatever I can to avoid getting sick – the hospital is a death trap, they say. I'm not surprised to find out our health is of no concern to the authorities. Yet, I'm worried. I wonder what I'll do if I run out of my heart medication, or if I can't stop my skin itching. I also wonder what I'll do about my right leg. It's currently held together by pins and plates after a break and I'm supposed to have the metal removed in a few months. The constant cold makes my leg and ankle ache, and I can feel one of the metal pins through the skin of my ankle. I understand why we should do everything we can not to get sick in here, but most of us entered this prison with pre-existing health issues.

Obaida comes back from his family visit. The first thing he does is approach me, telling me that his brother spoke to my wife. The first letter was delivered!

I am so happy to hear this and my heart soars high. They finally know where I am! This news gives me a glimmer of hope that I could leave soon. I know that my family and Australia will not leave me to rot here. They will get me out, they know I have done nothing wrong.

Lamisse

13 February 2018

Amgad, Yacoub and I are going to Tora prison today to see if we can visit Dad.

Amgad said we need to be there around dawn for check-in so I sleep over at my aunt's house, where Amgad and Yacoub still live – like many their age, they're unable to afford to move out.

Last night, after dinner, we sat in the living room, full of nerves and tea, lighting cigarette after cigarette. At around three in the morning, I retreated to the guest bedroom to get some sleep but lay awake, restless and full of apprehension.

At 4.30 am, we pile into the car and head to the prison. None of us have slept. As we speed along a highway nearly empty of traffic in the pre-dawn darkness, sandy walls fringed with barbed wire come into view.

'There's Tora,' says Amgad.

The Tora Prison complex is next to the affluent suburb of Maadi, an area I've frequented for yoga classes, expensive cappuccinos in private cafe gardens and beers at a bar with Bowie's face painted on the wall. It disturbs me that I've done all this over the past eight months with no idea that a graveyard for the living was a few kilometres away.

As we get closer, I spy the tips of guns pointing out of towering turrets.

We turn off the motorway onto a side street. Short, dilapidated buildings stand along a muddy, unpaved road. We drive slowly, looking for the visitors' entrance. At the time, I sat in the car thinking that what I could see was it, but the Tora prison complex is much larger than the small section I'd come to know: it spreads across about 1.3 kilometres of land and consists of multiple buildings, including its own courthouse.

Yacoub pulls up to an open gate and Amgad gets out of the car to investigate. He disappears from sight, leaving Yacoub and me to wait in silence. After a few minutes, he reappears and sticks his head through the open window. 'Visitor sign-ins don't start until six am,' he tells us.

We have an hour to kill. Unsure of where to go in this desolate area, we agree it would be better to find a cafe to wait at. Yacoub suggests we drive and see what's around. Amgad says he'd rather walk. Staying in the car with Yacoub, we roll down the street, glancing out the windows in the hope of seeing some shops. A few hundred metres away, at the south end of the street, there's a fruit shop, a kiosk, a sandwich stand and, thankfully, a shisha cafe. A couple of men are seated out the front of the cafe, dimly bathed in the morning fog and dawning light, gently pulling on their water pipes.

Yacoub turns to face me in the back seat and says firmly, 'Don't get out.'

'Don't get out of the car?'

'Yes, don't get out of the car. You wait in the car. I'm going to the cafe. Do you want anything?'

'That's ridiculous,' I protest. 'Why can't I get out of the car?'

'Because it's not safe. It's not good for women.'

'Seriously?'

'Yes, not at this cafe. You wait here, okay?'

Although I nod, I am fuming. In my first trips to Egypt as a young adult, I travelled with Dad – he fussed over me, fearful and over-protective. When I protested, he said I didn't understand, so I blamed him for my inability to understand: 'If you only taught us Arabic!' I would say. 'If you only taught us about Egypt. Why did you hide this from us?' At 17, I had not conceptualised that my own father carried his own wounds as a migrant, that he grew up as part of the Egyptian diaspora in Kuwait in the 1970s, was a uni student in Lebanon in early 1980s, then in the 1990s came to Australia, where multiculturalism masked the pressure to assimilate. Dad thought he was doing the best thing for us, but in my late teens, I saw him as a withholder and a tyrant.

Thus, his monitoring of my movements fed into my perception that being a girl was primarily the reason I couldn't do anything independently. Having him hover over me throughout my first trip at 17 only strengthened my resolve to come back to Egypt on my own. When I was finally on my own in Egypt for the first time in 2013, I had to admit Dad was right.

I didn't understand.

So, despite these visceral skin-crawling reactions to being told what to do, I acknowledge that Yacoub asking me to stay in the car could be for my own safety. I accept the way my cousins offer care. Now is not the time for a misguided war on patriarchy, though this doesn't stop me from quietly fuming.

Minutes later, Amgad strolls up and taps on my window. I wind it down.

'You want a sandwich?' he asks.

'What kind of sandwich?'

'Betingaan, fouul ...' he trails off, looking over at the sandwich shop. 'Batatas.'

'Oh yeah, I'll have eggplant. I don't feel like fouul,' I reply. He gives a jovial wink and trots over to the sandwich stand.

His approach – appeasement and humour – has dissipated the tension that Yacoub's more commanding style had inspired in me. At this point, my strategy of submission is making my palms itch. I hate being told what to do.

I long for a sense of control. Not over others, but over myself; I want control over my agency.

I sulk as I watch Yacoub from my car window, sipping coffee and smoking his shisha while sitting outside the cafe.

Amgad returns with a Sprite, a Coke and some sandwiches in small, clear plastic bags. To my surprise, instead of passing me my food through the window and sitting at the cafe with Yacoub, he gets into the car and hands over my sandwiches with the Sprite. Whether it's out of some duty of protection, solidarity or simply because it's cold, it doesn't matter; I'm pleased not to be sitting in the car on my own. In contemplative silence, we chew on our food.

The sun is in the process of making its full appearance and it brings the prison into pitiless view. My sandwich loses its taste and slides unnoticed down my throat.

That's the place.

Leaving the car parked outside the cafe, we head towards the visitors' entrance. Without footpaths, we walk on the road. The middle of the road is cut by a dug-out, narrow, winding chasm, almost full to the brim with decaying rubbish. Heavy sloping concrete barriers have been placed on either side of the chasm. Pedestrians back up to the top of the road to cross it or scale the barriers over the pit.

The pre-dawn ghostliness of the street has been transformed by the sun into a loud and busy street market. Wooden carts filled with produce occupy space along the road as women and men select from the array of fruit and vegetables. We pass a matted grey donkey tied to a post and a stall selling sneakers, rubber flip-flops and knock-off Crocs. Colourful plastic chairs are haphazardly lined up under a tree. A cafe has been carved into the ground floor of a stone building that faces the street. The front of someone's home operates as a milk bar, selling candy, water, chips and cigarettes. It is a piece of the prison economy in action: business hours of this street market coincide with visiting hours.

An open gate of black wrought iron leads into a large courtyard – this is the visitors' check-in and waiting area. Colourful chip and chocolate packets are scattered across the dusty concrete ground and the only people lifting cigarettes to their mouths are guards. Men, women and children – wrapped in dark colours and thick jumpers – sit on hard wooden benches underneath a canopy of steel and plastic. They all look sombre in the cold.

Are they all visitors too?

Amgad and Yacoub approach a leathery-faced, plain-clothes guard. Instead of giving him a silly nickname, my first reaction is to imagine this man as a child: Who was he before he became a guard at a prison? Why did he become a guard at a prison? Humanising him makes him less scary, but it also triggers a confusing sense of empathy: perhaps, I want to see him as human so I can be assured that he might see me – and Dad – as human too.

Amgad tells the guard that we're trying to visit Hazem Hamouda. He points to me and explains that I'm Australian and don't speak Arabic, and that they, as my cousins, are here to help.

The man takes this in and nods.

Then he outlines two rules to Amgad and Yacoub:

No visits before one month of imprisonment.

No visitors except for immediate family members: mother, father, sister, brother, son, daughter, grandmother, grandfather.

After Amgad translates this to me, I panic. Feeling desperate, I look at the guard then back to Amgad. 'But why? Why is that the rule?'

'I don't know.' Amgad sounds disappointed. 'We can talk to Saleh and see what we can do. It's also frustrating for me because he says me and Yacoub can't visit Hazem because we are his nephews. But I want to see Uncle Hazem, too.'

'Come back in a month,' the guard says emphatically, before shooing us away with his hands.

As we walk off, I cry: 'It's just so much bullshit! Why didn't Saleh tell us about this!' I'm struggling to comprehend the fact that Dad is behind those sandy, barbed wire-topped walls, and yet we can't get to him to confirm he's really there. Does he know we're looking for him? Would he guess that I've been trying to get to him?

I stare at the prison walls, convincing myself I can telepathically communicate with Dad: *We're here, we're here, we are trying to get to you, we love you, stay strong.*

I look away from the prison and down at my hands, starting an inner dialogue with myself: *These are my hands. I am here and I am real. I am really here staring at the place that Dad is in, the place that is a prison. The place is called Tora Prison. I am here and I am real and I am at Tora Prison.*

A walled-up numbness erects itself: a levee to protect me against the rising ocean of devastation that the prison is undeniably real.

This isn't the spot where I'm going to break down.

I have to stay in control.

Hazem

It's been 29 days since I got to El-Eraad. I'm finally on my way out, knowing that I won't be coming back to this place. I stand outside the building, the sunshine on my face and a clear sky above me. The guards gather prisoners from three different holding cells. In the open space, I feel myself coming alive, as though I have stepped out from a grave. Every moment outside the cell feels as precious as freedom itself.

All my belongings are in an old plastic shopping bag: a small face towel, a pair of white underwear, a T-shirt and a blanket. I'm also holding my ticket. It's a white card with my picture and prison ID on it. Every time we leave our cell, we have to take our ticket with us. I walk with the guards and other prisoners until we reach Building 4 in Tora Tahqiq. We wait to be allocated a cell. A couple of hours pass; time here feels irrelevant – things just happen when they happen and we have all become accustomed to this waiting. Three of us – Obaidah, who smuggled the letters out for me; Mohammed, a primary school English teacher; and myself – are told to follow the Shaweesh; one of the conscript soldiers working in Building 4 as a prison guard.

The Shaweesh is taking us to cell 1/1. As we are walking, I try to look around the building without being too obvious. The building is two storeys: the first floor is enclosed in mesh wire and steel bars;

on the second floor I count 24 cells, separated by a narrow corridor. There is only one gate to go in and out, and a Shaweesh sits on a dilapidated chair and desk. Beside him is a bench with four prisoners sitting on it. There's a toilet block just outside a steel gate, as well as a courtyard that looks to be about 20 x 35 metres – it is also covered with steel bars and mesh. There are two guard towers on watch at each corner, and a small room containing the water pumps that supply the complex. From what I've seen of the Tora complex so far, this prison is bleak and run-down. First established by the British in the late 1800s, the complex has since been extended upon by subsequent rulers and presidents. From the start, it's been used for political prisoners: from those against the British occupation, to those against the monarchy, to those against the President.

We are ushered into our cell. The door closes behind us. I look out at new faces and introductions begin. A heavy-set man introduces himself as ex-military and a Brigadier. He's part of the political prisoners who have been swept up since the start of election season. More people introduce themselves: one man says he's been accused of murder, and two other men tell me they've been in prison for four years as part of the al-Rabaa' case. The biggest mass trial, the al-Rabaa' case, contained over 700 men, ruefully still awaiting sentence four years after being placed in remand detention, in Tora Tahqiq.

It's surreal to meet these men; I've been following the case since it was opened. I offer my own introduction. 'I'm Hazem, from Australia. I'm part of case 977 and have been here about thirty days.' I found out the number of the case in the last hearing. At this stage, this number and the accusations I received while at the prosecutor's office are all the details I have about my case.

Tiredness and bewilderment leaves me with shattered nerves. The sound of unfamiliar voices grates at me. Adjusting to a new cell with new prisoners is stressful, and it's a particularly small and cramped space. The toilet is filthy, and there are only two small openings in the walls, both covered with mesh and steel bars. Little natural light or air comes through the cell, and the steel door has a small opening covered with bars, through which we can see the Shaweesh sitting at his decaying desk.

The men clear some room for the three us to put our blankets down on the concrete floor. It's freezing inside the cell, and there's only one blanket left after we've covered the floor. One of the men offers us a spare blanket and between the three of us, we'll huddle under the two blankets and try to sleep tonight. I've brought some leftover food with me; just bread and white cheese. I'm feeling speechless so I eat quietly, sitting on my blanket in my new allocated space. The men respect my silence and give me space. The cell has one of those dreadful exposed fluorescent lights and it remains on 24/7. In one of the corners of the cell, there is a handmade wire structure, coiled and connected to exposed electric wires coming out of the wall; it acts as a makeshift heater. While the exposed electricity seems dangerous, gathering any kind of heat in this cold trumps safety concerns. I fade out of the room and into my thoughts, surrendering to my imagination so I can envision that I'm home with my family, back at work, with friends. This escapism helps me to finally sleep.

The next morning, I'm awoken by the cell door being flung open, followed by a yell for everyone to get out of the cell. I quickly get up and head out to discover prisoners walking up and down the narrow corridor. I find one of my cellmates.

'Eh l'akhbaar?' *What's going on?*

'Da wa't tarayyod.' *It's time for exercise.*

Now that I'm out of El-Eraad, we get time out of the cell to walk up and down the corridor. I start walking, striding and stretching my legs.

I walk with my cellmate, bombarding him with questions about life in prison.

He explains some things to me and then tells me: 'It will take time but you will get used to it, the rules, the language in here ...'

This makes me panic because I don't want to be here. I want to go home. I don't want to learn these rules and this new prison language, I want to be in Brisbane. This is a nightmare and I'm waiting to wake up.

News has already spread that there is an Australian man in the building. While on my daily walk I'm approached by a friend from my time in El-Eraad. It's nice to see a familiar face.

Lamisse

Australia's Privacy Act is getting in our way. Whenever I've asked direct questions about Dad, they've stated they cannot answer me due to the Privacy Act; Dad needs to give them permission to speak to me. They're still only offering advice on what they can and cannot do, while reminding me to pass on any information to them. To get Dad's permission – verbal or written – they need to get approval from the Egyptian authorities to visit him in prison. Or I need to get a written authorisation from Dad when I see him in prison.

It seems insane to me that this isn't categorised as an exceptional situation that would allow us to bypass the Act. What if the Embassy is denied visitation? What if I'm pushed back again? Even worse, what would happen if we still didn't know where he was? How long would a person need to be disappeared for before you don't need their permission? No matter how pressing a situation is, it seems that laws are rarely ever suspended for civilians. Meanwhile, it's fair game when you're disappearing a human being or unjustly arresting them. Bitterness aside, I need to get past the Privacy Act as soon as possible. The Embassy says if I can get a written statement from Dad – should I be successful during my next visit – that would suffice.

We're all inculcated to give a certain amount of trust to authority, to believe that governments have answers. Throughout the early days of this ordeal, I harboured a desire for the Embassy to embody a kind of parental figure: that they would know something I didn't, would do something I couldn't. I wanted to trust them, to believe that they were there for me.

Thus far, the experience has been quite the opposite: one that consistently undermines whatever little belief I have in government processes. All I have to do is remember that during the search for Dad, the most useful information came neither from the Embassy nor the Egyptian authorities.

It came from friends, family and their networks. It came through a letter smuggled out of the prison.

*

At our next meeting, Saleh gives me a letter stating that I have special permission to visit Dad. It should provide me with an exemption to the one-month waiting period on visitors. Amgad is hyper with confidence, triumphantly stating 'This is definitely going to work!'

Though I'm hopeful, I dread returning to prison and facing its stony, barbed wire-topped walls. For those tasked with visiting a loved one in prison, it ought to be viewed as an additional avenue of psychological torture: the architecture is built to be menacing, the guards trained to be threatening. The natural response to danger, to entering a violent space, is the activation of your fight or flight response. While I cannot fight the prison, I sure as hell could run from it. Yet, to get to Dad, I must suppress my instinct to fight or flee – that is, my instinct to protect myself and those I love. So, to be forced into compliance, to suppress all my instincts at the prison, doesn't make sense to my body, which then produces a staggering amount of dysregulation: something which then manifests as trauma, as PTSD.

This violence is what is enacted upon prisoners, except that the suffering isn't restricted to visiting day. Layered upon that is the psychological distress that's caused by witnessing the suffering of a loved one, an experience exacerbated by feelings of being powerless to stop it. For prisoners, this inflicts feelings of deep shame and guilt, and I was yet to understand how much this guilt would shape Dad in the years after his release. The more I experienced, witnessed and learnt about the impact of trauma upon the body, the more the insidious elements of a prison's violence were revealed. Just as a person doesn't need bruises for there to have been domestic abuse, neither does a prisoner, or their family, need to be 'tortured' for there to be torture. The Embassy emails me a list of questions about Dad's case. I reply with what I know and it's all the same information: a reiteration of the process of court hearings every 15 days, my concerns about Dad's health, with the addition of mentioning the letter from the lawyer with the hope that it will work. I also inform them that Dad was due to go to court on 10 February, but had been taken on 7 February instead. I note that it is apparently common for court dates to change last minute, without the lawyers or families of inmates being notified. This tactic alienates the prisoners from their legal representation and the family members hoping to catch sight of their loved ones in court. Despite this, in their reply, the Embassy makes a point to recommend 'the lawyer keep a closer eye on Mr Hamouda's case'. The admonishment feels personal: How is Saleh supposed to do that? Did they not read my email explaining why the date change happened?

Regardless, it plants a seed of doubt – one easily sowed during uncertainty. I wonder if Saleh could do any more than he's already doing. I remain unclear as to what reasonable expectations I should have for both Saleh and the Embassy. Was there anything anyone could do differently? I don't know where the information about court hearings is sent, or how Saleh even gets the information about it. I don't know what court Dad gets taken to, or if I can attend, or what happens inside a court hearing. The opacity of processes makes understanding incredibly challenging, especially since it seems that the law is more of a malleable concept than a fixed practice. Every time I have had an expectation of a process – whether it is waiting 48 hours to be notified or the prison visiting protocols – it either hasn't happened or there's been misunderstanding, missing information or confusion.

At the end of my reply email, I decide to ask the Embassy if they have any information they could share with me, even though I know the Privacy Act still stands between us. I also ask if they have any recommendations for support services that families of the detained could access. In their reply, they advise me to contact Consular Services in Canberra, so that Consular Services can connect me to a toll-free call to Lifeline.

They might as well have started their email with 'R U OK?'

It hurts to realise I won't be as important as I want to be. I want Dad, me and my family to be wildly defended, radically supported and ferociously fought for. This is *huge*. It's completely life-changing and life-threatening. Yet, we are little but a diplomatic concern, an issue to be managed. A box ticked; a case noted. Paperwork filed at the end of the day.

So, why do I have all these hard feelings when I know it's just bureaucracy doing its job?

Lamisse

18 February 2018

Amgad calls to tell me they're downstairs and I crawl out of bed, throw on a dress, stockings, lace-up boots and an oversized denim jacket. My head is muddled and thumping. Last night, instead of staying at my aunt's flat, I went out and got as drunk as possible with some friends.

During the ride to Tora, my mind is occupied with thoughts of my family. I've been drip-feeding information to Mum by text. This is the tension: I'm on the ground, but Mum is in Australia with her imagination. Having such a wide space for speculation sends her into catastrophising. It pains me because I can't answer all her questions; I give her what I know and little else. I refuse speculation and grasp control by demanding we only deal with the facts, even if they are few. Even so, her anxiety spirals inevitably send me spiralling, and my own sanity is dependent on avoiding catastrophising thoughts. I need to know Mum can handle whatever she needs to handle without my help. This dynamic precedes the prison, having taken root in my youth. After all, an over-burdened mother with six children learning to lean heavily on her eldest daughter for emotional and material support would be of little surprise to anyone.

So, I convince myself that parallel action will be our form of working together: she deals with her side while I deal with mine, and we don't need to talk about it.

As the car slows to a stop by the prison, a lacklustre rage fires up inside me. The numbing effects of booze and sleep deprivation do the job I'd intended for them: it can't hurt when you're too tired to feel.

We get out of the car and make our way down the street past the garbage-filled chasm, the matted donkey and the carts of fruit and vegetables. We weave through the people in the courtyard and approach the sign-in desk. The guard behind the desk is in an official uniform, complete with a peaked flat cap. Amgad tells me to take out my identity documents and the letter, so I hand over my Australian passport, Egyptian birth certificate and the letter from the lawyer.

The guard glances at the documents, makes a note and hands them back. He says he must check something, that we need to wait. Then he leaves.

Amgad and Yacoub make their way to a bench and sit down. I follow and attempt to sit next to them.

'No.' Amgad stops me from sitting down. 'You have to sit on the women's side.' He motions to the benches opposite theirs.

Of course. I should have remembered that.

The courtyard is almost full and there are a lot of children running around, laughing and screaming as they play tag. Some other children sit quiet and wide-eyed.

All the women wear exhaustion on their faces like make-up. A sweeping glow of dark shadows under the eyes, a sallow pinch in tired cheeks and a glittering sag at the edge of the mouth. Full white plastic bags sit either beside the women or at their feet.

Most of them are covered, dressed the same way as my mother's friends: headscarves paired with jilbabs of navy, black and dark grey. Mum used to dress like this too; yet, in recent years, the sombre scarves were replaced with turquoise, pink and forest green. She forwent the heavy jilbabs for floral dresses, linen shirts and – gasp! – jeans. As a teenager, we'd battled over my desire to wear jeans. This was the noughties – skinny jeans were it. Though I wore them under dresses or with long shirts, she claimed they were not modest enough because they clung to my calves.

I see that I am not the only one who is noticing – I too am being noticed. Gazes flicker up and down. The more I see the eyes that flit towards me, the more I become uncomfortably self-conscious. I feel thrust into a sea of my mother's disapproval and a hot slice of shame cuts through me. Suddenly, my dress feels too short. My stockings are too sheer, calves too visible. Something must be wrong with my face: Do I have mascara smeared under my eyes? Can they smell the stale alcohol and cigarettes on my breath? Why did I think it was a good idea to go out last night? How am I supposed to face my father and reassure him that we can get through this when I'm such a mess?

The same guard from our first visit appears and Amgad tells me his name is Haytham. He's still in plain clothes; his heavy-set and strangely handsome face holds loose teeth and a raspy laugh. I have learnt that most of these guards are poorly paid with undesirable jobs. Poverty or conscription often brings men to prison for work.

Haytham is standing away from the sign-in desk, close to the gate, near the edge of where the canopy begins its rise over the seating. He calls us over. We get up from our wooden benches and walk towards him.

Amgad asks me for the letter from the lawyer and offers it to Haytham. He refuses to take it from him. Amgad hands it back to me.

Yacoub adopts a quietly desperate tone for his appeals to the guard. Amgad has lost his exuberant confidence from earlier; his shoulders sag as he interrupts Yacoub with his own pleas. The guard is gesturing intently, leaning forwards as he speaks.

I interrupt: 'What's going on?'

Amgad turns to me to answer: 'He says not today.'

'What do you mean not today?'

'He said not today. He said we have to wait till the end of the month, until 28 February.'

I'm gutted. 'Why? We've got the letter!'

'He says that's the rule. And he says that Hazem's papers say he was arrested on 28 January. This letter doesn't work because it says the wrong date – it says that he was arrested on the 25th. So, we have to come back next week.'

'What? But Dad *was* arrested on the 25th! That's when he was taken from the airport!'

Later, I found out that this wasn't how it went: the day Dad was taken from the airport was not the same as the day he was formally charged. The day he was formally charged was the day he was considered arrested, while the days before that were for the lawless black hole of airport cells and National Security interrogations.

Amgad shrugs and returns to the conversation with the guard.

Tears burn down my cheeks and my quick blinks fail to hold them back. I step forwards and shove the letter at the guard, saying the only word I know for this moment: 'Minfadlak!'

I point again to the letter as I pause to take a breath. I don't want my voice to crack. 'Ana eiza shoofi baba!'

My Arabic sounds pathetic; I feel like a toddler crying for their parent and I'm embarrassed that this is all I'm capable of saying. But it's all I have and I say it again: 'Ana eiza shoofi baba!'

Wordlessly, the guard turns away from me.

Amgad touches my arm. 'Lamisse, stop. Just let us handle it.'

'*No!*' I whip around, on the verge of telling Amgad to back the fuck off. But when I see his face, I don't.

'He's my uncle and I also want to see him. He's like a father to me.' He speaks softly. His eyes are wide and watery. I can't handle it. His pain reflects my own and I want to push it away and scream, 'No! He's not your dad! He's *my* dad! You're not sad! *I'm* sad!'

I catch myself before any of this gushes out of my mouth. I'm angry, but not blind. I want to attack, but since I can't direct my rage towards the guard, my cousin is in the firing line.

Holding my breath, I nod in response to Amgad's comment. 'I know,' I say.

I take a few steps back to wait, quietly witnessing my cousin's intensifying argument with the guard.

Disassociating, I experience my surroundings as though I'm watching an Egyptian film, without subtitles, on my grandmother's TV. Mouths move and sounds are made as I passively watch, disappearing from the present moment. I'm five and I'm in Cairo. My grandmother and I are watching a film together. On the screen, a woman lays out a woven mat to pray. A mean-looking man puts a snake on her prayer mat, hoping it'll strike and kill her, but the snake disappears. She finishes her prayer, saved by a miracle from Allah. I ask my grandmother if it's real, and she says it is.

The message I got that day was that prayer will protect you. Is that what I should do? Pray these guards away and pray Dad out of this prison?

Haytham begins ushering Yacoub and Amgad towards the gate, using the walking-and-talking tactic. I follow, trailing a few steps behind as I try to re-enter into what's happening. As Haytham talks, I listen in to the polite but firm tone he's adopted. The pitch is interrupted by impatient slippages in his voice that say 'you can fuck off now'.

We arrive at the gate.

The letter, the lawyer, the confidence and the promises that it'd work amount to nothing. We are defeated. Humiliation settles into our bodies. I wonder if my cousins are cornered and conditioned into predetermined ways of behaving within an Egyptian context.

In my struggle to extricate myself from the haze of interior distancing, it all seems unreal. I don't bother looking at my hands to undo this sensation. Instead, an ethereal sense of power comes over me, because when nothing seems real, nothing seems scary and everything seems possible. I feel like I'm seeing clearly for the first time.

Perhaps powerlessness is our true state of being; experiencing our powerlessness is painful at best, and traumatising at worst. Consequently, much of what we do is to avoid confronting our own powerlessness. Whether we pray to God, worship the strongmen of military and government, gather around cult leaders and life coaches or centre our life on revolution and activism, subconsciously, we are seeking to align ourselves with something we perceive as power. The very act of aligning ourselves makes us feel like we can *do* something; we experience our agency. When we experience outcomes – whether tangible real world results or emotional relief – we want to keep doing it.

Maybe my ignorance was a kind of power? Perhaps I could subvert the unspoken rules that shaped how my cousins navigated the world. Perhaps my not-knowing freed me from these invisible, yet collectively agreed upon, cultural scripts and expectations that tell us how we are supposed to speak and behave. Plus, if the minimum of agency is attitude – that is, our response to our circumstances – then I have agency. I can choose to reduce how much power I give to those who I think 'know'.

Surfacing from these reflections, I take a good look at the prison and move to a new thought: I need to do this alone.

Connecting to my rage, I visualise myself running headlong against all these barriers, like a battering ram. No more being placed on the sidelines to watch negotiations or be ignored. No more being told to wait in the car, to be quiet. I experience this rage as an almost physical break in my psyche, which has, up until now, been more concerned with self-preservation than attack. While something about my determination feels unhinged, I am certain.

I will do this on my own.

*

In working on this chapter, weaving together my written account with Dad's, I had a realisation: Dad wasn't even there.

While I was convinced that I was being deliberately blocked, Dad was still in El-Eraad. The holding cell. But I was in the section of the prison where he would *soon* be – Tora Tahqiq, the investigations wing of Tora prison. It didn't matter if I had a letter or not, whether I followed all the rules or not, whether I had my cousins with me or not; there was no father to see.

However, the emotional experience of this moment facilitated an important shift in my psyche. Despite my efforts to numb it, I connected to my anger. The experience of anger often arises in response to a sense of injustice (irrespective of it being perceived or real). Too often, we banish anger, especially as people socialised as women, but anger is a necessary and vital emotion. By connecting to my anger, I connected to my profound love for my dad and for my family. Many of us state that we'd do anything for those we love, but what happens when we're actually confronted with that request? How far would I go to get my dad back? The answer that rose from the depths of my inner being was petrifying. I would die for my family.

Death sounds dramatic, but there was no other way to psychologically put myself into a place where I could confront my terror of the prison and my fear of the power of the State. If the State was willing to kill for its own preservation, then I had to be willing to die in defence of the people I loved.

However, it is important to remember that we construct turning points to create linear narratives. While this was a genuine epiphany, the shift it initiated in my approach wasn't consistent. I would forget my commitment to fight again and again. Like a drowning person dunked by waves, I'd be swamped by fear and sink under. Something would push me, I'd surface and gasp at the air, remembering why I had to keep going. There'd be a brief reprieve and a remembering, then I'd be dunked again.

Forgetting, drowning. Rising, gasping, fighting.

Lamisse

24 February 2018

The brother of Dad's cellmate texted another letter to Mum. In the letter, Dad tells us he's been moved to a new cell, which he describes as 'dark, dingy and cold'. He said he doesn't have access to any of his stuff, including his medication, but that he is trying to 'keep in good spirit'. He mentions he's been treated badly. In their email, the Embassy wants to know how badly and ask me to get clarification when I see him. I plan to visit him in four days on 28 February. I joke about the fact that it isn't a leap year. I'll be going on 1 March, two days before my 29th birthday.

Though they've asked me to get details, I don't know if I want to know these details yet. Being disappeared is bad. Prison is bad. Aren't those two things enough to speak to someone being 'treated badly'?

Meanwhile, *The Age* published an article about Dad today.

Though DFAT advised us to keep this quiet, I've been uncertain if this is the best course of action. While I want to follow their advice, I have my own emerging opinions about what should, or needs, to be done. Keeping quiet feels counterproductive. While I fear losing the Embassy's support, there's got to be some kind of awareness raised about Dad's situation, a light shone on the injustice. It feels important to get the story out, to begin building a campaign and public accountability. I'd collaborated with a friend who was a journalist, provided the quotes and even checked the piece before it was sent to the editor. This was another friend I'd met in Palestine: an independent journalist who'd settled in Egypt during the short years of revolutionary promise. My trust in Australian journalists was especially low, so collaborating with this friend felt safe. I could somewhat trust that they'd represent us in the best way they could.

With Dad's plight now in a public space, people who know my family and I are making contact: the messages of surprise, worry and concern are touching but overwhelming. The article gives us public legitimacy. Mum calls to thank me for organising the piece: 'I'm getting more of the support that I needed to deal with this,' she says. 'People see that it's real.' While I'm also getting supportive messages, being in Cairo has meant I've already been around people who understand what we're going through. With Mum's isolation in Australia, the publicity and subsequent messages ease how alone she feels in the ordeal. Receiving these messages reminds me of how important it is to reach out to people experiencing hardship: sometimes you don't need to 'do' anything, people can be comforted by just feeling you care.

Despite these positives, when I read this news report on my family's current trauma, I'm disoriented knowing that it will still seem abstract to many of those reading it. The limits of space, convention, agenda and 'objectivity' may make events real, but it unmakes the humans at the centre – people gazed at, but not seen.

Meanwhile, online comments remind me of the persistent presence of racism in Australia. It throws me back to the War on Terror discourse I grew up with: the expectation to 'talk back', 'denounce' and 'explain'. Talk back to whom? To those who hid behind usernames and enacted anonymous discursive violence upon our existence? It was never up to those espousing racist vitriol to explain themselves, but for me to justify why I exist as I do. An existence that only exists because of how I'm framed, not because of who I am: these racialised discourses fashion a cage around the racialised, and then demand you explain the cage you are in.

It took me far too long to realise how I'd been duped into identifying with my cage, that I'd learnt to articulate myself through the language of my oppressors – the Islamophobes and bigots who demanded I use the language of the 'Moderate Muslim', or the well-meaning liberals who said they don't see me as an Arab but as an Australian, as though erasing my sense of self was a compliment. Why must bigots colonise my attention when my efforts could be put towards collaborating with those who care? The labour of appeal produced a feeling of being on the defence; back against the wall as my energy is used to fight, instead of build. I wish I could issue a public ultimatum: choose to learn, choose to care, or get the fuck out of my way.

I'm also preoccupied with my concerns over how Egyptian authorities will react to us going public. I've been warned that the Egyptian government doesn't take kindly to this sort of 'negative' publicity. What if they're angered? What if they decide to make an example out of Dad and his case? I need Dad to be known because public accountability is a powerful tool for our advocacy, yet notoriety can become a noose to hang yourself with. There are too many unpredictable elements to juggle and conflicting possibilities. There are several prominent prisoners in Tora, and friends talk about how publicity sometimes makes it worse for them. In my research, I read cases of inmates who have had their remand detention extended beyond legal limits, been denied visitors or, worst of all, been condemned to solitary confinement. The most prominent of them is Alaa Abdel Fattah:

a revolutionary who has been in prison for almost a decade. He's been subjected to some the most punitive of punishments, including extended solitary confinement without visitors, books or even a notebook and pen. His reflections and experiences are detailed in essays published online (and later, collected in his book, *You Have Not Yet Been Defeated*). Admittedly, plenty of men without public profiles have also languished in remand detention and solitary confinement, have also been on the receiving end of petty, punitive punishments.

In the end, prison is prison. Publicity or no publicity.

*

Within a week of the publication of the article in *The Age*, I kill the momentum. There are too many unpredictable elements to juggle and conflicting possibilities. The horror stories get to me: the fact I haven't yet seen Dad means I also can't make an assessment of what he's going through or where he's at.

Making decisions about someone else's life while being in the dark about their well-being is scary – Dad's already disenfranchised, one of the few things I could offer him is a say about publicity. What'll Dad think of being Googled and having this article come up? One that links him to terrorism? What'll that do to our futures? To Dad's future? Do we really need to add to this one article if we could end this without a public record? Or is it too late? I tell Mum I don't want to do this. No campaigns. No media. 'Let's get as far as we can without it,' I say. 'Maybe Dad can come home without needing to put ourselves under the media's glare.' I turn down a few journalists' requests, and then all goes quiet. The media moves fast. The article, and the Hamouda family, is quickly forgotten.

Lamisse

Thursday 1 March 2018

It's been 10 months since I hugged Dad goodbye at Brisbane Airport.

36 days since he arrived in Cairo.

32 days since his formal 'arrest'.

A few hours until I see him.

Last night, I went to my evening critical theory class, then promptly forgot anything that was discussed. University is becoming a struggle. My memory is a sieve; anything that isn't related to Dad and his case falls right through it.

When I get home, I resist the urge to go out. Instead, I cook dinner and watch Netflix until I fall into a restless sleep. I wake before my alarm, unsure of whether I slept.

Get dressed, down some coffee and skip food; anxiety zaps my appetite. Then I walk to the station to take a train to the prison. No cousins, no car. I can't remember if I told them I was going alone. Over the year, our relationship would go through ups and downs as I began to isolate myself from them. Guilt and shame for asking them for help, knowing I could be asking them to be exposed to harm with me, would be punctuated by the need for their support and the desire for familial connection. Through these waves of emotion, I oscillated between staying in touch and avoiding their calls.

The train goes directly to the prison. Station: Tora El-Balad. When the train arrives, I hold up my phone and take a photo to send to Mum. I want to show her this place, to give her imagination something real to latch on to, even though the photo is painful in its own way. Before I can send it, two plain-clothes security men stop me: photography is forbidden. My hands are shaking as I delete the photo and profusely apologise.

My route takes me from the station through a dishevelled square, circumscribed by rickety shops. The square is shadowed by trees with leaves blanketed by dust. I turn onto the main street, squeezing myself past idling taxis and micro-buses. The packed dirt road, with the chasm of garbage still plunging down its middle, unfolds before me.

I walk, looking for the courtyard where visitors do their signing in. I don't need to go far before I find the wrought-iron gates. As I approach, I feel my body start to stiffen. Swallowing the lump in my throat, I think: *Is this a bad idea? Am I totally stupid for being here on my own?*

No one is at the desk yet, so I take a seat on the women's side to wait. Nervously, I smooth down my pants. I've tried to dress more appropriately: a coat over a long cotton shirt over loose pants, a scarf looped around my neck and draped across my chest.

There are some women next to me; I turn and smile awkwardly at them.

'Assalamu'alaykum,' I offer.

'Walaykum'assalam,' they reply.

If only I could say more – ask them questions about the process or even engage in some idle chit-chat.

More people trickle through the gates and into the courtyard. I spot Haytham and one of the uniformed guards from the previous two attempts to visit Dad. They stride up to the desk that sits between the two sections of wooden seats. The uniformed guard takes the seat. Haytham stands beside him.

Men and women start lining up, so I do likewise. A lady with a kind face taps my arm. 'Ta'ly hena' she says, then pulls me into her line. It's men on the right and women on the left. Haytham moves between the queues, checking in one woman and one man at a time. Each person hands over their identity card. A form is filled in by the uniformed guard, with the occasional help of Haytham, who spells out names and double-checks details. Once people are signed in, they leave the courtyard.

I get to the front. The uniformed guard motions for me to hand over my documents. I have both an Australian birth certificate and an Egyptian one, so I give him the Egyptian birth certificate and my Australian passport. While he studies them, I look down at his form and see he's been listing the name of each visitor, alongside their identity number and, what I assume to be, the name of the person they're visiting. There are three coloured sheets to the form: white, green and pink. The paper is that thin carbon-copy type; the uniformed guard presses firmly as he writes, making sure the ink sinks all the way through.

He looks up from my passport and asks my name.

I don't want to speak with an Australian drawl, so I put on my best Egyptian accent, saying my name how Dad says it. Then I point to my name on the Egyptian birth certificate.

The guard then asks who I'm here to see.

'Hazem Hamouda. Huwa baba.'

He stumps me with his third question: 'Siyasi wla gena'ee?'

When I stare uncomprehending, he repeats himself.

I know he's asking me to choose between two options but I don't understand the meaning of either 'siyasi' nor 'gena'ee'.

'Mish fahma,' I say. How important is this question and what if I can't answer it? Maybe I've been too confident, maybe I do need my cousins here to translate.

The uniformed guard frowns, turns and says something to Haytham.

Haytham then asks me the same thing: 'Siyasi wla gena'ee?'

Whatever shred of confidence I had that I could get through this on my own is now burning under the heat of humiliation.

Reverting to English, I say, 'I am here to see Hazem Hamouda.' I point to my birth certificate, where Dad's name is written in Arabic so he can read it. Then I point to my passport. 'Ustraliya,' I say. It's presumptuous, but since Dad is also the only Australian guy in there, maybe there's a chance they'll have some idea who he is.

Haytham looks down at the identity documents, and then looks back up at me. 'Siyasi wla gena'ee?'

Frustration replaces humiliation. If I haven't understood by now, why keep repeating the question?

I shrug. 'Ana asfa, mish fahma.'

An orchestra of voices erupts around me as several people start speaking all at once, faces earnest as they attempt to help me solve this comprehension problem. Out of the crowd emerges a lady who appears to be in her mid to late 40s; short and stout, with a bright, stretchy hijab wrapped tightly around her face.

Brandishing her finger at me with the flourishing authority of a strict aunt, she looks up at me with confidence: '*Bad man* – ge'naee! Ikhwan – siyasi!'

A neuron fires off in my head: *Ikhwan? Siyasi?* Ikhwan means Brotherhood, shorthand for the full name of the movement: Al Ikhwaan Al-Muslimeen (The Muslim Brotherhood). So, does the word 'siyasi' have something to do with the Brotherhood?

I hazard a guess: 'Uh, siyasi?'

Haytham nods in approval and repeats 'siyasi' to the uniformed guard, who duly notes it. The people get back into line and I thank the lady as she steps back, looking pleased. Haytham proceeds to spell out our names, then he reads out my passport number. He hands back the documents. Much to my relief, he asks no more questions and shoos me off.

I stride away in the same direction I saw other people take. Walking with the satisfaction that I've overcome the first hurdle, I come crashing into the realisation that I have no clue what to do next.

At the same gates that I came in through, I pause to take in my surroundings again. This time, I notice there are two black iron doors that punctuate the seamless dull yellow of the sandy wall that hides the prison buildings inside. They look like portals. *Which one will I go through?*

I remember the haphazardly arranged chairs under the tree at the top of the street; it seemed like a kind of waiting area, so I make the decision to head there.

Winter rains have created slick mud patches on the dirt road. Tentatively, I pick past stewing puddles, the carts of vegetable and fruit sellers, the makeshift wall of plastic shoes and cheap sneakers, and the kiosk built into the ground floor of an apartment building. A bakery radiates the tantalising smell of fresh bread. I pass the now familiar muddy donkey, still tied to a post and facing a wall.

At the waiting area, a large tree creates a shaded canopy over plastic deck chairs in pink, blue and white. Tuk-tuks and taxis swerve past, almost scraping the legs of those sitting in the row facing the road. There is also a wooden desk. Arranged across it are boxes of chewing gum, men's razors, tissues and chocolates.

A woman sits behind the desk. With a worn, tough but friendly face, she's busily talking to people who approach. I choose a seat near her, then cross my legs and fold my hands in my lap, as though I'm casually waiting for the bus.

Every now and then, the lady pulls out white plastic garbage bags from under her desk and sells them to people. The person buying the bag then picks up a permanent marker sitting on a box of lighters and writes on the bag. They put the marker back and then walk off with the bag.

Other people go up to the lady and hand over their mobile phones. I assume she's scribbling their names on torn pieces of paper. She tucks the phone and paper into a freezer bag and slides it all into the desk drawer. Obviously, mobile phones can't be taken inside the prison. This is the woman who'll keep them safe. I'm absorbed by watching people move through motions that are yet to have meaning for me; I don't connect the movements of people getting ready for their prison visit to something that I also need to do to. Writing this, it occurs to me that I didn't ask anyone about what they were doing, nor did I ask for guidance on what was next. I just sat, watched and wondered: separated not by language or physical barriers, but by my own disassociated state of witnessing without connecting.

Behind the desk, to the right of the seated area, is a table with a stainless-steel hot water boiler, along with glass mugs, boxes of El-Rosa tea, instant Nescafé packets, sugar and CoffeeMate. It's another makeshift commercial enterprise; the man sells tea and coffee to people seated under the tree, delivering them directly into the cold, outstretched hands of his customers.

The iron door closest to where I'm seated has opened. I see Haytham cross the road, coming from the courtyard. He gets to the opening and stands outside of it. Visitors approach, all clutching their bulging white plastic bags with Arabic marked on the front. As Haytham yells names, people step forwards and trudge through the entryway. While I patiently watch and wait, the crowd diminishes in size.

As the last people are going through the door, the lady at the desk calls out to me. She asks me what I'm doing here, so I point to the prison and say, 'Baba henaak.'

Immediately, her eyes widen. 'Yalla rooh!' she yells, while making an urgent sweeping motion with her hands in the direction of the prison entrance. Her intensity pushes me off my chair and I begin my sprint across the dirt road. She calls out after me, 'Mobeel!', so I sprint back and thrust my phone at her. Then, I run across the road, take an awkward side-leap over the chasm and concrete barrier, and hurry towards Haytham and the open iron door.

The list of visitor names is scrunched in his large hands. Disapproval is evident on his face. As he speaks, I infer that he's asking me where I've been, telling me off for missing the fact that he had called my name.

I point to the plastic chair: 'Henaak!'

He launches into a monologue – presumably giving me instructions or a reprimand. Possibly both. Maybe neither. Embarrassed about missing my call, and afraid to interrupt him, I nod along, feigning understanding, all while hoping my obsequiousness will placate him so he'll let me in.

Maybe he asks me a question and I nod instead of answering. Regardless, I clock the moment that my polite pretence is up, as his face reveals that he knows I have no idea what he's saying. His speech peters out, ending with a tired, 'Mashy?'

'Mashy,' I parrot.

'Emshy, emshy!' he says, hurriedly ushering me inside.

Internally, I'm screaming at myself: *What the fuck? You're in! You almost missed it but you're in! Look at you! Look at this place! You're going to see Dad!*

I step through the entrance, then hop down a couple of steps. The sandy wall encompasses the entire complex; I assume there are separate entrances for guards and prisoners, and that these doors are just for visitors.

At the bottom of the stairs, I encounter a guard seated on a white plastic chair and holding a clipboard. He asks for my ID. I hand over my passport, my birth certificate folded and tucked into its pages. He doesn't open it. Just glances at it, nods then points to a small courtyard across the other side of a dirt road. It is crammed with people.

So, this is Tora: so far, it's a couple of low-set, dull ochre yellow buildings. Behind the courtyard crammed with people is another long wall and turrets; in the turrets, guards and their guns. To the right, the dirt road runs straight and long, and there's a large green military truck parked in the distance. On the left, the road and wall curve; the end of the road is cornered by the residential street on the other side. I know there is so much more than what I can see, yet I'm afraid of being seen to be staring too much. I drop my gaze as I reach the enclosed courtyard.

Nervous anticipation has my heart leaping over beats, my skin prickling. I want a cigarette: a quiet moment of leaning against the courtyard wall. I look around and notice a couple of men smoking outside the courtyard, but no women.

It's too full to stand inside the courtyard, so I hover at the entrance. There must be about 80 or more people crammed into this space. The lucky ones are sitting on granite benches along the walls. The smell of stale urine occasionally wafts through the air. After a woman steps out from behind a swinging wooden door looking both relieved and disgusted, I realise there's a toilet in the back corner. If I can smell it from the other side of the courtyard, what must it be like inside?

I start to wonder what the toilet is like in Dad's cell. Then I stop. I have to block off any thoughts of Dad's living conditions. If I don't, I'll catastrophise by filling in the blanks with all my anxiety. Remember to let go, to receive the prison as it is.

Everyone in the courtyard is facing a doorway with the kind of security setup you see at an airport. An aged conveyer belt takes up quite a bit of space, so the stand-alone metal detector creates the only entry point. In front of the archway of the metal detector stands a conscript with papers in his hand. I'm certain he's a conscript because he looks different from the plain-clothes guards and the uniformed guards: he's young and skinny, wearing a roughly made bottle-green uniform of thick cotton, and his black pleather boots are peeling. Egypt has mandatory conscription for men under the age of 30, and there are few exceptions to this rule.

He calls out names. Men's names. That's when I notice it's always women who get up and answer the call, hauling along their bulging white plastic bags and lifting them onto a conveyor belt. Then it dawns on me: maybe this is what Haytham tried to explain! That they call people by the name of their imprisoned relative.

Is this why I missed the call? Because I was listening out for my name, but they called me by my father's name? Thinking about this starts to creep me out.

It's like Youm al-Qiyama (Judgement Day).

The religious instruction I'd received growing up had included a minor detail: that on the Day of Judgement, we'd be called forwards to answer to Allah by our father's name. Remembering this, I imagine the courtyard as an assembly of wretched, dusty humans preparing to beg for mercy from the ravages of Hell.

And if I could beg someone for mercy to free Dad from this hell, I would unhesitatingly throw myself on this dirt.

I don't think about how people are here for more than their fathers: they're also here for their sons, husbands and brothers. A younger lady approaches me. Greeting me, she smiles warmly, pulling me out of my apocalyptic visions. She then invites me to sit with her and her family on the granite bench. I'm grateful to have a seat and a person to connect with.

'Shantitik feen?'

'Eh?' I respond.

She points to the full white garbage bags at her feet. 'Ah-heh.'

I look down at the bags. 'Eh da?'

'Akl.'

She opens the bags and shows me containers of cooked rice and meat, biscuits, bread, vegetables and fruit. I'm shocked by the amount of food in her bags. I'm surprised: Don't the men get fed inside? Why didn't anyone tell me I had to bring supplies with me? I was so focussed on getting into the prison, I didn't consider bringing supplies with me. The lady confirms that I need to bring food, as though she can hear my thoughts.

'Lazem tageebi akl li-babaki.'

'Ah … mish arfa …' I say sadly. 'Momken murra gayya.'

Her smile is gentle and empathic. 'Ma'lesh.'

I smile back, then lapse into silence, again thinking about what else I don't know and what I could bring.

My butt grows numb from sitting on cold stone.

Then I hear it: 'Hazem … Hazem Hamouda!'

I get up and yell, 'Aywaa!'

I place my drawstring backpack on the conveyor belt to be X-rayed. Then I walk through the metal detector. The walls of the room I find myself in are painted white, but stained and marked with graffiti.

'Bas?' asks a plain-clothes guard; he looks like a swollen bullfrog, chest heaving with each laboured breath.

'Na'am,' I shrug. 'Bas.'

The guard motions for me to go left.

I'm greeted by a sour, tight-lipped lady. She's standing by a desk tucked into an alcove sectioned off from the corridor.

She asks for my bag and I hand it to her. Pawing through it, she finds my wallet, then looks through each of its little compartments. She motions for me to come towards her, then runs her hands over my body, taking time to feel around my breasts. Her hands continue down my legs, swiping briefly between them, and I tense with discomfort. Satisfied, she gives back my bag and tells me I can go.

There's only one direction to go in – towards a caged corridor, where an iron lattice comes up from the ground, like a vine growing over our heads, connecting to the prison wall. All the visitors who were ahead of me are standing in this corridor, so I join them in waiting. At the end, two conscript guards stand and call our names. We trudge forwards. Every wintery gust throws up dust that flies at us like tiny glass shards, whipping at our exposed skin. Like most people in this procession, I try to turn away from the wind, hunching to protect my face from the flying grit.

The 80 or so people who were crammed into the courtyard are now squished into this passageway. Small, barred windows, just above our heads, carry out the conversations of people on the other side of the wall. Graffiti is etched onto the wall and scratched into the iron pylons. There's one piece of graffiti in English: *ashes to ashes / dust to dust / fade to black / the memories remain.* I write it down in my pocket-sized notebook.

Progress is slow. I don't know the time as I don't have my phone nor do I own a watch. I have no sense of how long I've been waiting; perhaps I've moved a metre in what has seemed like an hour. Judging by the sunlight, it appears it's been at least three hours since I stepped off the train at Tora El-Balad station. Restless kids climb the iron lattice. Irritated mothers pull them down before irritated guards can yell at the children. I'm tall compared to most people here, so I can see over people's heads to the end of the corridor. The young conscripts laze against the doorway. Every now and then, one of them cranes their head back to nod at whoever gives the instructions. After the nod, they face the passageway and call out a name, and a person, or group of people, steps forward and disappears around the corner.

The wait in the corridor drags on. There are no chairs. Children are quickly quietened if they get loud, and most impassively stare. Some people sag against the walls. Others chit-chat.

I notice a kid with large green eyes gazing into the distance. He looks to be about 12 or 13. A weariness hangs over him. His hands are stuffed deep in his pockets and his shoulders are close to his ears. He is with his family: a mother and some younger siblings. He could be the eldest son; a tired child charged with being a man while he's still a boy. I preoccupy myself by wondering who this kid is. *Is he here to visit his dad? Why does he look so stiff and tired? Does he go to school? What is his life like?*

I shift my gaze, glancing around at people in line as I wonder about who they are. After a while, I give up people-watching and listlessly look out through the cage of iron lattice. Time in this corridor feels like I'm dragging my knees through the heavy water of the sea. Visible in the distance, to our left, are some conscripts hanging around at the corner where the road curves. I watch them as they chat with each other. They share cigarettes, inhaling slowly while looking down the dirt road or back at the cage towards us. Their bodies are slouched; they all seemed bored, resigned to passing time with idle words and grey exhales.

I'm closer to the front now, and I notice that the two conscript soldiers keep looking at me; I can't tell if it's a sexualised gaze or an inquisitive glance. Every time I catch them looking, their eyes flick away in haste. I think about aggressively staring one of them down so he'll stop, but I'm too anxious, too uncertain about what the unspoken rules of interaction are in the prison. Best to let them look and studiously avoid eye contact.

At long last, Dad's name is called. I step forwards, past the two conscripts, following the path towards large double iron doors fitted into a towering wall at the bottom of some stairs.

A guard in a blue and white uniform cracks open one of the gates, and I slide through the gap into a shabby courtyard.

He closes the gate, turns towards me and asks for my ID. I riffle around in my bag and bring out my passport.

He takes it, and I wait for him to give it back. Instead, he tries to shoo me off.

'My passport!' I insist, panicking.

He shakes his head.

'No, my passport!' I don't move. My passport is my security blanket. *What if he loses it? What if it goes 'missing'?*

With a sigh, he explains, and I infer, that I can't have it back until after I've finished the visit. He walks away, leaving me standing there by myself. Hoping I've understood him, I let it go. As one of the last visitors to be processed, I don't have anyone to follow. Again, I have no idea where to go.

To my left are offices on a raised platform. A toilet block sits beside the offices. Beyond the toilet block is a row of low-set buildings that form a long L-shape before ending at a gate that opens into another courtyard on the other side. Through the open gate, a tree is visible. Quite close to me are three tables. Several plain-clothes prison officers are sifting through bags of food while a couple of visitors watch and wait. Some mangy cats hang out under the table, presumably waiting for scraps.

A plain-clothes guard walks up to me. He looks like a stereotypical Arab Dad, the kind who shows up on Egyptian sitcoms: a baggy knitted jumper, collared shirt underneath, a bit of a paunch and a thick, black moustache. He asks who I'm here to see.

'Hazem Hamouda,' I reply.

'Il-Ustraliya!' he says with glee.

He motions to a white-haired man in a blue uniform sitting on a plastic chair, nursing a notebook. The pen in his hand is poised over its pages. 'Go to him,' he says in English.

The elderly man on the chair also asks who I'm here to see and I repeat myself: 'Hazem Hamouda.' I swear, I've never said Dad's name so many times in one day. He writes Dad's name down in the notebook, then waves me away.

I wander back to the spot where I was standing before the guard approached me. It's near the gate, in front of the elevated office. Confused and uncomfortable, I'm still uncertain as to where I should go next, so I just stand there.

The courtyard is now quiet; the guards have left the tables and there are no more people having their bags of food searched. Some people dressed in what looks like green pyjamas – I think they're prisoners – are hauling the white bags from the desk to the courtyard on the other side, placing the bags somewhere out of sight.

The guards I can see seem preoccupied. A plain-clothes guard leans on a wall near me. He has slicked-back hair and vividly black eyes; the combination of his thin, angled features, smooth skin and glistening gelled hair gives him the look of a shark. In his hand, he holds a packet of Marlboro reds and a mobile phone. He doesn't look approachable at all. I stay where I am. I gently sway, shifting from foot to foot as my feet are aching from standing for so long. It was around 8.30 am when I bolted in; surely it is almost midday now.

In front of me is a covered passageway, tucked between a portable unit the size of a demountable schoolroom and a building – it could be the same building that forms the wall the iron lattice connects to on the other side. I saw other visitors walk through it, after their food had been searched. *Perhaps that's where I am supposed to go.*

Another plain-clothes guard walks towards me. As he gets closer, I notice he has light blue eyes.

'Enty bint Hazem?' he asks.

'Na'am,' I reply.

'Mashy. Estaniny hena.'

I wait in the empty courtyard, shivering, whether from the cold or because I'm nervous, I don't know.

As time passes, boredom overtakes my nervousness: *did they forget about me?*

Finally, the blue-eyed guard reappears. 'Ta'aly,' he says.

We go past the portable unit, through the covered passageway, and enter a small paved clearing in front of an open door. From the doorway, a cacophony of voices rolls out. It is the same space from which I could hear voices as I waited in the latticed corridor.

Instead of going inside, the blue-eyed guard firmly guides me to a wooden bench in the concrete clearing.

'Au'dy hena, abuki gay.' He walks off.

My heart jumps: *Dad is coming.*

Hazem

In the early morning, the Shaweesh comes to our cell door and shouts through the nadarah.

'Hazem Hamouda. Ziyara!'

I can't believe my ears! I have a visitor? Is it Lamisse? It must be! Am I finally going to see her today? I can't think straight! I don't know what to do! One of my cellmates shouts out, 'Congratulations, ya Hazem! This is very good news! You need to write a letter to explain to her what's going on. And you need to wash, freshen up!'

I snap out of my daze, and ask for a pen and paper. I sit down to write a letter for the family, and one for Lamisse, to explain things. I finish writing and another cellmate approaches me. 'Hide the letters in your clothes somewhere. They will search you before you go out, and if they find it, the letters will be confiscated and handed to National Security, and you'll be sent to solitary confinement for three or four days.'

Laughing to hide my spike of anxiety, I say, 'Yeah sure, that's nice to know! Thanks for the information.'

I only have one set of clothing. The clothes are a bit dirty, and I worry for a moment about not being clean enough for a visitor. Then I remember that I get to see Lamisse, and my concern over my clothing is subsumed by my excitement to see her, to have a visitor.

It's about 11 am when the Shaweesh arrives to open the door and command all those who have been called for visits to stand and step outside. Another cellmate of mine happens to have his mother and sister visiting today too, so I follow him outside. His name is Omar, he's only 19 – that's the same age as my own son, Harun. He's quickly won my heart and, like my own son, he is a gentle, kind and intelligent young man. Omar turns and reassures me, 'Emshy waraya, wa 'amil illy ana amiluh.' *Follow me and what I do.*

We go into the corridor and wait. A person comes striding up behind me, saying my name. I turn: 'Ayuwaa, da ana.' *Yes, that's me.*

He grabs my hand. 'Al-humdullilah a'salama, ana Mustafa Kassem. Ana Masri-Amreeki, ana hena min alfeen wa talatashar. 'Amil eh?' *Ah, thank God for your safe arrival! I'm Mustafa Kassem. I'm Egyptian-American, and I've been here since August 2013. How are you?*

He's particularly enthused to meet me, and invites me into his cell. He shares the cell with two men: a man named Ismail, who is 33, and Mohammed, who is 48. Like Mustafa, both of them have also been in Tora since August 2013. A lot of the men in Building 4 are from the al-Rabaa' case.

They both greet me with warmth. Meanwhile, Mustafa Kassem boils a kettle and makes me Nescafé. I haven't had a coffee since I was in Dubai airport! None of the other cells I've been in have had coffee as tea is often preferred.

The cell is particularly small, and given there are only three of them in it, they manage to keep it quite tidy. I notice their cell is also well-stocked; not only do they have a kettle, they also have a NiCr coil fixed into a ceramic body, which allows them to heat their food. There is also a Styrofoam box filled with ice that keeps items that would usually be refrigerated. There is even a fan, an MP3 player and a lot of books stacked in one corner.

How on earth did they get these things?

I don't hold the question to myself. I ask Mustafa and he laughs.

'Qisat taweela. Ishrab al-Nescafe. Ana eizak tukoon mabsoot la'ma tahshoof bentak. Khaleeha tukoon mabsoota, ulaha kolo tamam. Muhim enaha ta'raf innak fe aman.' *It's a long story. Enjoy your Nescafé. I want you to be happy when you see your daughter. Make her feel happy too, tell her everything is okay. It will be good for her and your family to know that you are safe.*

Mohammed looks at my clothes. 'Akhi, il-jacket mish helw. Khod il-jacket da. Ahly gabooh momken tilbiso. Mati'lash, il-kilaab mish hataraf inuh mokhtalif.' *Brother, this prison jacket you are wearing is hideous. Here, take this one. My family brought it for me a while ago. And don't worry, the bastards won't notice you've got a new jacket.*

I accept the jacket gratefully. 'Shukran, ya akhi.' *That's really kind of you, Brother.*

'Brother' is a common endearment used among men in the prison – like the way you'd use 'bro' or 'mate'.

Our names are called again. We need to leave to go to the prisoner visitors hall. It's around 12 pm, and all the prisoners from Building 4 who are receiving visitors line up in front of the first steel gate to get out. There are about 20 of us. We wait for the Shaweesh and the Mokhber to call our names and search us, one by one. I notice some of the prisoners are carrying white plastic bags containing clothes and plastic containers.

My name is called again.

I walk towards the guards as they mark my name down on a formal sheet, then they start patting me down. We are walked towards the visitors building, passing steel gates and prison guards. More prisoners join us from Buildings 1, 2 and 3. Once we reach the main yard, one of the guards opens a large lockup area, another *Habsa*

Khana: it's a steel-barred cage with a filthy toilet in the corner. Since we're all dressed in white, we look like sheep being herded into a pen. I follow, keeping my eye on Omar. Once we're inside, there's an explosion of chattering and mumbling between the prisoners as everyone tries to catch up with their friends from the other buildings. I feel like the new kid at school, watching all this commotion, but still excluded from it because I don't know anyone. I hover close to Omar as he chats to one of his friends from Building 3. Prisoners are often moved around to different cells, so it is during the daily walks, court-hearings and visitation days that we find chances to catch-up with old cellmates and friends.

My name is called again. The guards come up to the cage. The noise of the chattering fades and everyone turns to look at me. The guards open the door, and the prisoners shuffle aside to let me out. As I'm walking through, I hear some whispers: 'Who is he? Why did they call him?'

I'm greeted by one of the Mabahiz. His nickname is *Abu Tiyaaz*, Father of the Assholes.

'Bintak barah, warayah,' he commands. *Your daughter is out, come walk behind me.*

Lamisse

Sitting alone in the quiet courtyard, I can hear all the other visitors' voices coming through the doorway. It sounds noisy inside but part of me wishes I was in the same room as everyone I stood in line with. *Are Dad and I getting special treatment? Is it a privilege to sit outside?* We'd been given a separate space as Dad is a somewhat 'special prisoner'. The only other prisoner offered this was a former media personality, who we once shared the space with. After a few visits, I informed Dad I wanted to sit inside the cafeteria with everyone else. The solidarity and connection of being in proximity with the other families was important to me; plus, suffering shared is suffering eased.

The increasingly familiar scent of piss teases the air and I take a quick look around for the source. On an impulse, I bend forwards to look under the bench. My head hanging between my knees, I see a stinking, open drain.

Content with knowing where the smell comes from, I sit back up and keep waiting.

My father rounds the corner, a guard holding his arm. Dad is wearing a white zip-up sweater, white pants and white shoes like Crocs. I leap up from the bench and gasp, 'Dad!'

He doesn't respond; just looks at me, his expression blank. Then he turns to the guard and quietly says something. I freeze, unsure whether or not to approach. But then the guard lets him go and he walks towards me, wrapping me in a big hug. 'Lamisse!'

The guard walks away, leaving us on our own. I cannot believe I have Dad in my arms; that he's fleshy, warm and real. His earthy, spicy scent is comfortingly familiar and I want to keep holding on to my father because as long as we're hugging, we don't have to talk.

I have no idea what I'm going to say: what do you say to someone after all this?

We part and sit down.

Immediately, Dad's nose wrinkles. 'It smells so bad.'

'I know, we're above a drain.'

He bends over to look under the bench, his head hanging between his knees. 'I see,' he says, then sits back up. 'We should move the bench.'

'I don't know if we can,' I say nervously. I'm scared of doing anything except what I've been instructed to do. And what I've been told to do is sit here on this bench. 'Don't worry about the smell, it's not important.'

I put my hand on my dad's knee, hoping touch will get him to focus on this moment and not the drain. 'How are you?'

Looking up at his face, I can see his hazel eyes are darkened, wide and walled up. I recoil – Dad has his defences up. This face was familiar to me. Outside the prison, I knew this mood to be the one where you don't ask Dad for anything: not a lift, pocket money, homework help or permission to visit your friend. You wait until he's softened; until he is in a good mood, when he's put his defences down and he's ready to receive you. Otherwise, he cannot hear you. Not because he's hard of hearing, but because he's closed.

I am not a child and we're not at home. In this environment, why wouldn't his defences be up? Why wouldn't he be closed?

But can he take them down for me?

'Yes, I'm fine,' he says, then rattles off some small talk about how he's doing okay, that it's not that bad, and how he hopes he's only going to be in here for a short time.

'Tell me,' he says, suddenly finished with talking about himself. 'How's the family? How's your mum?'

His tone is short and sharp; I get the feeling we can't talk candidly. There's something brittle about the wall he's holding up and I don't want to break it. Even though we're alone, I wonder if the guards are watching us from some place out of sight. As much as it pains me to play into the pretence of being fine, it feels necessary for this moment.

So, I place some reinforcements in my own emotional walls and calmly reassure Dad. 'We're staying strong,' I tell him. I tell him everything is fine, and not to worry about us because everything will be fine, and no worries, we'll get through it, it's only a pothole in the road of life. My babbling, and the word 'fine' chime empty in my ears. Though I play along, I hate the pretence of strength: this is the first time I'm seeing Dad since I left Australia in July last year. Where's the space for tears, for the expressions of love and relief at finally finding each other?

I keep offering these rambling platitudes while I sit with the horror that has consumed us since Dad first disappeared. I'm thinking about the tears, the thrum of fear that's come to occupy our daily lives. I want to tell my father I feel small and scared, to confess that I don't know what I'm doing.

But I press on and confidently launch into an explanation of what (I think) the lawyer is doing. This prompts a slow thawing as Dad perks up and begins to offer his own thoughts on the legal processes. We compare notes on what we think we know about his case and our ideas about what to do. Then, Dad goes off on a tangent, talking about the role of the Embassy and being Australian, and I realise he doesn't know much about his own case. All the information he's gleaned has been from his brief moment in the prosecutor's office and two short, sham court hearings. He hasn't seen the Embassy or a lawyer yet. Since January, I'm the first person he's been able to talk to who isn't from within the prison system. I explain to him the challenges of dual national arrests in countries where they hold citizenship.

I remind him that he's stuck in remand detention until the accusations are either dropped or formalised into official charges. When they're formalised, he must then wait for a conviction. Remand detention isn't supposed to be for more than two years, I say. But there are some people here who have already been waiting for five, he replies.

Saying this, Dad only barely conceals his panic: he starts talking faster, pulling out theory after theory, bargaining with the air, me standing in as a witness, prosecutor and judge. As he spirals, I'm fading in my fight to keep up with him. In the cell, he's had so much – too much – time to think. It's too much speculation for me.

Once again, I just want to deal with facts.

And the overarching fact is: neither of us knows anything substantial about his case or what to do. We're both in the fallout of shock and we need more information.

Dad does a sharp pivot away from his case and asks about the letter and our search for him. The version of the story I give him is bland, truncated: we went to the courthouse, the airport and the police station and found nothing. I emphasise: 'If it wasn't for your letter, I don't know when we would have found you.'

Discussion of the search reminds me of the Embassy and the Privacy Act. I tell Dad that the Embassy will visit soon and that he needs to give them permission to share information with Mum and me.

From my bag, I pull out my pocket notebook and a pen. 'Write it here.'

'Write what?'

'That you give me permission.'

He scribbles down a note for the Embassy and signs it.

*

A loud and urgent whistle goes off. It startles me.

'It's the end of the visitation hour,' announces Dad.

The visiting area starts emptying out; a bottleneck forms at the top of the passageway as people fill up the small clearway, collecting their IDs as they're shuffled out.

Getting up to leave, I say: 'It's a bit chaotic, isn't it?'

'You should see inside,' comes Dad's dry response.

He stands and pulls himself to his full height, and for a moment, he towers over me. With his back ramrod straight and shoulders square, he looks tall and intimidating, like a grizzly ready to fight. I'm possessed by the urge to push him. I want my soft and loving Dad, not this; I want to be comforted and reassured.

Instead, I make a move towards the crowd.

'By the way, is there anything you need?' I ask before I move out of range.

'Clothes. I need more clothes. And food, anything. Just bring food. Nothing that spoils though, we don't have a fridge. And notebooks and pens. And books, if you can.' It pours out of him like he already had an inventory of needs prepared in his head. 'And a blanket,' he adds. 'It's cold. There's no heating.'

'I'll see what I can do,' comes my response.

I move back towards my father to give him a goodbye hug. I place my head on his chest. I can feel and hear his heart against the side of my face: it thumps rapidly against my cheek. It's all an armoured front: he's petrified, too.

Dad puts his face into my hair and inhales deeply – something he's done ever since I was a child. I tighten my arms around him. It's comforting and reassuring. The intimacy threatens the integrity of my emotional wall. This is why we need distance: no breaking down is allowed. I push away and out of the hug.

'I need to get going,' I say, turning to face the crowd and regain a neutral expression. I glance back at Dad. He's looking over the heads of the jostling people. I follow his gaze. He has locked eyes with the blue-eyed guard. The blue-eyed guard nods at him, as though to say, 'Yes, time is up. Wait there.'

I give Dad's upper arm a final pat. 'See you next week, okay? My visiting day is every Thursday from now on.'

'Okay. Next week.'

Leaving Dad standing by the bench, I slip into the crowd and start slowly moving along. Ahead, people are picking up their ID cards from a man who sits at an open window in the portable unit. I turn and yell, 'Salamu'alaykum, Dad. Love you!'

'Walaykum'assalam. Love you too,' he calls back. Then he sits down again on the bench, dropping out of view behind the throng.

I push my way past the people waiting for the return of their identity cards to get to the man who took my passport.

He's standing by the iron gates. When he sees me approaching, he sifts through a stack of passports on a concrete ledge. He wordlessly hands back my blue document with the kangaroo and emu etched in gold on the front.

Carried along by the crowd, I walk back through the big iron gate and make a beeline across the dirt road to the iron door. Up the stairs, I step through the opening and my feet land on the pavement.

The moment I stepped inside Tora, I forgot the existence of the outside world. Now, I'm disorientingly thrust back into it. The tuk-tuks still screech, the chairs are still cracked and dusty, the tree still spreads its leafy branches and the sky is still blue.

When I go to collect my phone from the older lady at the desk, I try to thank her. If she hadn't shooed me, I would have sat on that chair all afternoon and missed seeing Dad. It seems like she understands my earnest attempt at expressing my gratitude. She returns my phone and I leave.

I check my phone. It's just after one o'clock. Turns out I was in the prison for nearly five hours. Only one of those hours was spent with Dad.

Exhaustion sinks into my bones. I can't be bothered taking the train, so I trudge down the street towards the corniche, the long stretch of highway that runs by the Nile.

The Nile drifts under the bright afternoon sun, muddy and slow. I wave down a speeding cab, jump into the back seat and tell the driver my address. I lean my head against the window and stare out at the street whizzing past me in a colourful blur.

I feel hollow.

I check in with the hollowness and find anger.

Beneath the anger, I'm shattered.

Hazem

Abu Tiyaaz leads me to the main courtyard; we round a corner and she's sitting on a wooden bench.

Lamisse!

For that moment, nothing exists except Lamisse. Everything goes quiet around me and all I can see is my beloved daughter. I open my arms for a hug. We don't say anything and just hold each other. I keep myself composed as Mustafa's advice echoes in my head: 'Let your family know that you're safe.' I want to reassure her, even though it feels wrong to tell her I'm safe.

We sit down on the bench, and it smells terribly. Lamisse points out there's an open drain underneath us. She puts her hand on my knee and I hold her other hand as we talk. I give her an extremely brief run-down of what's happened so far, leaving out most of the details. I feel I need to be the strong father, to remain in control and not let her see how afraid I am. I ask her about what's happening with the family back home, and she tells me about the lawyer and how she's trying to figure out what we can do to get me out. It's business-like, the way we update each other.

I realised later that, perhaps, I was in shock. Even though I was so happy to see her, I felt I couldn't explain to her what I was really feeling ... what was really going on. Everything had been so strange and disorienting up until now. Seeing Lamisse there, in the prison, peeled something away from the edges of my consciousness as a roaring feeling began to surface.

This was all very real and not a terrible dream at all.

With the guard watching us, I am unable to give Lamisse the letters I wrote. Instead, I tell her as much as I can about my case and what I have analysed so far. She gives me a summary of the search for me after I ask about the letter I'd smuggled out. She mentions that the Embassy are going to try to visit.

The guard calls out to tell us it's time to wrap it up.

We stand up as people start coming out of the prison cafeteria. They quickly fill up the space where Lamisse and I are standing. I look out for the guard, and he catches my eyes and nods. I give Lamisse a goodbye hug. I don't know what to do, how to reassure her or myself. This all feels so surreal, and so horrifying. As Lamisse looks like she's about to disappear into the crowd, she asks me if I need anything. I quickly tell her the list of things I have written on the letter hidden in my sock. She turns back towards me and gives me another hug. I put my arm around her, but I'm looking at the guard, knowing that he's going to take me back inside as I grapple with the pain that I don't get to leave with Lamisse. I take a deep breath to try and calm myself down, and hold onto this moment for a second longer.

Abu Tiyaaz escorts me back to my cell alone. As we walk past the prisoner holding area, I can hear all the men talking. Abu Tiyaaz hands me over to a Shaweesh once we get to the entrance of Building 4. The Shaweesh then takes me through the building, back to my cell.

I walk inside. The door closes behind me. The happiness I had carried from seeing Lamisse crumbles into devastation. I'm actually here, trapped again. A hot itch spreads over my skin. My cellmates ask me how I am, how my visit with Lamisse went. I answer their curious questions and try to act normal, but I'm shattered. I feel utterly wretched and I drown in my anxiety. I ask for some space, and I go to my corner to lie down. Perhaps, I can sleep this feeling away.

PART TWO

'Everyone is subject to violence in prison, but overt violence is usually rare; walls, gates, locks, and hopelessness are usually enough to ensure the prisoners' compliance.'

– Alaa Abdel Fattah

Reflection

Though we started this project as co-authors, Dad soon stopped writing.

During those early days of drafting this book, we were constantly confronting the power of silencing through violence and fear, reacting to the cop in our heads. Or, as I characterised it in my journal, 'the security apparatus that had been installed in my chest'. That chest-binding paranoia was reminding me daily that speaking up could place us in danger. After all, that was the point of Dad's imprisonment: speaking will make you a target of violence. This is how the walls last beyond the prison; this fear is how you become complicit in maintaining the walls built inside you. This is one of the reasons why so many keep silent after they've been freed. Few want to take the risk of inviting more terror. The desire to move on with family and friends, to preserve access to a nation-state that still holds loved ones is strong. And it's understandable.

For all the fear that I felt, I felt something else more strongly: a raging, desperate desire to speak. The intense injustice of the experience couldn't be rectified in any other way: there was no court to go to, no pathways for compensation. All I could have was the truth as I told it, my refusal to be silenced. And while writing about these days required me to agonisingly relive them, once memories were within reach, I could displace them out of my head – and out of my body – by putting them onto the page. The catharsis became greater than the fear.

Thus, writing became my way of fighting to stay alive. Writing was how I could tear down the walls. Writing was how I wrote myself back into being. Writing was how I was made visible, while making visible those being made invisible. Writing meant that I no longer had a secret: I had a record.

For Dad, however, it was a different story.

For starters, I wasn't the one in prison – Dad was. While the impact on me ran deep, it is also vastly different to the enduring legacy it left in Dad. For Dad, there was no proxy through which to experience the violence. The violence was fast, vicious, sustained and direct. He was the one who suffered under the prison's daily humiliations. The passages he wrote, which appear in the preceding chapters, convey his deep shock – the scrambling to make sense of an onslaught of psychological and physical violence. What strikes me is his determination and desperation to grasp onto anything that could help him make sense of it all, epitomised by his demands for the most minimum of rights he believed he might have: the right to contact a lawyer, the Embassy, his family.

Inside those walls, the experience wasn't solely of horror. Friendships formed, thanks to the intertwining of fates, the camaraderie that weaves itself among men in suffering. Separated from love and belonging, they built bonds with each other. Once out of prison and back in Australia, Dad found himself grappling with survivor's guilt, adrift in a sea where few understood what he'd been through.

Since being released, he has remained deeply troubled by the possibility that he'd invited this horror onto himself and his family. He wanted to move on – to find a job, to get back to a 'normal' life – but that proved to be not so accessible. He acknowledged the necessity of the campaign to free him, but resented that he couldn't erase it from the internet, convinced that a simple Google from an employer would ensure he'd never work again. On top of all that, he struggled with the thought that this book could invite more danger, and it didn't matter if the risks were real or not.

Dad became overwhelmed. He reached the point where he could no longer write, even to empty his mind in his diary. It was as though the excavation he did – through the passages he produced – had uncovered a block inside him, and instead of trying to smash through it, he decided to respect it. Perhaps there's a reason it's there; perhaps it's protecting him. I expected him to withdraw from the book entirely, to tell me to stop writing, but he didn't.

We all have different ways of unravelling our silences. While Dad could no longer write, he said he would like to talk. So, I did interviews with him. They're interspersed throughout the rest of this book: his voice, his record, pieces he's willing to share, clear and determined, to be heard on his terms.

Saturday 3 March 2018

It's my birthday. I'm still reeling from the visit with Dad, burying my distress under the flurry of attempting to maintain a 'normal' life. This is what we're all trying to do. Saja is working full-time, Harun and Amira are at university, Jasmine is pregnant with her second child, Kareem has just started high school and Mum is in the middle, supporting everyone: caring for Jas and her 3 year old, parenting my 13 year old brother, and ensuring Harun and Amira are supported to continue their studies without worry. In a few weeks, these strained efforts of trying to keep everything together will collapse when Saja comes back from an overseas conference and quits her job.

I haven't organised anything for my birthday – messages come in but I don't feel particularly celebratory. However, a friend pops over that evening and gifts me watercolours, paintbrushes, a black felt-tip pen and a sketch book.

As he presents them to me, he says, 'You're really good at talking and words, but sometimes, you don't need words.'

What could lie beyond words? This sentence stays with me, demanding I notice what I'm neglecting to see, all that I am burying in the hope it will remain hidden if I leave it unsaid and unwritten. The gift is an oblique avenue towards what I cannot say; it nudges at the cracks in my defences, a gentle provocation to uncover that which I avoid looking at within myself.

I begin to paint.

*

An email from the Embassy appears in my inbox. They visited Dad last Thursday. They came in after I'd seen him.

The email contains some bullet points of information: they've asked for another visit and have sent a letter to the Commissioner of Tora Prison to confirm that Dad is an Australian citizen. He'd been registered solely as an Egyptian national under the details on his identity card.

They write that Dad has another hearing this week and they want details from me: When will it be? What time and where? Are consular staff permitted to attend? I'm confused by their request: why would I know if they can come or not? I message Amgad so he can ask Saleh, the lawyer.

As the week passes, I put off going to the grocery store – avoiding doing any shopping for Dad during the week allows me to push away the prison from my mind until I absolutely have to confront it. In between working on Dad's case – which is mostly continuing to do research and messaging Amgad to message the lawyer – I keep myself busy by socialising and going to my classes.

The local supermarket is open until midnight. I start my grocery shop for Dad at 11 pm on Wednesday – in less than eight hours, I'll be presenting myself at the prison entrance. Over the coming months, the grocery store will become a trigger. To compartmentalise the way prison creeps in to my day-to-day life, I will come to separate all our grocery shopping: Khair Zaman for Dad, Alfa Market for me; the prison street market for fruit and vegetables for Dad, the Dokki street market for me.

I have another restless night's sleep. In the morning, I double-check the groceries I'd purchased for Dad:

A box of rolled oats
A round of La vache qui rit cheese
Roumy cheese
Bosomat
Fino bread
Apples
Bananas
Mandarins
Biscuits
A couple of chocolate bars
Tomatoes
Cucumbers
Tinned fouul (fava beans)
Jam in a glass jar
Honey in a glass jar
A white jacket
Two pairs of white pants
Two white undershirts
A pair of white socks
A pair of boxers
A bottle of three-in-one shampoo, conditioner and body wash
Two Dettol soap bars
Hand sanitiser

I opt to take the train down to the prison again. It's a busy morning and there are no seats, so I stand. My white plastic bags of goods start cutting into my fingers. The train begins emptying the closer we get to Tora. Relieved, I snag a seat.

When the train pulls in to Tora El-Balad, I head straight to the courtyard and go through the job of signing in. After the first visit, I relayed the 'siyasi wla g'naee' story to Drew and Salma, and found out that 'siyasi' means political (in reference to political prisoners) and 'gena'ee' means criminal. Today, when Haytham asks, I no longer hazard a guess but confidently say 'siyasi' as I check in. Then I find a plastic seat under the tree and wait to hear Dad's name – not my own.

I'm called forward with Dad's name. Stepping into the prison complex, the courtyard is already packed as I'm once again one of the last people in. I squeeze myself into a gap on the granite benches, sitting for another long wait. Dad's name is eventually called by the conscript guard at the metal detector's entrance. I step forwards and put my bags onto the conveyor belt for the first round of inspections. I walk through the metal detector. The bullfrog guard is waiting on the other side of the scanner. He heaves himself off his chair and digs around in my bags. He takes out the glass jar of honey, the glass jar of jam. Then follows the bottle of 3-in-1 shampoo and the tin of beans. He indicates that I can take my bags and I reach over for the honey, jam, beans and shampoo.

He stops me.

I reach for them again.

He stops me again.

'But why can't I have them?' I demand in English. Then I correct myself: 'Leh?'

'Mamnoo'a,' he states without further explanation.

I look longingly at the goods I must forfeit. Why are they prohibited? The food I'm bringing in for Dad already seems so meagre when compared to the boxes of fruits, snacks, cooked rice and meat hauled in by other families.

I'm body-searched by the sour lady in the alcove. My handbag is checked. Once she's satisfied, I turn into the lattice corridor.

A woman comes up and introduces herself as Fatima. She speaks to me in English, informing me that she's an English literature graduate. Her satin hijab, tightly held together by pins, frames her fair, bright face. Softly spoken, she gently lets me know that she'd noticed my confusion about what items are allowable.

'They don't let in any glass or tins, only plastic,' explains Fatima. 'And only bring small shampoo bottles, not the big ones.' She adds that I should always bring cash for Dad because he can also buy things for himself at the prison canteen.

I'm grateful for Fatima's kindness. She asks about Dad and why he's in Tora. I tell her, 'Because of social media.' She nods in understanding and tells me she's here to visit her husband. He's also facing similar charges. He's been in Tora for four years. They have three kids. She says her kids don't like coming with her to the prison, that she doesn't pressure them to come even though she wants them to see their father.

'Oh, that must be so difficult for you,' I say, touching her arm.

We both go quiet. This is only my second visit and it's harrowing to think of people doing this for years … to think that Dad could be here for years.

Though Fatima is someone I can talk to, I withdraw, directing my energy towards keeping a lid on my surging emotions while we crawl towards the second set of iron gates. When I reach the gate, I hand over my passport, then give Dad's name to the elderly man with his notebook. Since I have food with me, I walk over to the wooden tables set up in the inner courtyard so my groceries can be searched again.

A guard with broad, rough hands and chipped fingernails reaches into the bag. He takes out the box of rolled oats, rips it open, then pulls out the plastic bag of oats and shakes it. Feeling the bag for anything that might not be oats, he stares at it before putting it back in the ripped box. I reach over and take the box out of his hands, attempting to smooth down the ripped cardboard. I put it back in the bag. The family beside me is watching another guard dig through their rice and meat with a crusty wooden spoon. He finishes and rests the spoon on the table. It appears to me that this is part of the accumulation of small abuses in a prison: nice things like home-cooked food don't make it to prisoners without being molested by dirty spoons and fingers.

Meanwhile, the guard in front of me opens the circular box of cheese triangles, followed by the bag of fino bread. Then he sifts through the tomatoes, cucumbers, apples and mandarins. He tears off the plastic packaging from the clothes and feels around in the pockets of the pants and jacket. He shakes out the socks and boxers. He dumps everything into a pile on the table and then tells me to put it away. I straighten out the clothes, doing my best to fold them neatly and put them back in their plastic packaging. I'm determined to counteract the indignity of the mess this guard is making, of his brutish carelessness.

The guard looks at the white garbage bag and asks me something.

The only word I catch is 'name', so I assume he's asking who all this is for.

'Hazem Hamouda.'

He repeats the question, then points to a bag that's being searched beside me.

With all the confidence of the ignorant, I say again, indignantly this time, 'Hazem Hamouda.'

Visibly perplexed, he draws my attention to the Arabic written in permanent black marker on a bag next to us. Then he yells for a qalam. A lady behind me pulls a black marker from her handbag and holds it out to the guard, who indicates that she needs to hand it to me.

I take it.

'Oktob,' he commands.

I pause for a moment, thinking about how to spell Dad's name. Hesitantly, I write هدومح مزاح, hoping it's right.

This is the last hurdle; even though it's only my second visit, it's been less of an ordeal than my first visit last week.

This time, I bypass the wooden bench outside – the one above the drain from the urinal – to join all the other visitors inside. My brief conversation with Fatima gave me a sense of comfort and solidarity. I want to prolong this feeling by being in the same place as the other visiting families, knowing that we're all in this together.

The visiting room is a large cafeteria. A single, long step runs through the middle of it, splitting it into two parts. In the corner near the entrance, people are lined up, waiting to purchase snacks. Long granite benches are arranged on one side of the room and a smaller square of granite benches sit in the middle: a square within a square. In the other half of the room, the granite benches are placed in rows, like a train carriage where people sit facing each other in blocks of eight. There's a metal door near the step that divides the room.

Families are crammed on the benches but respectfully so, always with precious space left between women and men. A couple of groups have spread blankets on the floor, upon which they've laid out food to create makeshift picnic sites. Some kids run around playing, squealing. Everyone seems to be talking: voices reverberate across the dimly lit, stony space.

A sharp sound of metal banging against metal cuts through the noisy room. Most of the children go running towards the sound, some yelling in excitement.

The door opens. Men dressed in all white start pouring through.

High-pitched chanting erupts from the children: 'Baba! Baba! Baba! Baba!' Some kids have climbed up onto a half-wall near the door, ready to jump onto their fathers. A lot of kids run giggling and squealing into their fathers' arms. Not all are so bold: there are a couple of kids hanging back near the door, quietly waiting. I see one kid has noticed his father, but his father has yet to see him. The child is frozen, staring, clearly waiting to be seen. When his father spots him, he scoops him up into his arms and the kid beams with unabashed adoration. The raw emotion of all these kids is too much: I clench my teeth to stop myself from exploding into tears.

Men keep streaming through the door like shadowy apparitions. In Islam, it's customary to bury the dead wrapped only in white cloth. Surely it's macabre to dress imprisoned men in white outfits?

At last, Dad's greying head pops out from around the door frame. He seems tentative as he scans the room. I've positioned myself away from the doorway, towards the back of the crowd. I call out and wave at him. He makes his way towards me and we give each other a quick hug.

As we scout the room for a seat, the volume is tremendous: conversation echoes off the walls, the voices of what I estimate to be about a hundred people eagerly trying to make the most of this precious hour. A family shuffles along one of the benches to make room for us and the man in white in the middle of them smiles kindly at us. When he turns back to his family, I notice that his spine is curved over, his body large and soft with disuse.

'We're cellmates,' Dad tells me, then puts his hand on the man's back as he leans over to say thank you.

It occurs to me how physically different my dad is to many of the men in this room. He isn't hunched or overweight. His skin isn't marked, scarred or deeply lined. He doesn't have the dark under-eye circles that settle in after too much stress, too many cigarettes and countless sleepless nights. He has all his teeth. In his face, and in his body, I see evidence of having lived a comfortable life in Australia.

In recognising these signs in him, I realise they must be evident in me. It reminds me we had a life before Egypt, before this prison. It all seems strange and unreal. I push thoughts of Australia from my mind.

I'm here now; that's all that is real, that's all that matters.

It's hard to hear Dad, so I lean in close, turning my head so he can speak directly into my left ear.

'I wrote a letter for your mum. Can you bring in letters for me? All the men get letters smuggled in. You can bring some too and give them to me when we meet.'

While he's talking, Dad reaches down to scratch his ankle but pulls something out of his sock. Then he takes my hand in his. I feel him slide two tightly folded pieces of paper into my palm. When I pull my hand away, I discreetly tuck them into my bag.

Dad leans back to access his pants pocket. He brings out a flower made of coloured tissue paper.

'A man inside made this for you. I told them it was your birthday this week so I could get this flower to give to you ...

because I can't, uh …' He trails off and looks around the room, making a sweeping gesture with his hands. 'Yeah … I can't really get you anything.'

Gently, I take the flower from his hands. Dark pink petals surround a yellow centre; they're cupped by a blue rim that turns into a blue stalk secured with a green band. I twirl it in my hands, touching the wrinkled paper petals. The brightness stands out against the dull greys and browns of the room. I'm swamped with grief. The vibrant colours symbolically evoke a reminder of the vivid internal worlds we all carry – and that all these men still possess despite the bleakness of prison. The flower is an insistence: an expression of the impulse to create, even in the most abject of circumstances, to remind yourself – and others – you're alive.

'It's really cool, Dad. I can't believe someone here actually made this …' On the verge of tears again, I don't finish my sentence.

'Yeah, there are some good guys inside …'

As much as I want to rest in the tenderness of this moment, it's not possible. While we need to remember our humanity, daring to come too close to our humanness hits upon the contusion of our dehumanisation in the prison: it hurts. Dad keeps jiggling his leg, a sure sign he's stressed. I look up and see that his eyes are darting around.

A guard I haven't seen before walks past us. Dad tenses. His shoulders lift to his ears and he leans forwards. 'I don't like him,' he spits. 'I don't like that one.'

I can't get a proper look at this guard; he has his back to me.

'He's not nice,' Dad growls. 'He's no good at all. He's a killer.'

The guard turns and retraces his footsteps. As he strolls past us, he nods at Dad. 'A'zayak ya, Hazem?' he says casually.

'Kolo tamam,' Dad answers tightly.

A quizzical look comes over the guard. I can't tell if he's genuinely confused or is feigning confusion over the undisguised hostility in Dad's tone. He decides not to question it and walks off.

As soon as he's out of earshot, Dad rages. 'I hate them,' he says. 'I hate them. I hate them so much. They're my oppressors. They're the ones keeping me here. Why should I smile at them and make small talk? They're not my friends! They're my enemies! That guy … he beat a man up! And that man died!'

There are many ways to die in prison: you do not need an official death sentence to be killed. And if you die in prison, your death will never be recorded as a crime. It can never be the fault of the prison – that is, those who run the institution, those who guard and police it. No, it's the fault of the prisoner for dying. For getting sick, for 'provoking' the guard, for refusing to eat, for protesting their conditions, for being alive inside these walls.

Dad lets out a heavy breath. 'It's so hard …' He stops himself. 'It's so hard …' He stops again. 'This place. It's so unjust.' I want him to say more, but he tightens his lips and shoots another angry glare at the guard. Then he sighs heavily, puts his head in his hands and makes a prayer in English, 'Ya Allah! Give us Justice!'

'Ameen,' I murmur.

My breath is shallow and I am literally sitting on the edge of the cold granite. I can see that Dad is overwhelmed, angry and scared. Hell, we both are. However, we're still on a time limit. Since there are no clocks, I don't know how many minutes we've already used from the hour. I'm stressing that I won't be able to give Dad the updates I need to if we end up in an emotional spiral. Adopting a measured tone, I talk to Dad about the lawyer.

'Maybe you should ask Saleh about my citizenship. There's an American here, and he said I should denounce my Egyptian citizenship as soon as possible,' Dad says.

'Hmm … no one has said anything like that to me yet … I'll ask.'

'I'm Australian, aren't I? My wife and kids are Australian; my whole life is in Australia.' He's working himself up again. 'I don't need to be Egyptian. I can give it up!'

'Yes, you are Australian too, Dad …' I try to be tactful. 'But … you're also Egyptian, and that's part of it. I'll talk to the lawyer and see what he says about the citizenship thing.'

I'm already growing tired of this tension of citizenship and the rights they allegedly allow and preclude: I need to speak to the lawyer and do more research before I agree to anything Dad suggests. Yet, relinquishing his Egyptian citizenship does sound like an intriguing possibility. I wonder why it hasn't been suggested before by the lawyer; I wonder if it could work.

I have one more thing to tell Dad.

'I didn't bring a blanket. I kinda don't know where to buy one.'

'It's okay for now. I've been given a couple from the other prisoners. I just wanted my own. Whenever you can get it, bring one for me anyway.'

'I'll try next week.'

'Inshallah.'

During the long pause that follows, a blade of anxiety slices through my chest.

'Don't do anything stupid, Dad,' I blurt out. 'Think of us?'

Weariness carves into his face as Dad looks at me, staring deep into my eyes. 'I won't. I think of the family all the time.'

Cast Your Voice

Seeking more information, I emailed one of few local human rights NGOs left in Cairo. Since 2014, NGOs were being shut down via laws that required them to register with the government and submit to oversight from Egypt's national security bodies. To receive foreign funding, NGOs required government permission. In a vaguely worded remit, all NGO work was prohibited from activities that 'harm national security, public order, public morality or public health'. New legislation further allowed the government to cancel a foreign NGOs licence at any time, and interfere with the day-to-day operations of an NGO, including choice of leadership to schedules for internal meetings. In a bizarre stretch, even relocating headquarters without informing authorities is a punishable offence. Failure to comply could lead to significant fines, operations being shut down, assets seized, travel bans and prison sentences of up to 25 years. In the previous years, Amnesty International and Human Rights Watch had their Egypt offices closed, while many local NGOs were shut-down, as various directors and staff of rights-based organisations were harassed and arrested. Among the many arrested in 2018 was Ezzat Ghoneim, executive director and human rights lawyer of the Egyptian Coordination of Rights and Freedom. In 2023, he and several other staffers would receive prison sentences ranging from 10–25 years.

A staff member replied to my email and invited me to the head office for a meeting. They sat with me for two hours and explained Dad's case: Case 977/2018, also known as, Mikamileen Itneen. They said it was a mass trial involving some 60 other defendants. It was known as a 'media case' as most defendants were linked, in some way, to an accusation of spreading false information. It started with the arrest of opposition party members from the Strong Egypt Party in February, after a television appearance by the party leader on an Istanbul-based station called Mikamileen. Mikamileen was a Muslim Brotherhood-affiliated television station based in Turkey. When the station conducted an interview with the leader of the Strong Egypt Party, Abdel Moneim Aboul Fotouh, the pretext for the raid was formed. While Aboul Fotouh was thrown into solitary confinement, Deputy Leader Mohamed el-Qassas was put into Case 977/2018. Then, the net widened: A Facebook post. A radio interview. A satirical Twitter account. A protest flyer distributed by university students. The scope for arrest was so wide, even simply having shared someone else's post could be used as 'evidence' – membership to an opposition party was irrelevant. All this was used as 'evidence' of having or spreading 'false information' and 'terrorist' sympathies. Though Dad was arrested in January, he was later moved into this case in February. Those also associated with his case would be people he'd meet for the first time in prison. The lawyer wanted to get Dad out of this mass trial and into his own case. He seemed to think that this would give him better ground to defend Dad as a unique case, given he's a dual-citzen.

During this meeting, I wondered if I'd ever be presented with evidence of what Dad had allegedly done online to warrant this arrest. The answer would be nothing: no evidence would be ever be shown in court, or shared with us.

*

Soon after I started making regular visits to Dad in Tora, I got a job as a copyeditor for the English news desk at a private media outlet. I had little experience, but I was a native English speaker with a tertiary education and that was good enough.

Walking to work, the streets were layered with election posters of President Abdel Fattah el-Sisi. The posters had been around for a while, but I had not paid them much attention. It was through my job as a copyeditor that I started to take notice of the fact that Egypt's elections were due at the end of March.

The 'democratic' process was a one-man show. At this late point in the campaign, only one political opponent was left; everyone else had been successfully intimidated, the party dismantled or taken into custody.

It's impossible to understand Dad's circumstances without understanding at least a bit about the Muslim Brotherhood. It was a widespread Islamic political-religious organisation established in Egypt in 1928. Over the course of its history of existence, they've had everything from community outreach to militant wings, social support programs and organisations forming in other countries. In Egypt, specifically, the Brotherhood has had a prominent and tumultuous history, going through multiple phases of persecution and freedom.

Most relevant to the current circumstances is the fact that in 2012, Mohamed Morsi – a presidential candidate affiliated with the Muslim Brotherhood – was elected President. This was an historic moment as it was the first time Egypt's president *didn't* come from the ranks of the military.

The 2011 revolution allowed, for the first time, the formal establishment of political parties regardless of affiliation or ideology; in this climate, the Muslim Brotherhood established the Freedom and Justice Party. To lead the party, Mohammed Morsi was required to relinquish formal membership to the Muslim Brotherhood, as the party contained members from across the religious, cultural spectrum of Egyptians. Morsi's presidency was fraught with difficulty.

Within the government, the cabinet contained 36 ministers, of which five ministers were from the Freedom and Justice Party. The rest of the ministerial roles were dealt out to a range of technocrats, many of whom were Independent. As Morsi sought to cut deals with the military and right-wing Islamic parties, many independent parties felt increasingly sidelined. After the approval of the 2012 constitutional referendum, those sidelined went on to form the National Salvation Front, headed by Amr Moussa, a former Secretary General of the Arab League.

For the first time, independent media and satirical political comedy had a role in the public sphere, as the civil space had expanded enough to explore ways to hold power to account. Public gaffes could be mocked, topical issues critiqued and explored. At the same time, life was tremulous and fraught: this was new territory within old structures. Economic disturbances, including petrol, electricity and bread shortages, alongside petty talks of banning alcohol and bikinis. Just because there was a new government and figurehead didn't mean the structures that fed, powered, employed, managed and paid Egyptians had changed. Egypt's economy remained deeply tied to the military, along with the security services and public broadcasters.

On 30 June 2013, protests erupted against the President and his government. By 3 July, Mohamed Morsi was president no longer. Defense Minister and army chief General, Abdel-Fattah el-Sisi, had Morsi removed from power. At the time, el-Sisi stated that he wasn't interested in the presidency, that he was simply a humble man seeking the best outcome for the Egyptian people.

However, in response to the removal of Morsi by el-Sisi, pro-Morsi and anti-military (note that anti-military doesn't necessarily mean pro-Morsi) protestors established the two primary protest sites: at Rabaa Al-Adawiya and Al-Nahda square.

On 14 August 2013, armed forces commanded by General el-Sisi surrounded the two protest camps and shot into crowds. Depending on the source, between 800 and 1000 civilian protestors were killed, possibly more; thousands were arrested. The massacre signified a bloody end to the revolution, sending a chilling message to Egyptians: protest and be arrested or killed.

At the end of 2013, al-Jazeera journalists Peter Greste, Mohamed Fahmy and Baher Mohamed would be jailed, sparking another wave of critical attention upon Egypt's new leadership. Elections were formally called for in 2014 and el-Sisi resigned from his military position to run for the presidency. With the promise of re-establishing security, and with little opposition, el-Sisi won. Soon after, the Muslim Brotherhood was officially declared a terrorist organisation and the 2012 constitution was scrapped. The 2012 constitution that had been passed by Morsi's government, crucially established Presidential limits of two four-year terms in an attempt to prevent another 30-year rule as had happened under Hosni Mubarak, the President removed by the 2011 revolution. Instead, el-Sisi introduced a new constitution that laid the foundation for passing a law that would allow him to rule until 2030.

The Sisi-fever that swept him into power quickly dissipated as the repression, which had begun with the Rabaa massacre, began to spread further and further into political and civic life.

For those affiliated with the Brotherhood, a religious organisation with an extensive following, many could be swept into the web of terror. From politically-active Brotherhood members, to high-school teachers, engineers, university students and charity workers. Amid it all were all those who had no affiliations as the repression further extended to journalists, media personalities, writers, poets, singers, songwriters, video producers, comedians, individuals who mistakenly took photos in forbidden zones and small-business owners, not to mention all those people who simply had the misfortune of finding themselves in the wrong place at the wrong time. The web of terror spread to people with Twitter and Facebook accounts, and people who'd marched in, or even watched, the 2011 protests. In 2013, a young man, Abdelrahman ElGendy, was arrested with his father after filming a protest from their car. In 2018, his smuggled essays started being published on Mada Masr, which is where I first encountered his story. His essay, 'Encountering Disability and Friendship in Tora', is one of the most devastating accounts of the intersections of violence faced by disabled people caught up in the prison system.

The online sphere became one of the regime's primary tools to track, arrest and jail citizens for online dissent. As the counter-revolutionary repression spread, civic life, both online and offline, was suffocated by increasingly invasive surveillance measures.

Tahrir Square, 2011, the Arab Spring: all needed to be erased from the collective memory. The pro-revolutionary graffiti not only needed to be washed off the walls, but out of people's hearts. Multiple tools were used to annihilate anything related to revolution: from collective terror instilled by the arbitrary violence of arrests and disappearances backed by draconian new laws passed in the name of 'security', to the re-writing of history in schools, universities and national memory. Within a few years, the civic and political freedom the revolution had briefly made possible was crushed.

I thought about all these things on my daily walk to work. On my way there each morning, I'd look at el-Sisi's posters, then picture the families I'd seen at Tora Prison. Once at the office, I'd order a coffee, and then get to editing the articles assembled from government press releases.

This is my polite way of saying I edited propaganda.

Before working at this news desk, the word propaganda would bring to mind Soviet posters, Uncle Sam's wagging finger and NewsCorp articles. It was crude and silly; awkward flexes of power that would be funny if they didn't actually work.

Propaganda was the exact word for it: the truth obscured by omission, bias, exaggeration. Sometimes, I suspected, we were publishing straight-up fabrications. Much of our information came straight from government sources. The journalists around me were smart; they could have produced intelligent, critical writing, but instead, it seemed they were smothered – pressed into reproducing stories that delivered the same government narrative in different ways day after day: el-Sisi is a great President, the military are good, Egypt is safe thanks to the President and aren't we doing better than ever?

As I skimmed the articles, I fought disinterest and disdain. Soon, I slipped into apathy. I was a mediocre copyeditor: sloppy and careless. My work often came back to me with red underlining and queries from the head editor.

As election day neared, the tagline 'Cast your voices' kept popping up in the articles, encouraging people to vote. I consistently altered it to 'Cast your votes'.

After a memo about it went around, none of the journalists stopped using 'cast your voices', so I also stopped correcting it.

Cast your voices, cast your votes, whatever – maybe I was the one who didn't understand.

*

At my next prison visit, Dad asks if I'd mind moving back to the outside bench instead of sitting inside in the noisy prison cafeteria. We drag the bench out of the shade and away from the smelly drain and place it in the sunshine. As we go to sit down, a harried mother bustles out of the cafeteria, pulling her small son by the hand. Ignoring us, she ushers her child over to the drain and tugs down his pants. He pees. She pulls his pants up and hurries him back inside. *Ha! That's why the drain smells.*

Sunlight angles past the corrugated iron roof that covers the courtyard, casting a gentle golden light across Dad's face. He avoids eye contact with me as he seats himself. His head hangs. It looks like he'd fall if his arms weren't wrapped around his waist, holding his body upright.

I wait, quiet.

Finally, he looks up.

Dad is crying.

'I'm so scared,' he sobs. 'I thought they were dead, the bodies under me. But then … they moved. They moved!' This story is starting in the middle; I've no context for these bodies. His voice breaks and his head sinks back down.

Dad speaks again, softly and into the ground. I lean forwards to hear him, resting my hand on his back.

'I thought I was going to die. And I was so scared, I wasn't ready, and I saw the light, I saw Allah, and I was so afraid. I wanted my family. I wanted my mum. I thought …' He breaks off and holds his breath, trying to control his heaving chest but his breath shudders out.

He continues: 'I thought I'd never see anyone again … I'm afraid that I will die here. That I'll never see my family again …'

I don't know what to say so I put my arms around my dad. I bring his head to my chest and rest my chin on his head, and I stroke his back. He held me this way when I was scared; now I'm holding him. He's shivering. His breath is uneven. I hold him until he pulls away. His face is red and tear-streaked. Another sob escapes him and he resumes speaking. It's all jumbled and I cannot properly follow what he's saying: Bodies. Blindfolds. God. Confusion. Razors. Criminals. Prosecutor. Light. Scared. Death.

'I'm so sorry, Lamisse. I'm so sorry …'

Desperate to soothe Dad, I tell him it's okay, that he doesn't have anything to be sorry for. The rest of the visit passes in a blur; I've never seen my dad cry before and I'm shaken by how broken he looks, how afraid he is. Helpless, I cannot stop his suffering. I cannot ease his pain.

The People (Don't) Want

Monday 2 April 2018

Coffee in hand, I take a seat at my desk. Election results are being announced today. On my computer screen, a notification pops up that another article for review has come through. I open the file: it's a press release from a foreign government congratulating el-Sisi for his win. The public announcement hasn't been made yet: I set it up so the article will be released later.

A large flat-screen television is behind me. I swing around on my swivel chair to take a look. Footage from the election booths rolls across the screen; it's mostly elderly and middle-aged folk lining up to cast their votes. The demographics on screen speak to a publicly denied reality: disillusioned young people refusing to vote in an election where the outcome is already guaranteed.

The results arrive before long: 92% for el-Sisi and 3% for the fumbling opposition Moussa Mostafa Moussa. The other 5% of written votes went to a man who was never a candidate and not on the ballot paper: Mohamed Salah, Liverpool Football Club's star forward and captain of Egypt's national team. The fact that a sporting celebrity garnered more votes than the opposition leader becomes a national joke.

Then the re-elected President el-Sisi appears on the screen; the television is taken off mute. I watch for a while, observing his every expression. Not one of my colleagues has said a word yet, neither one of celebration nor defeat: it's just silence. Are they listening intently or lost in thought?

I think of Dad. He and many fellow prisoners have been saying that an el-Sisi election win will hasten their release. These are the bargainings of people without agency: attaching hope to arbitrary events and dates in the unfounded belief that those things will edge them closer to freedom. I start to feel dizzy, so I get up and head to the bathroom. Locking the door and closing the lid of the toilet, I sit down and lean forwards with my head in my hands.

I shut my eyes and take a mental journey to the prison: I wind through the iron portal embedded in the sandy wall, past the courtyard and down the corridor. I step through the large iron gates, pass the guards checking food and arrive at the cafeteria. Imagining that all the detainees are there watching the television as el-Sisi makes his victory speech, I picture moving through the room, giving each man a hug of consolation: Sorry, this is too big. Sorry, we lost. Sorry, the revolution is dead. Sorry for this life. Then I find Dad and take his hand. I want to stay in the cafeteria with all these men, sharing our grief.

I open my eyes and I'm still in the toilet, alone. All I can think of is how I have to resign – I can't edit another sycophantic word about the President in this place.

*

Shortly after the election, I fall ill and spend nearly a week in bed: sweating, sleeping and drinking litres of water. A few days pass in a daze. When I finally start to feel lucid again, I check my phone to see what I've missed and see that it's Thursday.

I'm supposed to be at the prison.

The prison is only 15 kilometres away, yet it feels like a thousand cavernous miles of distance. Without a visit, I can't get any information on how my dad's doing. I can't scan his face for injury, check his skin and eyes for signs of ill-health, make an assessment of his state of mind. *Is he doing okay or is he falling apart?* I can't hug him to get a sense of his weight and how much he's lost. Without my visit, he'll have to rely on the prison food and the generosity of other cellmates. The prison food is gross: watery beans and rice cooked by tired, deprived conscripts.

Most of all, checking on Dad during the weekly visits reassures me that he's still alive, while also being a source of morale for him. I'm his only link to his life before – and after – prison. There will be an after; there must be. I live with the daily dread of receiving a call to inform me that Dad is coming out of prison in a body bag. Lying in bed, knowing I'm missing a visit, I ruminate on this thought, and it begins to eat me alive with fear. I fear that by missing one visit, I could put his life at risk, and that his death could then be my fault.

I return to my attachment to telepathy. Perhaps 'God' can take him a message. I need to believe something, anything.

I speak out loud to the room: 'I'll be there next week, Dad. I was pretty sick but I'm feeling better now. I'll be there for you next Thursday, okay? Stay strong. Love you.'

*

For a brief while after I quit the copyediting job, I feel a sense of liberation. I have a pile of university work to sift through, and part of me knows I'm in deep denial about how much I'm struggling to keep up. I want to believe I can still have a life – that somehow I can cling to the dreams I came with. Unwilling to face how much I'm deluding myself, I continue to go to classes, party and pretend I'm holding it together.

During the two-hour bus ride home from university, I put on my headphones and stare out the window. The love and curiosity this monstrous city once inspired has been replaced by apprehension and terror. For a decade, I had been in love with Egypt; visiting whenever I could, carrying dreams of carving a life among its chaos and smoothing its syllables onto my tongue. Every time I flew over the city, on the descent into Cairo airport, I would be flooded with the joy of coming home. I wanted to mark myself as an Egyptian, to line-up the feeling in my heart with physical evidence that I belonged here. Now, I felt betrayed, overcome with a feeling that mirrored the realisation of finding yourself in an abusive relationship: *Why is this happening? How did I not see the signs? I love you, why are you hurting me?* Such questions swirl through me, and in my internal dialogue I speak not to a partner, but a country.

From behind the glass, Cairo appears like a shadowed dystopia, stretching up from the ground to tower over me. I get out the sketchbook gifted by my friend. I've taken to scribbling in this sketchbook when I'm anxious – I carry it around with me almost everywhere, along with the pens and watercolours. Creating repeating patterns of dots and lines is self-soothing. My pen sometimes connects me with a memory, a jagged-edged trauma that hasn't seen the light before, helping it emerge. These moments are bewildering, and they're happening more often. Constantly worrying about Dad is wearing me down: how can I be mourning him when he's still alive? I never knew that nostalgia cuts deepest when the past you imagine is still possible as a future; I do not long for a person that's passed on, but a human being that could still live, and God, I hope he does.

Along with Dad and the prison, I dream vividly of painful break-ups and slices of childhood violence; strange, symbolic nightmares often repeating around the distressing experience of my teeth falling out. It feels like my brain is purging – as though to make room for the new trauma, it is forcing me to free up some psychological real estate by facing what I'd buried. The skeletons in the closet are thumping at the door, stumbling out. As new horrors overlap with old, my mind increasingly feels like a terrifying space.

In my journal, I keep circling around the same theme: the foolishness and naïvety of having believed that I never believed I would be touched by violence like this. In this realm of realisation, all the trips I'd taken to Egypt suddenly look grossly entitled: What had I really learnt from those visits? Had I been picking out only the nice, exciting parts for myself and ignoring the rest? Had I unwittingly engaged in a vapid experience of developing my own diasporic practice of colonially possessing 'the East' for my own ends? How much had I played the 'I'm Egyptian' card as a sort of self-justification, perhaps projecting the misdemeanours of whiteness and orientalism onto others so I could deny it within myself? Who am I? What have I been doing? How much have I failed to understand? How much have I failed to feel?

Is this the violence that Dad was afraid of? Is this what he tried so hard to protect us from?

*

In 2013, five years before Dad's arrest, protests against President Mohamed Morsi thundered beneath the balcony of my apartment in Heliopolis. The place I was living in – my grandfather's flat – was next to the Presidential Palace, which had become the second biggest site of protest after Tahrir Square. I was back from a two-month stint in the occupied Palestinian territories. Crossing over at the Taba–Eilat border in Sinai, I had taken the 12-hour bus ride back to Cairo, then a taxi home from the bus terminal. I trudged toward my street, eager to put down my heavy backpack and sleep. Outside the sports club at the end of the main road, a stage was being assembled. As I turned to go into my street, I came up against concrete blocks daubed with fresh graffiti. I wasn't completely aware of the political climate I was in – my attention had been consumed by navigating life in the West Bank, and I had pushed Egypt to the back of my mind, thus missing the momentum leading up to the 2013 protests. Squeezing past the barriers, I concluded that there was going to be some kind of festival the following day. I took a few photos of the graffiti, then lugged my stuff up the stairs to my flat.

In the morning, I was woken by the sounds of chants, vuvuzelas and an MC hyping the crowd. I went down to explore and found myself in the middle of a protest. A huge poster of Morsi as a sheep was suspended from the tramline wires. A fight broke out next to me. Someone shoved me from behind and I hit the ground. A stranger pulled me to my feet. It was the man who'd pushed me out of harm's way. 'Get out of here; it's not safe for women,' he said in English.

I took his advice and made a beeline for home.

The noise of the protest was relentless. Closing the windows and shutters barely muffled it. Yet, it was a buzz: I was captivated by the energy, thrilled to witness the coming together of so many people – this echo of 2011. A couple of days later, I headed down to Tahrir Square with an Egyptian friend, who freelanced as a journalist. We walked through the crowd, from Tahrir Square to Qasr El Nil Bridge, where two bronze lions sat at the entrance of the bridge. From there, we watched military helicopters fly over us to the cheers of the crowd.

'Fucking idiots.' My friend spoke quietly, his anger barely concealed by his hushed tone. 'They just got rid of the military two years ago, and now they want it back?'

Up in the sky, the helicopters were fading from view. I didn't know what to say to him. It was all so big, so beyond me and my small existence.

While many members of my extended family supported the military's return to power, Dad had been devastated to see the protests against Morsi. 'It's democracy,' he'd said, during a discussion with me over Skype. 'It doesn't matter if you like or hate the party elected; they must serve their four years. And if you want change, you vote them out.' I wanted to believe it all worked like that, but I knew – just as he did – that rulers could change the rules and that democracy wasn't so simple. After all, the democratic system guaranteed you a process but not necessarily your rights: when someone voted in didn't represent the rights that you wanted, there was little you could do about it apart from protesting or waiting for the next election.

Plus, it was hard to trust in the possibility of the next election in a country with a history of dictatorship.

On the fourth day of protests, I was sitting in a cafe in the bourgeois suburb – and tiny river island – of Zemalek. My journalist friend was writing to the BBC while I scrolled through news reports and caught up on messaging friends. The music stopped and a voice came on: the military, represented by General Abdel Fattah el-Sisi, had heard the people's protests. Morsi would no longer be President.

People argued: was it a coup or another revolution?

Near my flat, the protests turned into a street celebration. I watched from the window, disappointed for my revolutionary friends and afraid of what this all meant. I got a phone call from Dad: 'Get out of the country. It's going to get dangerous. You need to leave; you need to come home. You've seen enough and I'm not supporting you to stay in Egypt any longer.'

I wanted to stay, but knew I couldn't without Dad's permission: I needed his support, both morally and financially. Though he wasn't in Egypt with me, I relied on his advice and cultural insight; I'd often call him, telling him things that had happened and then asking what it meant, or what I should do. Since I'd been overseas for seven months, my savings were finished, so Dad had been helping me out. Out of money and in the middle of uncertainty, I knew I had to listen to my father. Resentfully, I flew home to Melbourne, all while plotting ways I could go back to Egypt without being beholden to my father.

A few days after I left, Cairo went under a curfew. Military checkpoints were installed around the city. A month later, the military shot protestors at Rabaa al-Adawiya square.

In my room in Melbourne, I read the news of the massacre. I scrolled through pictures: pools of blood, white shrouds and wailing families. As I was crying at my desk, my boyfriend at the time told me to stop looking at the news. 'Why can't you just forget about it? You're here safe in Australia. I don't know why you keep checking this stuff if it makes you so upset.'

I understood the concern, but he didn't understand: I couldn't forget what was part of me.

Suspicion

Groggily, I haul myself out of bed, then put on some clothes, grab the groceries for Dad and head out. I order an Uber, giving up on the crowded train. I want air-conditioned comfort and convenience.

When I arrive at the prison around 8 am, I find the courtyard is empty and no guards at the check-in desk. Fuck, I've over-stretched my hand in gambling on time. I shouldn't have snoozed the alarm.

Gripped by panic, I hurry to the desk under the tree where Umm Baha sells white bags and stores mobiles. I make a fumbling attempt to ask what visitors can do if they're late. She points to a guard coming up the street with pink, green and white papers in his hand. I dump my groceries beside her desk and run up to him.

A couple of men jostle in front of me and shove their IDs at the guard. Seems I'm not the only latecomer haranguing him for attention. He takes the IDs one by one, grimacing as he records the names. I elbow my way to the front, insistently handing over my ID to the guard too. When he takes it, I melt with relief.

Despite the stress, I now know it's possible to check in late. Future visits become defined by knowing that I can skip the sullen courtyard wait in favour of chasing the guard for a late check-in.

With so much on the line, you'd think I'd have been organised, that I'd have behaved in an urgent and focused manner. On the contrary, I moved like I waded through wet cement. Every Thursday morning, my body screamed, 'Protect yourself! Don't go!' Without exception, I'd have to dig for the energy to override the internal protest. Operating on autopilot worked best: don't think, just do. Even if you're slow, even if you're disorganised, even if you're hungover and even if you're late, just get there and then deal with what happens next.

*

Over successive Thursdays, I accrue other small but important pieces of information that help make the visits go more smoothly.

One morning, after check-in, I'm seated and waiting under the tree to be called. A lady sits beside me and asks me for the time.

'Temanya w'nous,' I tell her after checking my phone

She looks confused, then smiles and we resume our quiet waiting.

Her reaction makes me uncertain whether she'd asked me for the time or something else. On my phone, I write down a transliterated version of her question in my notes app. I later find out she'd asked, 'What page are you?'

Since we don't get anything like a number or a pass, it turns out that knowing which sign-in page you are on is useful: the amount of pages indicates how busy the visit will be, and by knowing your page, you can estimate at what point you'll be called to come forwards. If you manage this right, you can sit for longer under the shade of the tree, instead of having to leap up as soon as the iron door is opened. Standing by the iron door waiting to be called means standing on the street without shade or seating. As summer approaches, avoiding prolonged exposure to the sun is vital to surviving the slow process of getting in and out of Tora. On those searing days when I forget to bring a hat, much to the bemusement of other visitors, I wear a white plastic bag on my head to give myself some shade.

Though the number of visitors fluctuates each week, I come to recognise a few regulars who, like me, almost unfailingly show up every Thursday. There's Umm Jaleel, whose son, Omar, shares a cell with Dad. There's three families from Alexandria who make the weekly trip to Cairo to see their sons. They wake at 3 am, travel three hours by train to Cairo, and then take another train from the central station to Tora El-Balad. Sometimes, they invite me to join them for a morning coffee under the tree. Other times, they're quiet and withdrawn. They all bring their children with them – from teens to toddlers, they come to see their older brother.

'Umm Jaleel's husband is in prison too, but a different prison,' Dad tells me during one visit. 'So, she's going to prisons twice a week with the kids. Once to see her son here, and once to see her husband in Wadi Natroun. Imagine what that must be like for her.'

Wadi Natroun is another prison allocated for political prisoners. I've heard it's an awful, isolated place out in the desert. That's the thing about ruling with fear: there must always be the threat of something worse. It's easier to subdue a prisoner when they fear there's a place that's worse than the one they're in.

Dad openly considers marrying my younger sister to Umm Jaleel's son. I've met him several times during the prison visits; he's a lovely person, polite and gentle in manner. He'd been involved in some kind of anti-government actions at university, and now he's in prison sharing a cell, instead of classes, with some of his uni mates.

Regardless, I view Dad's suggestion as completely absurd.

'You can like a person without needing to marry them to your daughter,' I say to him.

'What? I have four daughters and none of them want to marry a nice Muslim man!' He feigns exasperation and throws up his hands.

It's a discussion we've had countless times on the outside. Moments like this – of reaching for the familiar, for the selves that existed before Dad's imprisonment – punctuate prison visits that are usually laden with talk of Dad's case and fraught with fragile emotions. I know this conversation isn't really about my sister; it's about Dad trying to still experience himself as a father by imagining his daughter's wedding, and seeing himself as still having an important guiding role in her love life. Sure, it's a patriarchal imagining, but I'm not going to offer my critiques of his ideas on marriage during a prison visit.

Frankly, I want my father to be present at any of our future weddings.

*

April drags on into May.

Though I'm trying to follow instructions, the path I see unfolding for Dad and me in Egypt is disheartening. The judicial system is showing itself to be painfully sluggish, a Kafkaesque labyrinth of confusing instructions and indifferent judges. Dad keeps getting his 15-day detention period renewed. The lawyer keeps telling me we should hope for a 'nice judge'. I fear that after the tenth hearing in July, we will spill into the 45-day renewal phase. If so, Dad could end up staying in Tora for another two years without a charge.

I dedicate time to composing emails to politicians, human rights activists and journalists. How many years could pass in this harrowing way if I can't figure something else out? I've got to try: Marise Payne, Penny Wong, Anne Aly, Julie Bishop, Graham Perrett. I don't know, I'm striking out people in Foreign Affairs, people who might have sympathies towards us, people around our local electorate. I feel stupid for trying to get one single little citizen onto a Minister's agenda, but I have to try. The email responses slowly drip in: mostly receptionists acknowledging they've received my emails. One politician does suggest I get in touch with the Egyptian Embassy in Australia. It seems like a ridiculous suggestion, but I do it anyway: maybe it will generate some leads. Unsurprisingly, they don't reply. Later, once there's media attention on Dad's case, they'll release a statement backing the decisions of the regime.

Dad's asking himself similar questions. He's begun talking about hunger strikes. It baffles me that he'd suggest this when he's only been in prison for four months.

Look at that sentence – a real thing I thought and said at the time: 'You've only been in prison for four months.'

Four months in prison is already too long, but – much like the manufactured belief that it's not *that bad* because there are worse prisons to end up in – comparison is unavoidable. There are men who've been in Tora for years, still waiting to see if they'll be charged. There are returnees: men under investigation for a second, third or fourth time. Once you're in the crosshairs of national security, it can be hard to escape surveillance. If there's a particularly tense political time, men already known to security will get swept up, regardless of whether they've been politically active or not.

With all this swirling around me, who is my dad to be upset over four months? It is painful to write about how regularly I minimised his suffering by telling him to wait, to be patient.

'We need to exhaust all our options before you do something so drastic. We still haven't done a campaign, we haven't tried working with a lawyer outside of Egypt … There's still more we can do to try to get you out before we consider something like that.' To me, the hunger strike was one of the last actions taken by the desperate: the wail of those starved of justice, protesting a surplus of cruelty.

Earlier in May, Dad moved cells. In his new cell is the only other dual citizen in Tora currently: the American-Egyptian Mustafa Kassem.

In five years, neither President Obama nor Trump has succeeded – or had the will to succeed – in getting Mustafa Kassem out. He is desperate, Dad says, but is still waiting on the outcome of his case, and if he's sentenced to more than five years, he'll strike.

I see how impressed Dad is by Mustafa's strong convictions, his willingness to take a stand against the injustice committed against him. Even though I find it distressing to discuss the pros and cons of a hunger strike with Dad, I'm quietly confident he won't do it: he isn't going to risk death when he still thinks he has a good chance to live.

In the meantime, as I wallow in self-pity, anger and uncertainty over what to do about Dad, a human rights activist in Sydney offers to connect me to a producer at *The Project*. 'It might be good to reconsider engaging the media and publicising your dad's case,' she writes in an email.

The idea of re-approaching the media repels me, but I know she's right, so I accept her offer. Publicity could help. If I could get attention on Dad's case, perhaps some politicians will pay attention too. I resent what 'going to the media' entails: the loss of privacy and control over our narrative. I don't want to relinquish control to a mediascape that has spent years profiting off Islamophobia. How am I supposed to trust what editorial angle is taken, how a clip is cut together? Our trauma distilled into a soundbite, a headline. I don't have the energy for online trolls, an unforgiving and racist public's Facebook comments.

Reflecting on this, I drill down deeper into myself: if I'm to go in front of a camera, I'll have to be likeable, which I fear I'm not, and generate empathy, which I fear I can't. I'll have to reduce a bunch of complex and sensitive details into an interview that both informs and entertains. The media triggers my fear of being misunderstood, and that in the misunderstanding, my humanity will be lost again; I will come out wounded again.

There's a history of such wounding for us Muslims. I cringe at how we have to perform the role of the moderate Muslim, how we have to use a vocabulary not of our own making but adopted from a public discourse fashioned to depoliticise us, how we gut ourselves of our politics and our beliefs in the effort to make ourselves appear 'safe' and 'non-threatening', that we have had to play a game of convincing people that we are 'just like you'.

This exposure messes with my fragile sense of self: there've already been comments on how my siblings and I look, that it's lucky we're 'half-Australian', an 'articulate' and 'beautiful family', that we have 'good English' and an absence of visible Muslimness. It's implied that we ought to be grateful to be a family that's integrated into whiteness through our mother, that this proximity makes us more appealing. While these comments sound superficially complimentary, there's racism in them: an invisible line drawn between an imagined 'us' and 'them'. Would we elicit as much interest if our English was broken and my four sisters and I chose to keep our heads (and/or faces) covered? How could I assert my individuality without falling into the trap of distancing myself from my community and denying another person's humanity? What is with the ossified idea of a 'Muslim'? It's boring, limiting and erasing of the complexity within a global community of 1.2 billion people.

On top of that, my mind is full of speculation and mounting paranoia, thanks to the high-stakes, opaque circumstances of Dad's arrest mixed with my limited knowledge of large, complex systems like law, media and politics. How am I supposed to figure all this out and keep Dad, myself and my family, safe in the process? I can only try and hope my efforts don't cause a backlash, that they don't send Dad to the dreaded Scorpion wing or solitary confinement, and that exposure doesn't result in more prison time for him. In the end, it isn't the media I fear most – it's making a decision that could make everything worse.

What I've come to understand since is how hard I was trying to make sense of what made so little sense to me; I was still reeling from the randomness of the violence, of being flung into a world I was wholly unprepared for. By putting myself in the centre, by believing the decisions I made could influence what happened to Dad, I could regain a sense of control and order. What I now believe is that I had little control – only the delusion of it. Yet, that delusion of control was necessary: it drove me to act, to make choices about Dad's case, to attempt to bring about the changes needed to free my father, all in the belief that my actions could make a difference.

The other truth is that the systems that held him are characterised by the arbitrary and the opaque. Their processes are led by people working in suboptimal circumstances. Clerical workers have shitty days, make errors and lose paperwork. Lawyers say we have to hope for a 'nice' judge. Underpaid government workers will thwart you if no bribes cross their palms. There's also luck and timing, both good and bad. Making a decision is all trial and error, and always hoping it isn't the wrong one.

Regardless of this system and how it worked or didn't work, I had to believe in my agency and find some kind of logic. Most of all, I had to refuse despair: I had to believe that it was possible for me to free my father.

*

The activist reaches out to her contact at *The Project* and pitches our story. A couple of days after our email exchange, she forwards me a response from the producer: 'It sounds like a very challenging situation, and without knowing Lamisse's father's background, one that would need substantial evidence/paperwork to counter the government's argument for imprisoning him.'

Dad has just gone through his seventh court hearing. Eleven men were herded in front of one judge for five minutes. The judge renewed them all for another 15 days, Dad included. Since there's still no evidence, there's nothing to refute. I can't even brief a lawyer, let alone provide the producer with substantial evidence/paperwork.

I want to write, 'Well, fuck you, you stupid asshole producer who doesn't know shit.' But acting out like a defeated, angry teenager would only briefly feel good. I can't lash out; I have to stay contained and keep doggedly trying to get through to people.

Anyone facing a terrorism charge is going to be tainted with guilt. Even so, the positive is that the producer has responded, and I can't let an opportunity to get media coverage again slip through my fingers. Pushing my anger aside, I write an 800 word essay of an email, earnestly outlining Dad's situation, complete with hyperlinks and references to cases of other Egyptians in remand detention.

Writing the email stirs me up. *Wait, why* am *I fighting so hard for Dad?*

The following week, I arrive at Tora dragging all my pent-up suspicion and anger with me.

Dad and I find a seat in the cafeteria. I'm tense and preoccupied with my hostile emotions. *Should I be trusting Dad so blindly? What if he's lying to me to get me to back him up?* Such deceit would be humiliating. Once again, Dad's knee is jiggling. He's stressed after being sentenced to another 15 days and is talking himself in circles around his innocence. It's irritating me.

Unable to hold it in, I lash out at him: 'But are you innocent? Did you say anything online that would get you into trouble? What did you say on Facebook? Really?' I stare at him, furiously scanning his face for answers. 'I need to know! Are you even telling me the truth? I don't understand how they can do this. Why are you even here?'

My father flinches. Shock washes over his face, then hurt. 'No, no, I didn't … I don't know … I don't know what it is … I don't know …' He looks terrified; his body folds over, scared and defensive.

Immediately, I have the answers to my questions. My anger flees. Ashamed, I berate myself for losing sight of my dad, for allowing suspicion to cloud my vision. I can't disbelieve what I'm witnessing in the prison, what I know of my father and the injustice he's facing. Is this how toxic narratives turn us against each other?

I drop the anger and soften.

'I believe you,' I reassure Dad. 'I'm sorry for lashing out. I believe you; I really do.'

After I leave the prison, my mind is whirring the whole taxi ride home. I wasn't magically inured against suspicion and hostility, especially in a circumstance of all-consuming fear. I too was raised with the myths that justify the existence of the criminal justice system; myths that allow human beings to be selected as undesirable and disposable.

Even if Dad did express hatred of el-Sisi's government and ongoing support for the former president, Morsi, and the Brotherhood, I would defend him. If Dad has dissident opinions, then so what? Who defines 'dissident' except those who've pinched the power to define? It's been five years since Morsi was President, five years since the military regained its stranglehold on power. During those five years, Morsi has been in solitary confinement, facing the death penalty. What power does a man have left when he's been removed from the world and told he's going to be killed?

I have to fight to refuse the logic of criminalisation; I have to refuse the prison and its very existence. I have to refuse it in order to hold on to my own humanity and the humanity of everyone else trapped inside its brutalising claws. It is an effort to remember self-worth, and the worth of others, in a place designed to make you feel as though life is worthless.

This effort to remember: is this why the families around me quietly insist on their dignity through stoic kindness, and why the men share their food and make paper flowers?

Smuggled Goods

At the prison, the sour-faced lady reaches straight for my string backpack. She rips open the Velcro pocket at the front, which she's never looked through before. The pocket was cleverly disguised as a pattern on the bag. She's twigged that it's more than a collection of swirls, that I've been using it to smuggle in letters for Dad.

With a flourish, she pulls out two tightly folded letters. One is a transcription: I've painstakingly written out Mum's long text message, which included a love poem. Being scribe to their intimacy is a jarring insight into the emotional pain Mum is carrying as she approaches their 30th anniversary alone. The other contains information about the case – details I haven't had a chance to give Dad during the noisy hour-long prison visit. Seeing the letters in her hand, I go blank: I'm petrified of getting into trouble or getting Dad into trouble.

She shakes the letters and says something. I start apologising, unaware that a small bribe would smooth it all over. When no money is forthcoming, she rips up the letters and bins them.

Mournfully, I tell Dad the sorry tale. His response is that instead of letters, I should smuggle in an MP3 player for him. 'Then you don't need letters. You can get voice notes loaded onto a micro SD card and I can listen to them …' He says it's what the other men do, hearing the voices of their family gives them a feeling of still being connected.

The night before my next prison visit, I buy an MP3 player. It's a fake, small, square, lightweight, blue iPod shuffle. Instead of metal, it's plastic. Perfect.

At home, I look for things to download: I start with Islamic lectures and the Quran as read by Mishary Rashid Alafasy, Dad's favourite reciter. Then I add two audiobooks: Malcolm X's biography and George Orwell's *Animal Farm*. The internet is sluggish, so I leave my laptop on overnight as it all downloads. I text Saja: 'Remember to send in voice notes for Dad, I'm going to the prison tomorrow.'

Around midnight, an email arrives with the voice notes – all in MP4 format. I find a website to convert them into MP3s, but discover that each three-minute clip will take half an hour to transfer. It's late and I can't sit at my computer for hours converting files. I prioritise the ones from Mum and Nana, my Dad's mother, before going to bed.

*

Visiting Dad is now routine:

- *Early rise.*
- *Train to the prison bringing everything except the fruit and vegetables.*
- *Buy fruits and veggies from the carts outside the prison. It's a bit more expensive, but much more convenient.*
- *Buy bananas from the man always dressed in a thawb and turban, vegetables from the man and his wide-faced, bashful teenage son. The son is sweet and polite, though*

he tries to hide his boyishness by mimicking the same detached, roughness of his father.

To get the MP3 player in, I've worn my thickest padded bra, the kind that takes your breasts up a cup size. It's a bra I bought in a fit of insecurity, but have rarely worn. However, for this purpose, it's ideal. I ran my hands over my chest several times before leaving, poking and squeezing around. I can't feel the MP3 player and I'm fairly certain the sour-faced lady won't be able to feel it either.

In the prison cafeteria, Dad gives me a long hug. While in his embrace, I dig into my bra and pull out the MP3 player. We sit down, hold hands and he takes it from my palm then tucks it into his sock. Sometimes, I wonder if all this furtiveness is necessary; if the guards do notice, do they chase prisoners for a bribe later? In a later visit, I ask Dad about this and he confirms that they do.

'Headphones?' Dad asks.

'Oh, shit. I didn't buy any.' Here I was, feeling so triumphant for bringing in this MP3 player that I completely forgot to buy him headphones.

Dad looks disappointed. 'Well, how am I going to listen to this?'

I sheepishly reply: 'I'll bring some next week?'

*

In the prison cafeteria, one of the imprisoned men holds his newborn son in his arms. He gets up and walks around, showing off his miracle to the other men. His love fills the dank, granite room with the forgotten light of joy. His wife stays seated. She watches them roam the room and cries.

There's another man sitting in the back corner with his wife. His two children play on a blanket on the floor. He lifts up a piece of ripped cardboard, holding it in front of their faces. From my angle, I can still see them. He then lifts his wife's niqaab and their mouths meet, softly.

It's a tender kiss.

He leans in, hungry. His hand grips her thigh.

I look away, shy to have witnessed their stolen embrace.

There are no conjugal visits anymore. They were stopped under Mubarak, a long time ago.

Ramadan

16 May 2018

It's the first day of Ramadan. It's already searingly hot, the temperature sitting at 40°C.

It had been my intention to travel home for Ramadan. I'd planned it before even leaving for Cairo. It's nearly one year since I left – a perfect pause during my first year of university.

But, of course, neither Dad nor I are going anywhere.

Mum calls me and says this Ramadan is impossibly sad, that she has no motivation to cook. According to Mum, no one wants to gather at the table tonight because they'll only feel the emptiness of Dad's chair. For us, Ramadan has always been about togetherness. Yet, over the next weeks, Mum tells me that everyone breaks their fast individually, prays alone, wakes up by themselves at dawn for breakfast and prayers, or not at all. She says it's lonely.

After every Consular visit to Dad, I get an email update while Mum gets a phone call from Canberra. Her updates are all similar: they've talked to Hazem, his health seems fine, he wants some more books and they'll visit again next month.

During the last update, Mum lost her temper over the phone. The month prior, the *60 Minutes* crew were arrested in Lebanon; after two weeks in prison, their release was secured and they arrived back in Australia. After watching this case unfold, Mum yelled at the Consular Operations Officer: 'How did you get them back but you can't get my husband!'

The Officer responds, 'Well, the laws are different in Egypt.'

Mum lets me know she's also recently received a visit from the AFP, the Australian Federal Police. The two officers stated they were performing a 'welfare check', and they expressed concern for our circumstances. Then they asked if Dad had left a phone or laptop behind, and Mum said no. The phone and laptop had been taken by Dad to Egypt, both of which had already been confiscated by National Security. Mum was suspicious, saying she felt like they were fishing for information. When mum told me their names, I realised I knew one of the officers who visited; I had met him while working for an Islamic organisation in Queensland.

*

I don't fast.

I sip on water while lining up at the prison, ignoring the guilt I feel at drinking in front of fasting people. It amazes me how those around me don't pass out from dehydration in the summer heat. Of course, I know the resilience of the body while fasting; I know I could physically do it too. I just don't want to – why invite the challenge? It's hard enough just being here with a bottle of water.

Dad's fasting, but I worry for him. In the past five months, he's lost so much weight that he's the same size as he was in his twenties: the skinny, lanky young Dad who used to flex his biceps to the beat of the music to make me laugh. He might be as skinny now, but he's got less muscle. During visits, when I hug him, I can feel his spine and shoulder blades through his thin cotton shirt.

Dad says the good thing about Ramadan is that he no longer feels obliged to eat during the day. He says he's using Ramadan to practise for a hunger strike. He says that, even before Ramadan, he was preparing himself by reducing how much he was eating, that he'd fill his gnawing belly with water instead of food. Is that true, I wonder, or is he just hungry because he doesn't have enough food?

When Dad is eventually released, he is 23 kilograms lighter than when he went in. He joked that prison was better than *The Biggest Loser.*

*

So much life is compressed into the visitor's hour. Witnessing the unfolding stories of other families over the last five months, it is during my second Ramadan prison visit that I lose my composure, breaking down while waiting in line to leave.

Leaning against the iron lattice, I sob uncontrollably. Women try to shush me. I'm rupturing the collective stoicism, the shared self-protective mechanism, the silent agreement that we all stay strong while we're here visiting the prison. This week, I can't absorb it anymore: the sight of tired mothers and their kids, thoughts about all the empty chairs at dinner tables where fathers, uncles and brothers were supposed to sit. The years without touch, without intimacy; of seeing your children grow in weekly, one-hour increments.

It's not Ramadan that undoes me – it's not as if every prisoner observes the holy month or is Muslim. It's family I find myself yearning for. I miss the rhythm, the syncopated beat of what Ramadan has meant to me and my family. A month focused on introspection and connection, symbolised by the act of breaking fast together.

It's a bitter, lonely time and I'm tired of feeling so isolated. I wish I could at least spend more time with Dad, that there was some kind of special iftar visit. Amid all this hardness, I crave love, softness and safety.

At his next court hearing, Dad's sentence is renewed again, as feared. This is the ninth renewal.

Unbeknown to me, for the week of Eid, the one-hour visit is often truncated to 20 minutes. When the whistle goes off after 20 minutes, I'm crushed. I cling to Dad, sobbing.

How dare they rob us of our precious hour when we already have so little?

Lamisse

Dad is due for the final 15-day hearing at the end of June.

This is what Amgad explained to me back in February. Dad would first be moved through a potential total of ten hearings, at 15-day intervals. There's hope that maybe he'll be released before the 10th hearing.

After the 10th hearing, if Dad's remand detention period is renewed again, he goes into the next stage: hearings scheduled at 45-day intervals, and the possibility of two more years behind bars.

Saleh, the lawyer, informs me I can attend the 10th hearing as it's going to be held at a court outside the prison complex. The courthouse is in Tahgmo' Khamis, the same suburb as my university.

*

For the courthouse, I'm early. The taxi drops me off in a dustbowl parking lot – sandy and unpaved. The courthouse is supposedly nestled near this parking lot. Saleh isn't here yet. I need to wait somewhere nearby. I spot a McDonald's. Walking through this shadeless lot under the baking summer sun, I feel the sweat gathering on my face. It's a relief to retreat to the air-conditioned quiet of the always-the-same interior of a Macca's. As I wait for Saleh, dread pumps through me like petrol from a bowser: thick, nose-curlingly acrid. *Hold it together, try not to slip in this oil spill of anxiety.*

Taghamo' Khamis is a sprawling noveau-riche neighbourhood built on Cairo's north-eastern edge. Amid the malls and mansions are pockets of dilapidated housing for the poor and working class. Affluent areas always have accompanying zones for workers and their families: the folks who clean, cook, serve, build, fix, drive and nanny.

After a 20-minute wait, Saleh phones. It's a struggle to decipher where he's asking me to meet him, but I finally understand. Abandoning my burnt cappuccino, I head down to the courthouse.

Curved concrete barriers form a protective wall in front of the courthouse. There's a gap in the concrete barrier manned by two guards, and people are queuing to get through. I see everyone holding IDs, so I take out my passport and join the line. Seeing Saleh on the other side of the concrete barrier, I wave. He approaches the two guards to have a word with them, then I'm waved through.

Saleh pulls out a handkerchief from his suit jacket and wipes his brow. Despite the heat, he's in a three-piece suit. At the courthouse entrance, we're stopped by two more guards and there's another exchange. Saleh turns to me. 'They will not let you in, but this is not right. You are allowed to come in.'

My heart quickens, nervous I'll yet again be denied.

'Wait,' says Saleh. 'I will go inside and speak to someone.'

He sprints up the steps, disappearing into the courthouse.

The guards turn away, distracted by other people approaching to get into the courthouse. There's no shade or seats outside.

The sun is bright and blinding. A soreness settles over my right shoulder. I can feel my feet swelling in my sneakers.

A large, blue steel prison truck drives slowly past. I can see the bars on the top rectangle window. That's what Dad's described, how he's been transported in one of these trucks each time he's taken to court. It's a shock to realise he could be inside.

The minutes drag. *Everything takes so goddamn long.* I start pacing up and down. All of a sudden, Saleh is calling my name, waving at me from the top of the stairs. 'Come! Come!' he yells.

As I jog over, he pounds down the stairs and mutters something to the guards. 'Let's go!' he says to me, tilting his head towards the courthouse. The guards step out of the way.

'So, what changed?' I ask as we head up.

'Only Egyptians can come in. I had to prove to them you are Egyptian.'

The same old story, I think to myself.

*

The courthouse is cool, dark and dry. Wooden floors, decor ageing and run-down. Desks plonked in corridors like unplanned train stations for wandering carriages of people searching for the right room.

Employees, like listless station masters, hold their cigarettes idly in limp hands, darting eyes watching all who pass. It's all men, in various shades of grey, brown and green – polyester suits and pants, dusty black and tan shoes that are lace-ups or loafers.

We need directions to the courtroom where Dad's hearing will be. 'Where is the room for case number 977/2018?' asks

Saleh repeatedly, searching for an answer from one of these indifferent employees.

We go up more stairs, along several corridors and come to a halt in front of some doors. Saleh enters the room, then he hastily steps back out. 'No, not this one.'

Back into the corridor we go. Down more stairs, through more corridors, until we arrive at another island desk in the middle of a hallway. The same question, another answer.

We re-enter the maze of stairs and corridors. I follow Saleh, disoriented, struck by the irrelevance of time in the void where one lacks agency. Saleh turns a corner and stops before a set of heavy double wooden doors. He pushes one door open, and it swings into the room. He pokes his head inside, then pulls back and swivels his round face towards me. 'Okay, this is the one.'

I scan the wooden benches arranged in rows on either side of a corridor. The space is sparsely lit; sunlight steals in through unwashed windows. Dust tinges the room grey. Colourful rubbish is washed up at the shore of the judge's bench. Cigarette butts are bunched in corners and rolling around on the floor. A few men sit on the benches on the right of the room, occasionally tapping their feet on the wooden floor.

As the other men in this space are all sitting on the right, I move to the left, shuffle in between the benches and take a seat. Saleh tells me to wait, then walks to the front of the room. I pull my phone out of my bag. My thumb hits Instagram, and I mindlessly scroll through colourful images. In my peripheral vision, I can see two figures approaching. Two guards come into full view, leaning over the bench in front of me.

'Ya ustaza. Eiza tikalimi babaki?'

'Eh?' I respond, confused.

'Babaki, henaak. Mish eiza tikalimi wla eh?'

The guard gestures to the left of the room, and I see an iron-latticed wall painted white. Behind the lattice, I can see shadows of white moving. White prison uniforms. *Dad!*

'Akeed. Akeed!'

'Lah.'

'Leh?'

I don't understand the guard's response. He tries to explain again, with more emphasis in his low, gruff voice.

'Eh?' I say, and look over at the iron-latticed wall with desperation. Why would they just tell me Dad is in there in that cage and then stop me?

The guard looks at the other guard in exasperation. He turns back to me and opens his hand, pointing to his palm.

'Floos!'

'Aah … mashy!'

I dig into my bag, fumbling for my wallet. I pull out ten pounds and offer it to them. They shake their heads. I pull out another ten pounds. They silently accept ten pounds each, then move aside to let me pass.

I walk over to the painted iron lattice and peer in. 'Daaad?' I call out.

'Lamisse!' comes a voice from the crowd. Dad emerges from the rear of the cell and starts walking towards me. I move closer to the iron, hoping to curl my fingers through to touch Dad's hand. The guard yells, and I freeze. He motions for me to stand back. I clasp my hands behind me, but I don't step away. The guard doesn't object.

When Dad reaches the lattice, I see that his hands are cuffed in front of him.

'I was allowed to come to the hearing,' I say, hurried and breathless. 'How are you? Are you okay?'

'Yeah, we've been here since seven am. No water and no food …' he says.

I count 12 men in the cell. There's a bench at the back. Some men pace in the small space, some sit on the bench. A couple of others are huddled in a corner in conversation.

Dad and I make small talk. Then we chat about the lawyer and our hopes for the hearing, but we're both distracted and stressed. The conversation is stilted. Dad sees that my eyes keep wandering to the judge's bench, where three men are sitting.

'The judge is inside, in the back room behind that bench … See that door?' He indicates with his head. 'That's where we will go to have our case heard … in a back room.'

My eyes widen. Dad continues, 'The guys on the bench are thugs – or, as they say – "security".' The word 'security' falls out of his mouth in a mocking tone.

The three men sitting at the judge's bench are in casual clothes. I focus on the balding one wearing a knitted jumper. He possesses the most disinterested, bored air. Pulling out a cigarette, he rolls it around in his hands, then lazily lights up, slowly blowing the smoke upwards. The other two men are younger. They too smoke, but with speed and purpose; they stub out their cigarettes hard on the bench, crushing the butts. When the balding man is finished, he flips the butt over the edge and onto the courtroom floor. I'm both amazed and horrified by his cavalier attitude; it makes visible an utter disdain for the law. I don't understand how a lawyer is meant to do anything in this place.

'I should get a chance to talk this time,' says Dad, hopeful. 'I haven't been able to say anything for the last nine hearings. It's just been in and out, in and out.'

The guards who took the bribe start pointedly staring at me. I lose track of what Dad's saying as I look back at them; one of them gestures for me to step away.

'I've got to go back to my seat. I love you, Dad.'

Dad nods. 'I love you too.'

As he returns to the group huddled in the corner, I watch him shapeshift from father to inmate. I can't describe it fully, but it's in his body language. I've noted it before in the sound of his voice at the prison: it's the way he shapes the vowels in his Arabic. It sounds distinctly different from the light musicality I'm familiar with back home, the tone he uses when he speaks in Arabic with my grandmother. This way of speaking is harsher, wider and sprawling, echoing what I hear around me in Cairo. Every time I see this shift, it takes me by surprise. I glimpse the man who is in prison, a man who's different from the father I see every visiting hour. It alerts me that this experience is changing Dad, that he's embodying someone we may never know: that person will emerge with him, and neither he nor us may know what to do with him. *Will he come back to himself or will we have a different dad?* He can't not be changed by this; after all, it's already changing me.

Back in my seat, I get out my phone. The screen stays black. I don't even have the will to distractedly take a spin through Instagram. Instead, I stare at the floor, twirling the phone in my hands. I toy with the idea of taking a photograph; perhaps I can send it to Mum or make a post on Facebook to show people where Dad is, where I am. But – no – it feels too risky to do, too painful to share. So, I don't acquire any emotive court photos; soon, I'll wish I'd done so – especially when the media campaigning takes off again.

An hour passes. Now I wish I'd brought a book, though I know from experience it's useless to try to read. According to my bookmark, I'm halfway through *Pedagogy of the Oppressed* by Paulo Freire, but I couldn't tell you anything about it.

There's a commotion at the prisoners' cage. A door is opened by a guard. The men shuffle out, all handcuffed to one another. They scuttle like a chain gang of ghosts across the front of the courtroom, hurried along by impatient guards. They swerve behind the bench and are swallowed into the back room. Dad's salt and pepper head is the last go in, the last body on the chain.

Following Dad, Saleh hastily steps through the door. It closes behind him.

The courtroom goes quiet.

While I wait, I am an empty, blank statue. I cannot breathe. I cannot hope. I cannot move.

The door re-opens. I glance at my phone and see that 15 minutes have passed. I spring up from my seat. Saleh is at the door; Dad is standing near him. The guards tug at the chain of men; Dad is yanked with them as Saleh rushes after them. Suddenly, Saleh swerves and dashes back towards the judge's room.

I scream out: 'WHAT HAPPENED?'

The men begin disappearing through another door; the angle that they're walking at looks like they're heading downstairs.

'ASK SALEH!' yells Dad, and then he too, disappears. The door shuts behind him.

My head spinning, I collapse onto the bench.

Saleh is beside me. I didn't notice him leave the judge's room. He leans over and speaks in English.

'We will have a decision in a few days,' he says. 'The judge will decide and tell us.'

'Why not now?' I feel petulance creep over me.

'Because he needs to decide.' Saleh pauses. 'That was too quick. He was too quick with those men.'

'Yeah … that did seem very fast.'

'Yes … but we will see. I spoke for your father.'

'Okay, that's good.'

What else can I say? I don't know what to ask or what I can ask. Saleh interrupts the protracted silence.

'He will go back to prison now. You will visit him this week?'

'Yeah, Thursday – youm el-khamis.'

He nods approvingly. 'Okay then, let's go.'

This is the longest conversation I've had with Saleh in English, I could see it was a struggle for him, so I appreciate the effort. Getting to my feet, I pick up my bag from the bench and sling it over my shoulder. We trudge out of the courtroom, out of the courthouse and back to the street with the concrete barrier cutting the world in half.

Saleh walks me to the split in the solid grey wall.

'I'm going back into the court,' he says.

'Okay. Thank you for today.'

He shrugs. 'No problem.'

I walk through the cracked slit of concrete and into the windy, gritty car park. My heart feels like a boulder shackled to my feet, dragging metres behind me. I reach the main road and order an Uber. It arrives quickly, and I gratefully slide onto the leather seats and into the soothing air-conditioned coolness.

I sit back, close my eyes and imagine what jumping off Qasr El Nil bridge would feel like. These suicidal thoughts are coming more often, and I'm running out of ideas for fending them off. All I know is that I need to act: motion keeps them manageable; a sense of agency diminishes their power. If I just sit helplessly watching this spectacle of cruelty, I'll lose it. I wonder how Dad is doing. If I feel like this, how the hell is he psychologically surviving?

Hazem

Sitting down with Dad to understand what he went through that day, I was curious about many things: the procedures that he underwent, what he thought and felt, the perspectives of the other men in the case with him and what the judge said in that room.

Seeking to fill in these gaps and visualise Dad's experience, we started at the beginning.

> **Hazem:** In the morning, we go to the Habsa Khana [holding space] in Tora around 7.30 am. We stayed there till about 8.30 to 9 am. More people ... more prisoners came in ... There were probably more than 50 or 60 people at least – the mood was very, very tense. My main conversation was about whether someone has gone to court, and trying to ascertain what to expect. Most of the time, the conversations would go around hope ... Because you're taken to court to see a judge and not the District Attorney's Office, they say you have a good chance of being released ... So, we all had the same sort of offerings: apprehensive, anxious but nevertheless, hopeful. Basically, we're all handcuffed, then the process is that a Shaweesh would come in to open the steel gate and then start calling our names. He would state the case number first. So, for me, he said: 'Case

number 977! Hazem Hamouda.' When we were called, we would just walk to him and he would check our names again, then he would hand us over to another Shaweesh, who would do the same process again before we'd be taken to the truck. This is all done in the sight of the warden and his deputy. There are also National Security guys and Mabahiz [officers] there, watching. Some of those guys would just come over to us and say stupid things ... But we just laughed at them.

Lamisse: Like offensive things?

Hazem: Not really offensive. It's more of a sarcastic attitude.

Lamisse: Like what?

Hazem: For instance, there was this specific Mabahiz who would always say things like: 'Oh, you guys look pretty cheerful today!' or 'Hopefully you had a good time here!' You know, this sort of sarcastic attitude.

Lamisse: Ah, okay ... Like as if you'd just had a hotel stay.

Hazem: Yes, and teasing us for hoping we won't come back. Then, once we stepped out of the building, there would be guards with machine guns.

Lamisse: Do you have guns pointing at you as you're walking?

Hazem: No, no, they would be just carrying guns.

Lamisse: Okay ...

Hazem: They're always in the vicinity ... You can see that they're just watching you as they hold their guns. If something happens, if someone runs, then there are orders of shoot to kill.

I'm surprised to hear this said so casually, but Dad doesn't flinch.

Hazem: Once we were in the van, they would lock the gate behind us. And the truck was very filthy ... This one we took to the court, as I recall, had a spare tyre inside. And, as usual, it smelt of urine.

> Bearing in mind, we're all dressed up in white. So, by the time we got there, our clothes are dirtied from the steel benches. The truck would then take us to various parts of the Tora prison complex, where it would pick up different prisoners from different sections.
> **Lamisse:** Would they all be political prisoners?
> **Hazem:** Yes, yes. The whole lot. As we pick up different prisoners from like, from Scorpion One, then Scorpion Two [the solitary confinement wings], then we would go to Mazraa', then to Istiqbal ... Then to the reception area; that's another place that holds prisoners. This all takes at least a couple of hours ... And remember it's June, it's pretty hot and we're all stuffed inside ... no air-conditioning.

Dad goes on to describe arriving at the courthouse:

> **Hazem:** As we approached, I hear a lot of shouting outside. I was alerted to the fact that they are the family members of those who are inside Scorpion One and Two. They have been denied family visits for years, and the only way for families to get a glimpse of each prisoner is when the truck is turning into the district building of the Prosecutor's office in Taghamo' Khamis. Since it's secured all the way through, this shouting happens just as we're turning.
> **Lamisse [intervenes]:** But it's not like you're going to be let out of the truck at this point; you're just turning into the place where the truck will be parked, right?
> **Hazem:** Yes, the men inside are just shouting from that little steel mesh window at the top of the truck ...

The image of the truck passing me by as I sullenly waited for Saleh takes on new meaning. So, I repeat what I've just heard:

Lamisse: And that's the only way those men and their families can contact each other?

Hazem: Yes, all the men just keep yelling: 'We're okay! We're okay!' I found out later that, most of the time, no one knows who's shouting. It's just a comfort because no one can see anyway. The men said the families considered it like this: if they just hear a voice that says 'I'm okay', then they could think that it was their son or their husband or their brother ... It was very emotional for me to witness that. I teared up actually, quite a few times, whenever this happened.

Dad goes into a reflective pause; I'm silent, trying to contain my own emotions.

Hazem: But anyway, once we get inside, the truck stops and we're shuffled out, handcuffed to each other in pairs. There were a lot of guards with machine guns and a lot of people, a few plain-clothes police officers as well. This time, we would be sarcastic and say things like: 'Why all of this? All this effort just for us?' It was overkill. Way, way exaggerated. For those prisoners who had been there a while, especially the Scorpion ones, they were pretty chill. They used to laugh – intentionally – in front of the guards, and they would also say sarcastic things to them as well. But still, it is built to intimidate you ... to try to break you down, to create anxiousness and trauma intentionally. We were then walked down into a carpark area that was under the building. It was dark and dingy, full of rubbish and parked cars ... As we walk through the cars, we arrive at a basement underneath the main building. Once inside, on the left-hand side, is another Habsa Khana. Inside of those cells were criminal prisoners. They had men and women mixed too, which was very distressing. It was overcrowded, way overcrowded – there were too many people. There was shouting and a lot of profanities. There was food everywhere, food wrappings … And the urine, wow … it's amazing. Always in these places, the smell of urine and other things was always just horrific! Especially because there were no toilets.

Lamisse: Wait, so they're in these holding cells and there's no bathroom for them to use? Do people just pee on the floor?

Hazem: Yeah, they could be taken to bathrooms, but they have to be escorted. And most of the time the Shaweesh, or the police officers or the soldiers there, they just can't be bothered. It's like, 'Ah, fuck it, just do it there. Just do it in the corner. Or here is a bottle – just pee in the bottle or on the floor.' [Shrugging] What can you do? You think this is about giving people their dignity?

Lamisse: I know, I get it. It just still baffles me.

Dad smiles wanly.

Hazem: When we entered, the Shaweesh had a list of all our names. We're still handcuffed, but I actually peeked at what was on the paper. That's when I've seen, for the first time, a paper with my name on it and the case number. Remember, you don't get given any kind of paperwork. There was also a description of the case that says this was a case for the media arm of the Muslim Brotherhood.

Lamisse: So, they're accusing you of being part of the media?

Hazem: Yeah, media. Yeah, it said media arm … in Arabic, obviously. Which was interesting, like, what were these people on about? Me? Media?

He scoffs then continues:

Hazem: Anyway, we waited a bit, then climbed about four stairs to enter into a cage-like space. Saleh showed up straightaway. Then he started telling me, 'It's going to be okay. It's going to be all right.' He said, 'Look, this is definitely the way now, we're on the safe side of the court. They'll be able to make a clear assessment that you have nothing to do with anything ...' So, it was comforting to hear that. Then you appeared! At that moment, I was thrilled to see you, and even the other guys who were with me were happy to see you too. So, you gave us like a glimpse of hope. We took your presence as a sign that said, 'Hey, this could work out!'

Lamisse: You really do cling on to anything as a symbol of hope.

Hazem: Yeah, we do I guess – you have to find anything to hold onto. So, finally, the clerk came and called us out from the holding cell. We walked behind them without knowing where to go, and we were ushered into the door behind the benches. There were guards inside with batons in their hands. They stood in front of us like a line, maybe seven or eight of them, literally just backing us against the wall to create a barrier between us and the judges. The judges weren't sitting on any bench, they were sitting at desks. There was one prosecutor, three judges and a clerk. You could see one of the judges had all our files, and that he was just handing over these files as he tries to explain who are we. As he's handing them over, it seems to me that the judges didn't read our files beforehand but just now, in this moment. Then I hear him saying, 'Hazem Hamouda file.' The judges just shuffled and looked at the files, and shuffled the paper, and then one of the judges on the left looked at us, and he said, 'Does anybody want to say something?' I immediately shouted out, 'Yes. I have no idea why am I here! I have tried to talk about my health issue. And that there's … and I don't know why I'm here and I'm also Australian and I shouldn't be here!'

Lamisse: It sounds like you just tried to blurt everything out.

Hazem: I did. But the judge looked extremely confused, then he said, 'Okay, okay, okay …' So dismissive, like he didn't want to even listen. It was like the question was just a formality; we weren't actually meant to respond. That's when Saleh went to him. He spoke quietly, but I did catch that it was along the same lines, and he requested that I be released on bail. But the judges didn't respond at all to him. Then we were all ushered back outside; Saleh, too, was ushered outside along with the rest of the prisoners … Then we all had a feeling that this is not going well, and that feeling really affected us. We were asked to go outside and then … I can't remember … Wait, we went back to the holding cell underneath … Yes, that's right, we went straight down and I didn't get a chance to talk to you – I just yelled at you. Once we went down, we stayed there for a few hours. We didn't come out until about five or six o'clock in the evening.

Lamisse: But you guys were out of the judge's room by, like, two!

Hazem: Yeah, then we stayed for another three, four hours. Mind you, all we have is just water for the whole day from 7 am until whenever we get back to Tora – no food. Handcuffed, walked again through the car park back to the truck, the whole place is dark, quiet and empty. We did the same trip back into Tora, dropping everyone at their section or whatever their buildings are. Once we get back to our section, we still don't know what our verdict is. But we know that among the people transporting us, one was an administrator and he carried the paperwork that had the ruling inside it. Now, he doesn't disclose any news to us, not until we're back inside Tora. Before we'd go back to our cells, we'd be body searched. At that point, I can't remember if it was myself or someone else who shouted: 'What's the verdict? What did the court say?' And he looked at the paper and said casually, 'Ah, 45.'

Lamisse: What? Just like that? With that tone of, 'Yeah, too bad'?

Hazem: Yeah, just casually he says 45, and that's it. And with a flick of his hand too, like it's rubbish or irrelevant information. At that moment, my heart sunk. This is when it hits you: that nothing is what you think it is, that there are other things going on in the background, and we have no idea what that is. That this is not a trial. And if it is, it's definitely not a *fair* trial. It's not even a fair hearing either. And I never understood why you would have a whole court day. For what? What did they base their decisions on? There is no defence. There is no evidence ... There is no ... there's nothing.

Lamisse: Like the process is a performance ... to try to legitimise what they're doing.

Hazem: You know, I have never had any conversations with the court – at all. This hearing was the only time I actually managed to speak ... In all the other times, I was told to be quiet ... I was always just told to be quiet.

Exposure

Presuming Dad's been renewed, as I haven't heard from Saleh or anyone else, I am back at the prison for my weekly visit.

I get to the cafeteria and wait for the men to come out. Dad comes out with them, looking tired. We sit down together and he immediately informs me he's been renewed for another 45 days.

I then tell him I have a piece of good news to share: my talks with Channel 10's show, *The Project*, have resulted in securing an interview. The interview is scheduled for mid-July, about a week from now.

*

Preparing for the video interview, I place the laptop in different spots around the apartment, checking the camera to see what looks best: I choose to set myself up in the dining room so that only a white wall and a sideboard will be visible behind me. Then I fiddle around with the lighting, bringing a lamp from my room. It's daytime; I don't need it. I'm just nervous.

I quickly do my hair and make-up and put on a striped T-shirt. Despite my fussing around with the location and lighting, I don't think too much about what I'm wearing and what it conveys; it's more important that I feel comfortable and myself. Then I sit at the dining table and wait to be called by the producer.

When the call comes in, the Australian accent takes me by surprise. It's been over a year since such a strong drawl hit my ears.

The producer hands over to host Hamish McDonald. He gives me a quick brief. Because I'm not in a studio during the recording, I won't be able to see anyone at the Australia end; I'll only hear what's happening.

While they finish setting up, I sit there, quietly waiting. I think, *I'm going on television to talk about my dad's case.* I haven't prepared notes and wonder if I should have. Figuring I know the case well enough by now, I'll speak from my heart.

The interview mostly goes well: the questions are clear, and though I'm nervous, I feel confident in what I'm saying.

Then Hamish asks if my dad could be a terrorist. *Huh?* I bat the question away with a laugh.

The question is disorienting and alienating. I hate that it had the power to make me feel guilty and defensive, reminding me that Dad is presumed to be one before he isn't. I hate *The Project* for needing to even ask.

I just want us to be believed without question.

After the interview airs, a journalist friend texts me.

'I watched the interview. You can't laugh during an interview like that. You've got to stay focused.'

Stay focused. Stay serious. This is not a laughing matter. Terrorism is not a joke.

*

The interview goes online after it's screened on TV.

Mum texts me: 'I'm so glad you did that interview. It's a good reminder to people here that this is real, and it is still happening."

More real than when it was reported in the newspaper? There's a paradox within the media coverage we're getting: on one hand, it opens us up to the sting of questioning and suspicion. Many comments on Facebook and Twitter are nasty and unsupportive, racist and rude. On the other hand, it adds weight to Dad's plight. The publicity lends legitimacy to our suffering. It's cynical, but it deems it worthy of being noticed.

However, the support reminds me that we don't have to suffer in silent, harrowing isolation. It's the first step back into the spotlight, and I'm scared but hopeful. More hopeful than last time.

When I take the news back to Dad, I leave aside my criticisms and fears to give him a positive summary of the interview and its outcomes. I see that it gives his morale a boost: he isn't forgotten, he's being seen.

The Lying Daughter

A couple of weeks after the interview goes to air, I arrange a consult with a new lawyer.

Dad's unhappy with Saleh and insists there must be better lawyers out there. Saleh can't access Dad, no lawyers can access their clients in prison – they all wait to catch them at court. As such, the only time they've spoken is in court, in the brief moments while waiting for a hearing to start. Dad has lawyer recommendations from other prisoners. In response, I promise to ask for recommendations from friends. Perhaps it's prejudiced of me, but I'm reluctant to use the lawyer of a man who's been in Dad's situation for five years.

Looking back, I recognise that Saleh was a good lawyer. A bit chaotic, but then again, he was working in chaotic conditions. Lawyers struggle a lot in Egypt, especially the human rights ones. They're slogging it out in opaque, corrupt conditions. Most lawyers aren't well paid, particularly if they're working to represent prisoners. They too, are obstructed from doing their job, waiting to catch their clients in those brief, thieved moments in court.

I organise a consult with a new lawyer for the afternoon. I arrive at a discreet office snuggled into the second floor of an apartment block. The lawyer comes in, greets me and takes a seat at his desk. He pulls out a packet of cigarettes and lights one.

He speaks English. There's very little small talk and he gets down to business, pulling out a notepad and a pen. With painstakingly neat handwriting, he maps out everything I'm saying.

About 10 minutes in, he looks up and says, 'But the President doesn't put anyone in prison who isn't guilty. He always has a reason.'

This isn't a shocking statement, though I immediately know this is not going to be the lawyer for us. Many Egyptians support the narrative that life is safer in Egypt now that Sisi is in charge (safer for whom, is always the question to ask), that he's a good leader who protects the Egyptian people, and that the War on Terror is necessary and legitimate. I'm never sure if they truly believe it deep in their hearts, or if they say they believe it to survive. I'm angry, but I can't ignore what is between the lines of what the lawyer is saying: why rock the boat? Align yourself with the state for your own good.

Still, I feebly protest: 'No, but Dad isn't guilty. They're saying he had stuff on his Facebook, but I checked his Facebook and there's hardly anything on it.'

The lawyer frowns, pulls out his phone, and finds Dad's Facebook page. He scrolls through his feed and pauses. Then he holds up the phone screen so I can see. It's one of those pixelated memes that have Arabic writing and flowers on it: the kind your relatives share on a WhatsApp group chat.

'Here, see, it's a du'aa. Why is he putting this on his Facebook? Why is he referring to other Muslims as his brothers?'

I stare at him blankly. *What's wrong with that? Why is that cause for suspicion?*

He powers on. 'Here, that isn't good. It sounds too religious. It sounds like Brotherhood.'

This sounds so ridiculous: how can something as inane as the word 'brother' now be evidence of a predilection for extremism?

'But he's just making a prayer on Facebook,' I say. 'It doesn't mean anything …'

'It does. Why does he have to say it on Facebook? Make the prayer to God, not to Facebook.'

The lawyer leaves Dad's Facebook page, appearing satisfied he's found a piece of potential evidence. He keeps scrolling, though I'm not sure through what.

'You are here,' he announces.

'Where?' I ask, confused.

'Here.' He turns the phone around to show me the screen.

There I am. It's a screenshot from the interview with *The Project*. My striped T-shirt, my curly hair. It's an Arabic news article.

The lawyer flips back to the search results and scrolls through, showing me that there are multiple news articles featuring the same screenshot.

'I can't read Arabic; what is that about?' My heart is thumping; I can feel the blood pulsing in my fingertips.

He opens one of the articles, traces his finger under the Arabic headline and translates: 'It says, "The Lying Daughter of the Muslim Brotherhood".'

I want to laugh and pass out at the same time. He keeps reading the article. 'It says you went on television and said things that are not true about Egypt and your father.' Of course, they're watching. But the proof that they are still sickens me, spiking my paranoia.

Then he pauses, and looks up at me. 'Why did you do this?'

Why did I do this? Did he really just ask why did I do this?

I'm in danger of choking on my own saliva – the question shocks me. Why wouldn't I do this? Am I the only one who thinks it's crazy to arbitrarily arrest people? It's bewildering having to manage the Australian context and the Egyptian context, and I don't know how to bridge the two. Of course, the State has to speak back. Of course, they have to set the record straight – according to their record. Propaganda, free speech … Whatever it is, they're allowed to do it. And I am allowed to speak publicly, but this … this is something I feared. The accusation loaded in his question is punishing; am I not allowed to speak?

Then again, I want to laugh. It's also entirely ridiculous. 'The Lying Daughter of the Muslim Brotherhood'? *Me?*

I can't be in the room anymore. I tell the lawyer I have to go. He nods and puts away his phone, then a sympathetic look crosses his face. 'If you need anything, even if it's not about your father, ask me.'

Offering help is a common thing that Egyptians do at the end of conversations. I can't always discern as to when it's a genuine offer or a habit of politeness. One of my early lessons in Cairo was that when a taxi driver tells you, 'You don't need to pay', you shouldn't get out of the cab feeling amazed and happy about a free ride. It's a dance: you're supposed to insist on paying until the driver accepts your offer, and then you pay them with a generous tip.

There are many dances in Egyptian conversation, and I have no idea how to navigate any of them. My communication patterns are, to me, culturally Australian.

I thank the lawyer and decide it's more likely that he's just being polite.

Afterwards, I hastily message Mum: *I'm not doing any more media while I'm still in Egypt. I knew it, I just can't risk it.*

And with that, the second round of potential campaign momentum collapses.

Don't Get Sick

It's now August, and Dad's health keeps deteriorating. He's covered in a strange rash; it flares up at night and he can't sleep from the hot itch that comes over him. At the visits, he scratches at the side of his groin. I ask him what's wrong and he says the rash is not only over his hands and his legs, but also on his inner thighs, his behind and his genitals.

I bring him scabies cream and Dettol soap with which to disinfect himself. It's not scabies. Since I have psoriasis myself, I have a couple of bottles of MooGoo cream I bought with me from Australia. I bring him one, thinking it could help if it's eczema.

But it's not eczema either.

It's only after Dad gets out of prison that it's diagnosed as neurodermatitis: a stress rash.

Dad also keeps complaining about the ache caused by the metal pins in his ankle. One of them is visible through the thin skin over his protruding ankle bone. He broke his leg in a soccer accident in 2017, and had his shin and ankle pieced back together in a six-hour reconstruction surgery. He was due to have the metal removed three months ago. He's been persistently asking for permission to have the surgery at a hospital outside of the prison, but his requests are denied.

His medical assessment in the prison consists of a doctor glancing at his ankle and saying that it's not that bad.

During this time, Mum finally secures power of attorney and gets access to Dad's medical records. At this point, we're functioning under the belief – the hope – that evidence can help our case. We submit the medical reports but get nowhere.

Dad pithily summarises his feelings about it during one of our interviews: 'No rights, no value. If you're a prisoner, then you're nothing.' At best, he said, you'd get prescribed painkillers, antibiotics and steroid creams. When he reflects on this, he flares up: 'We all know these things can have serious side effects! In the long run, they can break your body down further.'

Outlining the process prisoners go through to access the hospital, Dad suddenly complicates the narrative when he describes walking through the room where prisoners recover after an operation.

Hazem: I was on my way to the clinic and I walked through the room where prisoners rest after an operation. It looked like a field ... a field ...

Lamisse: A field hospital during a war?

Hazem: Yes, exactly! Yanni, their arms are up and you can see the blood crust on the wrappings. The smell is horrific. I can't believe people actually survive this. But again, as I found out later, for some of these people ... this is actually a privilege.

Lamisse: What? To be in hospital?

Hazem: Yes, to be in the hospital and to actually get medical treatment. Numerous times, I was told that I don't understand where these guys come from, that I don't understand just how poor they are. For them, this prison is first class. It reminded me that so many Egyptians don't have access to proper healthcare, and that the prison, and what is offered there, *is* healthcare. So, yeah … the sort of … the irony of it … it's just amazing.

Lamisse: I guess it is some kind of shelter, food and healthcare …

Hazem: Yeah, being inside was like always living with these contradictions. Honestly, there were some people who actually appreciated the prison environment. By that, I mean for the first time they were away from poverty and hardship … They were just sleeping, eating, drinking and socialising. For them, it was a break. It was like a better life …

To imagine such poverty is heart-wrenching. Dad shakes his head and states, 'They trade their freedom for their basic needs … that's how poor they are.'

Love (in a Hopeless Place)

Dad is renewed for another 45 days. I can't deal, neither can Dad. Our visit passes in thinly masked fear and tension.

Escaping into a party one evening, I find myself in an intense conversation with a new friend. Since the political space has been so violently foreclosed upon, it seems that everyone in my generation knows someone in prison. He talks about friends inside, the 2011 revolution and the 'collective PTSD' among him and his friends. I appreciate his candidness as we connect over the prison, mental health and the struggle to survive the woundings. Then, he pulls out his phone and opens his Instagram.

'Here, look at this.'

It's the Instagram account of a man in Tora. For the first time, I'm seeing the inside of a cell.

I scroll through the blurry photos of a dark, concrete cell, lined with blankets, pots and pans hanging off wires; I can smell the cell just looking at these photos. It's incredible that this guy is running an Instagram page from prison on a smuggled phone. Men in white sprawl in various positions: some sitting against the wall, some lying on their sides with their heads resting on their palms. Then there are photos of inmates' drawings: sketches of flowers, of shadowed, haunted faces.

All I've known is that Dad's cell is three metres by three metres. That there's a tiny window covered in mesh. That he hasn't seen the night sky since being taken from the airport. That the only time he sees the sun is through the mesh overhang during his daily walk as the light weakly filters through.

Now I know what it could look like, I feel sick all over again.

Dad's cell, however, had a mural painted on one of the walls. One of his cellmates is the young artist, Shady Habash. He'd directed a music video for a satirical song that made a dig at President el-Sisi. Those in the project didn't think it was a big deal. Their arrest was a surprise. And those who'd escaped arrest were forced to flee, seeking asylum in Europe. In the cell, Shady had drawn a large, circular moon, shadowing it with craters. Above the moon, Shady printed in block letters: The Dark Side of the Moon. Descending into a deep depression, in what would be his final letter, Shady wrote, 'Prison doesn't kill, loneliness does. I need your support, so I don't die.' Denied visitors and court visits due to coronavirus measures, with a renewal that would keep him in prison beyond the legal limit of two years, Shady allegedly ingested hand sanitiser. He passed away on 6 May 2020. He was 24 years old.

*

By September, the overextended summer is ending, and some friends and I decide to close it by attending a music festival in Sinai. I didn't re-enrol at university and I don't have a job: my stretched savings are primped up by occasional freelance copywriting work.

In Sinai, at the festival, I meet a guy called Thomas. Thomas emanates positive energy. On the rooftop, where we sit and have pre-drinks with mutual friends under the night sky, he's warm and talkative. At the festival, he gives out high-fives and cruises around with a constant groove in his step. There doesn't seem to be a pretension about him: he's just a dude having a good time.

I envy him and his lightness, his joy.

While joy flows, fear stiffens.

A hard pinch on my ass from a man in a volunteer T-shirt at the festival reminds me that women shouldn't be fooled into thinking the words 'safe space' really means safe. I skulk around the festival, pissed off. I can't relax and enjoy myself. Everything appears hostile: the music too loud, the crowd of party-goers suffocating.

I don't want to be here.

*

Back in Cairo, a friend takes me to a dance class at a studio. Knowing I'd hated the festival, they suggest that if I want to dance, I should try out the studio's open sessions. During the class, I feel myself reconnecting with my body, unearthing the reality of how much I've disassociated from myself: this comes at a cost.

The hard shell of distance starts to collapse between me and my emotions. After my second dance class, I feel unstable. I ditch plans for dinner with my friend and head home. Hysteria softly combs its fingers down my cheek, provoking me to break.

Arriving home, I head straight into my first panic attack.

Alone in my room, my breath refuses to flow. As anyone who has experienced a panic attack knows, there is always the moment when you're convinced if you don't take a breath soon, you will die. I erupt into a choked scream, my whole body shaking as I enter an out-of-body state: a bird's-eye view of watching myself shivering in the corner of my bedroom, like a cowering, howling street dog.

While distressing, that first panic attack alerted me to something important: I needed release. If it wasn't for the dance class, if it wasn't for sinking back into my body and meeting the pain that sat there, I wouldn't have entered into conscious awareness of what lay behind the numb depression. I began to understand that I couldn't save up the pain and 'break down when it was over'. No, if I kept holding to that belief, I wouldn't just break down: I'd become so brittle, I'd break.

I found the space to release and process in movement. But it was unfailingly hard – as much as I knew I needed it, I battled my conscious unwillingness, my fear, of discovering the secrets my body hid.

*

Now that our friendship circles have overlapped, I start to see Thomas around Cairo more often. At social gatherings, his warmth and kindness are hard to ignore. Though I like him, my defences are up. I ungenerously presume his time in Egypt must be an exotic blip on his white middle-class radar, that he'd go back to Germany and I'd be a footnote, a fling. Knowing he lives within the expat bubble, I believe that my harsh reality can't meld with his, that there's no point. Guarded and scared, I'm uninterested in having my time, body and emotions wasted when there's so much on the line.

However, Thomas puts a lot of effort towards making me feel safe and comfortable around him. He is consistent and persistent, and I start trying to put aside my suspicion and distrust, to allow myself to receive the care he's offering. As I accept, I reciprocate and open up. We fall in love.

Still consumed by the feeling that the stakes in my life are too high to waste my time, our relationship moves fast. I tell him that I don't have time for slowly figuring things out, demanding to know if Thomas is committed to going through these hard times with me, to understand that – right now – there's nothing more important than my dad and my family; that this means he, and our relationship, will come secondary to the mission of getting Dad out of prison and back home. He doesn't hesitate to accept this, and it surprises me he's so willing to take it all on. A romantic at heart, he believes once this is behind us, we'll build a beautiful life together.

Though we're very different people on paper, together we form a foundation of emotional safety, a sacred space for vulnerability, love, compassion and deep care. This is what I had been craving, and with Thomas, I feel that I can drop my armour. I find comfort in his arms on the days the world seems unbearably hopeless and terrifying. I'd lost sight of the future, but through him, I find a rope that ties me to the world that could exist after Dad's ordeal ends. A glimmer of hope takes root. The hope of an earthly afterlife.

Desperate

During today's visit, Dad is agitated. He's frustrated. He's itching. His leg hurts. He doesn't sleep from the heat and the itching. He's hungry. He's tired. He's bored. He's depressed. Meanwhile, I'm anxious; I can't stop talking, rattling off my own desperate, hopeful words to keep Dad's sinking spirits up. It ends up in a verbal battle as we heatedly debate strategies, wondering what else we can do.

'It'll be all right. We've still got other things we can try. Maybe I can go back to doing media stuff, maybe I shouldn't be so scared. We still haven't got a lawyer from outside Egypt; maybe we need to do that. What do you think? Should we go public? Again? Do we need more open advocacy, Dad? Do you want this in the media? If you really do, I'll do it. I'll just push through and do it. Should we keep trying to find a new lawyer? Maybe we really do need someone else and not Saleh? I'm not sure, what do you think? Should we—'

Dad interrupts my rambling with quiet words, his head low. I lean in to hear him.

There's a military man who helps prisoners, he tells me. He's an ex-prisoner himself, and he's known to the other people inside. Apparently, he can help us.

The threads of faith I have left for anyone or anything in Egypt does not extend to the military. I express my hesitation over this idea, but Dad insists. He says he'll get this man's number off the men inside and give it to me at next week's visit. He says he wants me to meet with this military guy and see what he can do.

I can see Dad is desperate enough to think this is a good idea, and I don't want to disempower him by vetoing his decision.

While my mind is busy trying to rationalise Dad's wishes, my skin curdles in anticipatory fear.

*

The following Thursday, Dad slips me a note. It's got a phone number on it and a man's name. I've been harbouring an ill-feeling about this all week, while simultaneously hoping it's just a fleeting, desperate idea from Dad that won't stick. I'd hoped we wouldn't have to discuss it again, but now this guy's number is in my sweaty hand.

Dad and I get into an argument. I realise this lead is giving him a sense of agency. He's trying to exert control over his circumstances by telling me what to do because it's his idea and his contact. Part of me feels compelled to comply, to let my dad experience decision-making power over his fate, and accept my new position as a messenger between this man and Dad.

But I still urge Dad to revisit other options – like an international legal counsel, like a different Egyptian lawyer. Hell, let's go guns blazing to the media again: third time lucky.

Dad stands firm. I can do all that, he argues, *and* I can speak to this guy. Then my father does something he's never done before: he pleads with me. 'Just meet him and see what he has to say. See what he can offer.'

Over the course of these prison visits, there's been this undercurrent of tension as the power dynamic between us has undergone an irrevocable shift. Since Tora, I've worked out my own system of navigating and surviving this country. Prior to Tora, I'd have blindly trusted Dad's judgements about Egypt, acquiescing my power, because this was his home turf. Now, I'm the person Dad must rely on.

However, if Dad needs to experience his agency by asking me to do things for him, then I should do it. Despite my misgivings, I figure that the best thing I can do right now is stop arguing with him, and agree to contact this man.

After the visit, I still feel uncomfortable. I call Mum from the cab and tell her what Dad's asked of me.

She backs her husband. 'Try everything,' she says. 'Just try everything. You'd rather know you did all you could than sit there thinking what if … what if this guy could have helped?'

I'm tackled by the guilt loaded in the 'what if' question. What if I don't do this and I lose a chance to get Dad out of prison? I imagine future statements like 'What if you had …' or 'If only you just tried …' I hear it and I know – but at what price?

I'm haunted by the suspicion that Mum and Dad are becoming emotionally blinded by desperation. Desperation is corrosive. It rusts you into snapping; it's adrenaline-fuelled and unsustainable in a long-term battle. To me, desperation is fear-based, and fear clouds your reasoning. Decisions made from a place of fear are often the wrong ones. Keeping a clear, steady head feels crucial to survival, crucial to making the right decisions. The desperation of my parents feels like it's undermining my efforts *not* to be desperate. I hate theirs because it mirrors my own; it mirrors the fear I'm so desperately trying to keep away. As it is, I barely keep my cramped fingers gripped over it.

In the end, I accept that I'm desperate too. Irrespective of whatever I think or feel, I do have to try everything.

I contact the military man when I get home.

He says he's been waiting to hear from me.

The Avocado

The man asks me to meet him at a military club in the suburbs.

Military clubs are exclusive, gated compounds for army members and their families. They're used as venues for weddings, birthdays, graduation celebrations and meetings. They house hotels, restaurants and cafes. They have gardens and playgrounds and swimming pools and gyms and fitness tracks. Some are humble; others are illustrious, marbled and gilded, with sycophantic waiters, cleaners and service staff.

Existing, as I do, in the tedious liminal state between foreigner and Egyptian, I've previously had trouble getting into military clubs. So, as I drive towards the club, I'm nervous and wonder if they'll even let me in.

When the cab pulls up, I see the club is one of the more modest ones. I've been instructed to mention the name of the military man I'm meeting to the soldiers at the entrance. I do so, and the soldiers wave me in without even a request for proof.

The club's grounds are impeccably clean and green. A luxurious water feature sprawls at the front of the central building. To steady myself, I grip my backpack straps and stride across the granite walkway. Inside, the décor is all Louis XIV style, complete with gold-trimmed furniture.

A large 50-something year old man in a grey suit greets me. Sticking out his hand, he introduces himself. He smiles, the small close-set eyes in his sagging pugilistic face crinkling at the corners. Then he leads me to a table in the nearby cafe and asks what I'd like. I choose coffee.

The military man's questions begin: what am I studying and so on. His English is good enough to hold a conversation. I lie and say I'm studying teaching. It's easier than having to explain that I've dropped out from a Gender Studies degree. I pepper my speech with phrases like 'Ma'shallah' and 'Al'hamullilah' in an effort to mark myself as a respectful, well-raised Muslim daughter.

After some time, he pauses and looks at me confused. 'Are you Muslim?'

The question catches me off guard.

'Yeah …' I respond hesitantly, wondering how much I should say, 'I was raised to be Muslim, but I don't really practise …'

'Good,' he says assertively. 'I am atheist.' He pauses, then adds, 'Religion … it's all bullshit.'

Surprise bolts through me. Shocked at his boldness, I'm embarrassed I assumed he was a pious Muslim man; it hadn't even crossed my mind he might be Coptic or irreligious. As the surprise and embarrassment fade, my paranoia makes an appearance. *Shit, does open religiosity spark suspicion? Did I just incidentally add weight to the accusation of Dad being a Muslim-Brotherhood-supporting-alleged-terrorist by trying to mark myself as a good Muslim daughter?*

Now, my choice of behaviour doesn't feel like the polite thing to do – it could be dangerous. It makes me aware of the slippage that's been occurring between all these masks I wear: the Muslim mask, the 'Australian' mask, the 'Ana Masreya' mask. Have I ever been convincing to anyone, or are the masks more about convincing myself? Who am I? Why am I so inconsistent, so performative, in who I show up to be?

The man hasn't finished: 'But why?' he asks. 'Why do you still say you are Muslim?'

'Uh, well … my parents. My dad, he's religious, and Mum – well, she became Muslim and is very passionate about her faith. So, it's important to my parents. And I guess, because of that, it's still important to me too. Mostly, I want my parents to be happy. I don't want to make them sad by saying I'm not Muslim.'

I figure it's better to retain the mask of dutiful daughter than to open up about my contradictory spiritual convictions.

The military man accepts this and relaxes. He proceeds to elaborate upon his statement that religion is bullshit. I listen and nod. He gets on a roll: outlines his views on Christianity ('also bullshit'), the Quran ('it's all made up') and prophethood ('it's a joke'). He is steadfast in his disbelief, faithfully committed to his disdain for all religions.

As the man starts up on his contempt for the Coptic Church, I ask myself why he's telling me all this. I'd rather discuss why we're here, but I can't rush him or stop this boring conversation. To find out what he can offer, I have to be patient and polite. I keep smiling and nodding, feigning interest.

I take a sip of my cold coffee. It's burnt. *Should you drink a bad coffee slowly or get it over with as fast as possible?*

There's a lull as he runs out of anti-religion-ranting steam. I fill in the silence with a limp response: 'Well, that was interesting … to hear your views on that.'

He nods. 'I can talk to people for you.'

'Okay …' *Is this the conversation I've been waiting for?*

'I can talk to people.' He adds, 'I am like *avocahdor* for your father.'

'Sorry?'

'I am *avocahdor*.'

I feel myself blushing. I know he's unlikely to have said this, but I have to check because it's what I've heard. I say, 'Sorry. Did you say you are an avocado?'

He frowns. 'I talk to people. I am AD-*VOCK-KAY-DOR* for your father.'

'Oh, advocator!' I burst out laughing, relieved to have a reason to ease my tension. 'Oh, I'm sorry. I heard avocado, and I was so confused.'

He doesn't share my laughter; his expression stays stony. 'Yes, this is what I said,' he says sternly. 'You must listen to me, Lamisse.'

With that reprimand, I go still and quiet. 'Yes, sorry. I just didn't hear you properly.'

'We will need papers.'

He explains what papers he requires. It's a comprehensive list: all the family's IDs and Dad's CV. He says he wants to paint a picture of our family, of Dad's history in Australia. He says this will help people to see that Dad isn't a terrorist, but a man who legitimately has a family in Australia, a man who has lived and worked in Australia as long as he says he has.

I don't know what people he's talking about, but I assume they're important somehow. I agree to bring all the documents to him.

The meeting comes to an end. He walks me out and waves down a cab for me.

From then on, while I use the military man's name and honorific when speaking to him directly, away from his presence I only ever refer to him by one name: The Avocado.

At the prison, I give Dad a rundown of the meeting.

Dad tells me to keep going. He's positive The Avocado's got it under control. I lack the energy to dig further into this statement, to understand why he pins such hope on this man. I've said that I'm uncertain enough times for it to be known, no need to harp on; since Dad thinks he's got it 'under control', then I shall comply.

'He'll give you a price,' Dad says. 'When you find out, tell me what it is.'

I swallow and respond, 'Okay. If you say so.'

Al-Yad

The Avocado asks to meet every week.

In our second meeting, I express my doubt about his ability to get Dad out.

'No, it will be soon. You get the papers to me and we will get him free.'

It's a request in the tone of a command.

I have held off from translating our documents and handing them over to him, reluctant to give all that information when I still don't trust him. He gives me a list of questions to ask Dad. He says I'm to write down Dad's answers and then bring those answers to him.

*

On the third meeting, I give him a paper with Dad's scribbled answers: It's such a weird list of questions.

Have you ever made public comments regarding:

- *New Suez Canal*

  No.
- *New cities and developments in Egypt (e.g. the New Capital)?*

  No.

- *Tiran and Sanafir islands?*
  No.
- *Ethiopian dams?*
  No.
- *Egypt and international aid?*
  No.
- *Food prices and the IMF loan/inflation?*
  No.
- *Turkey and Qatar?*
  No.
- *Egypt's relationship to Israel?*
  No.
- *Camp David?*
  No.
- *QIZ [Qualifying Industrial Zone]?*
  No.

It's a strange set of questions as these topics expand into everyday conversations about Egyptian politics. Though Dad denies it on paper, he's talked about these things. In fact, we'd talked about them together, many times over the years. Why wouldn't you discuss New Capital? Why wouldn't you express concern over rising food prices and inflation? What's wrong with an interest in international relations or discussing regional politics?

The Avocado continues to badger me about getting the documents ready and handed over before Dad's next court hearing. He says they'll be handed to 'someone big'. He then tells me that these papers will help convince a judge to release Dad.

Dad asks for the price, but The Avocado hasn't given me any numbers yet. Skirting on the edge of the world of bribes and bargains feels Faustian. At the same time, I suspect that The

Avocado is a small fry: a parasitic fish trying to feed the sharks in return for favours, all while bargaining and extracting from other desperate fish.

I want to hate him, but there's also something pathetic about The Avocado; I can't hate someone whose life has been lived in a shark tank. In such circumstances, we all like to imagine we'd be one of the 'good' or 'righteous' ones, but who are we to ever say that with such conviction?

*

I get the documents translated at a quirky office, where A3-sized posters of automated emails from the Bill Clinton Foundation hang on the walls, alongside a certificate from Hansard University. It's bizarre. I google Hansard University on my phone. It doesn't exist.

The documents are translated and returned to me within twenty-four hours.

It's twenty-four hours too long; The Avocado wanted these documents yesterday.

I think my procrastination is a maladaptive form of protest.

*

When I meet up with The Avocado again, two weeks before Dad's next hearing, he scolds me over how important it is that I listen to him. Between his disapproving clucking tongue and my father's insistence that I continue dealing with The Avocado, my patience for demanding men is wearing thin.

Contrary to my internal backchat, I'm still trying to act acquiescent, obedient.

We're going to a meeting with an 'important man': the important man he'd hinted about in our first meeting. The Avocado says that, because I was late with the documents, he almost couldn't make an appointment for us today, but the important man was gracious enough to fit us in. I don't feel particularly grateful for this graciousness.

We leave the military club, hail a cab and head to the important man's office. We arrive at a nondescript apartment block in the suburbs. Apart from a small kiosk, there's nothing around us except more nondescript buildings. The plainness makes the area feel oddly desolate. We take an elevator up to an office, where The Avocado is greeted by the receptionist with familiarity.

The office is decorated with wood panelling. Multiple portraits of the same man sporting a thick, greying moustache and aviator sunglasses adorn the walls. We seat ourselves on heavy, studded-leather armchairs. A couple of hours pass. Finally, the important man emerges. He nods at me, then greets The Avocado. The thick moustache is greyer in real life.

The Avocado gives the man the papers. Among them is Dad's arrest certificate. It was a lot of effort to get it. I'd made copies to keep for myself. It will turn out to be the only legal document I ever receive from the Egyptian state.

The important man doesn't look at the papers. He enfolds them in his hand and calmly says, 'Twenty thousand pounds.'

That's two thousand Australian dollars.

For this amount, he says, he'll do us the honour of reading Dad's case, and then advise us on what we will need to do next.

Oh so gracious, I sarcastically think to myself. Though this deal reeks, I agree to pay in instalments of $500.

After the meeting ends, I hand over my first payment.

*

A couple of days later, The Avocado rings to say we need to urgently visit the important man. Apparently, he's read the papers and wants to talk.

I cancel my plans and meet The Avocado at the military club. The two of us make our way to the important man's office.

We wait five hours to see him. The receptionist keeps us hydrated with a steady flow of tea and coffee. By the time the important man summons us to his office, I am beside myself with boredom.

Today, he greets me directly. In English, he asks how I am and compliments me for being such a good, loyal daughter. My skin crawls. *Please hurry up and get to the point.* I look down at my feet and say, 'Thank you.' He seems satisfied, or perhaps he observes my discomfort – I'm not sure – but he doesn't say anything more. He switches to Arabic to talk with The Avocado.

After a few minutes of them chatting, The Avocado turns to me and says, 'Okay, let's go.' I stop staring at my folded hands and look up. The important man smiles and rises from his chair. He shakes hands with The Avocado, then nods at me. Five hours for five minutes.

In the corridor, I'm itching for answers. 'What did he say?' I ask.

'Wait,' he says. The elevator arrives, we step inside. The Avocado presses the button to go down.

Then he speaks. 'He said ten thousand dollars.'

'What? Pounds?'

'No. Dollars.'

'Australian?'

'Yes, dollars.'

'Australian dollars?'

'Yes, I said dollars.'

We walk out of the building and onto the street. He waves down a cab.

I turn to him, heart racing. 'Okay, so ten thousand Australian dollars?'

'Dollars. I said dollars. You don't have American dollars in Australia?'

'No, we have Australian dollars in Australia.'

'Okay. It's ten thousand *American* dollars.'

I climb into the back of the waiting cab, astonished at their brazenness. Once I'm in, The Avocado plonks himself beside me on the red and white leather seat. I find it unsual because he usually sits in the front.

The cab takes off.

I burst into tears.

'Stop! Stop!' The Avocado is thrown by this. He raises his voice, full of urgency. 'Don't cry, this is good news!'

His words make me cry harder. *This is not good news at all!* I put my hands over my mouth, trying to contain the noise coming out of it. I face away from The Avocado, looking out the window while I continue with my muffled crying.

The way these men so casually exploit vulnerable people like me and my family disgusts me to my core. I'd rather Dad stay in prison than give these opportunistic rats anything more than the $2000AUD I've already agreed to.

My tumbling thoughts pause: But would I? Do I really believe that?

I picture the prison, and what Dad looks like inside it.

What's the price of freedom?

But what's to stop them from gouging more? Who's to say the price stops at ten thousand? I feel bewildered, distraught and overwhelmed; I don't know what to do. My weeping intensifies.

'I said STOP!' The Avocado yells. 'WHAT IS THIS CRYING!'

His sudden yell shocks me into silence. I gulp. 'Sorry.' I clamp down on my jaw, gritting my teeth as I hiccup, pushing the hysterical sobs down into my belly. I frantically think of a reason to explain the tears away. 'I was just feeling sad for my dad.'

He softens. 'You're a good daughter,' he croons, and awkwardly pats my shoulder.

*

The Avocado attends Dad's court hearing.

Dad gets renewed for another 45 days.

The Avocado blames me, says it's all because I delivered those documents too late, that I'm not doing enough to help my dad.

I want to tell you that I told him 'Fuck you', but I didn't.

(Dis)Trust

After the court hearing and Dad's renewal, The Avocado tries to keep stringing us along by claiming Dad is a spy, and that I will need his help to deal with this additional complication. With a scoffing laugh of spite and incredulity, I dismiss the claim. A terrorist, a spy – what's next? Cannibal? The Avocado sought to frame a trip my father and I had taken to Jerusalem as 'evidence' that Dad wasn't just any spy, but an Israeli spy. Egypt may hold diplomatic relations with the state of Israel, the history of conflict between the two nations remains culturally and politically embedded on both sides, manifesting as suspicion, distrust, racism and a heavily-policed shared border. Thus adding the word 'Israeli' before the word 'spy' means one is more than a spy, they're a traitor. With this absurd accusation, the transparency of his lies becomes undeniable. Vindicated for harbouring doubt in The Avocado's promises, in my next visit with Dad, we agreed to cut the charlatan out.

Since this experience, I've had many questions about The Avocado. I wanted to know more about Dad's side, particularly why he felt compelled to push us down the grimy path of bribes.

Hazem: It was, as you said, part of that control, the feeling that I've got to do something from the inside, the question of 'What

> can I do?' I believed maybe this could work. But the risk is that someone can be hurt. Unfortunately, it was you. Because I had no idea what was going on outside between you two ... Those weeks were some of my worst weeks in Tora for my psychology ... I see now they were capitalising on vulnerabilities, capitalising on people's desperation. By doing this, they are, in my eyes, scum. When I deeply reflected on this later, from the moment I gave you that number I regretted it. I regretted it so much.

Given that a prison is a place you'd do anything to escape, why wouldn't you consider bribing your way out? I understand Dad, I do. Just as I did at the time. Yet, acquiescing my own power to go through something I didn't want to do in the first place, that left bitterness. But how are we to survive in such a predatory system without succumbing to desperation?

> **Hazem:** ... I felt that the sheer pressure and negativity of being in this place [Tora] created an impediment to my ability to be rational. I was emotionally consumed to the point where I was irrational ... I couldn't read situations clearly or communicate properly. The best advice that I was given from day one was to be quiet. I should have listened to it. Don't do anything. Just sit and freeze and follow. Nothing in this place makes sense anyway, and the moment you are going to use your mind, and the moment you're going to think about everything around you and what you could do, you're gonna fall into a trap. But we're desperate in this place. I was so angry, so desperate. And I felt massive guilt: some days, I was so scared that someone would harm you that I wanted to rip the door off and get out to stop you. I couldn't, though; I had to wait the week before you'd visit. And then you'd come, and I'd have hope that this could work ...

but that's what they do: lift you up, give you hope, then crush you down. On an emotional and psychological level, this hurts so much. The material aspect of it is negligible.
Lamisse: I remember this feeling of being in, like, so much constant danger that I felt I lost the ability to discern where the real danger is because everything feels so dangerous … After this experience, with The Avocado especially, my paranoia went off the scale. I wondered who else would try to exploit our desperation, and how I would be able to tell who I can trust. I even started thinking my friends were probably informants. I lost so much trust that I became afraid of my friends …
Dad: There were so many of informants inside. They'd offer to wash my clothes, serve me tea, and then they'd ask questions, pretending to be a friend. I hated that. I'd say 'Stop, don't touch my stuff', or I'd tell them to go away. It's just another way of interrogating, to try to buddy up and be your friend, to loosen your defences and get you sharing thinking that he's your mate …
Lamisse: But isn't that how you got the number of The Avocado in the first place?
Dad: Well, he'd been in Tora himself, and a lot of people still talked about him. Even though he'd been inside, people believed he still had powerful connections. His number had been passed on to different men and some had been freed … But now, when I look back, I don't know if they were freed by coincidence or because of him. It didn't matter; what mattered is that it seemed like proof …

The Fourth

On 8 September, the men of the al-Rabaa' case receive their first verdicts. They've all been waiting in prison for five years. A spokesperson for Amnesty International describes it as 'a parody of justice' stating, 'It casts a dark shadow over the integrity of Egypt's entire system of justice and makes a mockery of due process.'

Of the 739 men in the case, 75 are given death sentences. Though many of them can appeal, it still means years in prison with the spectre of death hanging over their heads. The rest are given sentences that range from 5 to 25 years.

I skip the prison visit the week the al-Rabaa' verdicts are announced. I can't bear to look at anyone who might still be reeling from the news that they, or someone they love, has been told they'll be killed. I worry about how the guards may be responding to the heightened emotion that must be circulating among the people inside.

The next time I see him, Dad confirms that it was a good idea to skip the previous visit. He doesn't say why. I don't ask.

In a later interview, Dad discusses how the al-Rabaa' case was at the centre of everyone's attention from the day he arrived in prison: 'The case of all cases,' he says.

> **Hazem:** All the prisoners were emotionally and psychologically invested in the fates of the al-Rabaa's defendants as it would set the tone for everything to come next. It was to be the litmus test for how the government would go on to treat political prisoners. This heightened emotion around al-Rabaa' did not escape those running the prison: as such, whenever members of the al-Rabaa' case were called for a hearing, the prison would instate emergency measures by locking everyone in their cells for the day and bringing in extra guards.

On the day the verdicts arrived, men in the prison banged on their doors shouting: 'Murderers!' Dad says he was so shocked he couldn't even yell. Instead, he chose to 'hold it all in'.

> **Hazem:** There was a group of us who wanted to show that we were strong, and they could be strong too and not give up. That there is hope because the verdicts can be appealed ... Many of us worked hard to give the guys [men who had received the death penalty] hope, to not give up, that this could not be the end ... But 75 death penalties ... That's when we realised, whoa these guys are coming in heavy.

In 2018, at least 717 people were sentenced to death. In 2019, more than 32 executions would take place; in 2020, that would jump to more than 107 people. While executions are a direct way to kill a human, there was many ways a state can murder without needing a noose and an executioner. Back in Tora, the devastation was manifold.

> **Hazem:** The men given five years were to be freed since they had served their time, having spent five years in remand

> detention. Then there were those who were devastated by the prospect of another 10, 15, 20 or 25 years behind bars. For those guys, especially if they were married, they were devastated they had to face so many more years of separation from their families. Devastated isn't enough to describe how down their mood was. There's also unhappiness about the fact some of their friends would be released so, it's like a double whammy: you face the loss of your life, your family and your friends – these are friends you've built relationships with over those five years you're inside. So many of them had high expectations that they'd also get five years and be released, but not even a quarter of them did ...

Those who were to leave faced many challenges too: reintegrating into their families and society, catching up on technology and finding work and dealing with probation restrictions, all while living with the fear that they could be taken again.

Meanwhile, Mustafa Kassem, Dad's Egyptian-American cellmate who'd been part of the al-Rabaa' case, receives 15 years. He declares a hunger strike. He asks Dad if he'll join him and Dad says he cannot. After Mustafa declares his intent to strike, Dad and the other men are moved to a new cell. Hunger strikers are always isolated. As a diabetic, Mustafa only consumed water and juice; he had stated to Dad that he often feared being abandoned during a sugar coma. A hunger strike isn't about trying to die, it's about trying to live. Hunger strikers enact their defiant, autonomous will to stay alive by taking ownership of their death.

Dad wanted to share a few words about his friend:

> I met Mustafa early on, because – like me – he was a dual citizen. We clicked straightaway. We had a similar background as both of us had left Egypt and had lived in the West. We were

both interested in similar topics, so we never really ran out of conversations.

As a dual citizen, he had some privileges. He also had a very supportive family and he was a kind and generous person, so he was always sharing his food and the other things his family brought him. In the beginning, we weren't in the same cell, so whenever I would go for my daily walk, he would call me over and give me something. He often had cake, and sometimes he'd just give me the whole cake! Then, he'd also pass on salmon and tuna packs. He'd give me porridge if I ever ran out before my next visit from Lamisse ... I was moved to his cell later, and stayed there for about five months until he went on strike.

Just before I left prison, he had already lost half his weight. He was literally just skin and bones, and he was struggling. I knew that he was sick. I knew that if *he* did not stop, if I didn't hear that he had broken his hunger strike, then eventually his body would give up. It was just a matter of time. So, when I was out of prison, I followed all the news about him, and others, as much as I could: from media to social media ... anything that was put out on the internet.

When I heard the news that he had passed away, I realised that, in some way, he was actually left to die. I felt very sad. Very, very sad. But, as much as I knew that he'd experienced such immense injustice, I was comforted by the fact that he stood up for what he believed in. He had really strong convictions, even if it meant using his life to say: no, this is unjust, this is oppression. But also ... he lasted so long: it was like he was trying to give them every chance to save him, but they didn't.

Mustafa was on a hunger strike for over a year before passing away on 14 January 2020.

Al-Sarsur

The October breeze comes through the terrace, cooling the living room. I'm lying on the couch in Thomas's apartment, reading a book, when I get a call. It's a number I don't recognise, so I answer cautiously. 'Hello?'

There's a delay, then a distant voice. I don't recognise the voice until it urgently goes: 'Lamisse, it's your dad. Hazem!'

Stunned, I jump off the couch and start pacing. My forefinger plugs into my left ear so I can hear without distraction.

Speaking rapidly, Dad says, 'Call your mum, give her this number. I can wait for her to call me back for only a few minutes. Quickly!'

Mum doesn't pick up.

After ten minutes, she calls back. I give her the number. She tries it but then calls back disappointed: the moment has passed; the phone rang out and Dad didn't call back.

At this point, my parents have not spoken to each other in ten months. There was little talk of Mum coming to Egypt. We agreed early on that, unless it was crucial, she couldn't leave my youngest brother nor my elderly grandmother, as both of them needed her care.

However, we now know Dad has access to a phone. This is game changing.

A few days later, Dad calls me again. Mum, refusing to miss out a second time, immediately answers my call to tell her to call Dad. She rings and gets through.

From that point on, my parents had a lifeline to each other. The phone is called 'the cockroach', al-sarsoor. It is as small as the pointer finger with a thin rectangle screen only big enough for numbers. Dad would call from this smuggled phone whenever he could. He'd get an allocated 10–15 minutes while standing in the toilet-shower block, as the other men took turns looking out for guards while waiting for their turn to call their loved ones.

The men took big risks with those calls. Any prisoner caught with a mobile phone would get a month in solitary confinement.

Omar Atef was another one of Dad's cellmates. He'd been in prison for four years, arrested at 25 for belonging to a political youth group. In early 2019, Omar would be dealt two big blows: a few days after being sentenced to 10 years imprisonment, his close friend, Ahmed Adegawy, was executed. The following week, Dad found Omar in the bathroom, bleeding after having taken a razor to his wrists. He called on the other men in the cell to help and several arrived with towels, wrapping Omar's arms. As they tended to his wounds, Omar cried out: 'Sibny, sibny – khalini a'rooh!' *Leave me, leave me – let me go!* Several months after Dad's release, Omar would be caught with the cell's mobile phone.

While in solitary confinement, Omar took his own life.

Al-Sarsur

October is consumed with the stressful ordeal of trying to work with an Australian lawyer. The episode ends with the lawyer coming to Egypt, contracting food poisoning, and missing the meeting with the Embassy, as the week is lost to him puking in a five-star hotel. On the lawyer's final day in Cairo, he calls to cheerily tell me he's feeling well enough to visit the Pyramids, and asks if I'd like to go with him. I don't go.

I am deeply disappointed by this lawyer; though he offered to work for us pro bono, he asked that I pay for his trip to Cairo and the stay in the hotel. He said the trip was necessary to be able to meet with the Embassy and get wind of what was happening on the ground. While he could not help being sick, the disastrous outcome left me with the bitter feeling that it had been a waste of money and time.

Heart heavy, I drag myself to the prison to update Dad on two things: that the lawyer didn't work out, and that I think I'm going to have to go back to Australia. Maybe I'll have a better chance of finding some answers to this madness at home.

Broaching the topic of returning to Australia with Dad will be hard. Without me, there's no one to care for him.

When Dad comes out, I can see he is feeling low. He tells me how hard it is to stay hopeful; he's struggling to stay afloat … to stay motivated to survive.

He adds, 'And then I get these thoughts … to end it … I wouldn't, but I've never had those kind of thoughts before …'

My breath leaves me. I have to hold us in this moment; I will wait until the next visit to tell him my plan. I can't dismiss such a confession.

'Me too, Dad. It's normal; it's normal to think about suicide.'

I pause.

It's essential to name it, to let the word linger. I believe that the word needs to live between us for a moment for its weight to be fully felt. It is a word that needs visibility, so that we can take in what it really means.

Dad doesn't say anything, so I keep talking: 'I realised that I don't actually want to kill myself, though. I just want the pain to end; I want to escape.'

At this, Dad's eyes become wide and animated. 'Yes, that makes sense! I just want this to be over too.'

I put my hand on his knee and he puts his hand on my hand. We sit there in silence, absorbing the pain we're both feeling.

I break the silence. 'It's really important to remember that it's not that you want to die, but that it's a response to unbearable pain, and to remember that the pain will end.'

Though I'm talking to Dad, I'm also talking to myself.

The pain will end.

It must.

*

Over the past months, I've developed a habit of eating Kentucky Fried Chicken after seeing Dad.

I skip breakfast, have a tea or coffee while I wait for the gates to open and our names to be called. Then I sip water throughout the long wait and snack on chocolate with Dad. By the end of the visiting hour, my exhaustion kicks in and I drag myself out of the prison, into a cab and straight to KFC.

It's the practice of the KFC near my house to only employ deaf and mute people. While I don't let myself think too hard about the chicken, it makes me feel good to be there. I want to believe that the people working there have hope. I want to believe that the world isn't bleak and abusive, but that, sometimes, it gives people a chance – even if it's inside the brutal capitalist enterprise that is the fast-food industry.

I also like the fact that I don't have to speak. There's no stumbling through English or Arabic; there are only hand gestures and smiles. My order is always the same: a box with a Zinger burger, fries, coleslaw, three pieces of chicken and a large Sprite. I hurry home with my warm, oily cargo, crawl into bed, and watch a Netflix comedy special as I drop chicken scraps to the house cat. The vague disgust I feel at being overstuffed and bloated feels better than the empty shame and sadness I carry with me from the prison.

I often lie there afterwards and wish I were doing something more profound, that I could say I found God and had epiphanies, that I gained solace and certainty in something spiritual.

Instead, I take solace in stand-up comedy. It's so good to laugh; for the absurdity of the world to be made manifest, for heavy things to be made silly and light.

At this time, it feels like there's no *reason* for what's happening. So, I'm not looking for answers. Cruelty is just cruelty. I'm not going to justify it, rationalise it, interpret or explain this pain away, look for a 'Higher Power' or find meaning – yet.

Right now, it hurts and that's it.

*

In the following visit, I tell Dad about how I'm thinking it's time to go back to Australia. He's distressed at the prospect of me leaving but he agrees: we need to try something else.

In the days after the visit, I book my flights for mid-November, which is in three weeks' time. Informing the Embassy that I'll be going to Australia for a month, I tell them that I'll be using the time to make another plan for moving forwards with Dad's case, then I'll come back to Egypt in January.

The downside of coming back is that I'll have to re-enter Egypt through Cairo airport. That airport is now major trauma-trigger territory: I worry that what happened to Dad could happen to me. What if they have a file on me? What if they're watching me? My paranoia knows no bounds; it just spills and spills and spills.

Thomas picks up on all this and comes up with a plan: he offers to fly me from Australia to Austria to spend the new year with him and his family. That way, we can spend some time together, and return to Egypt together, meaning I won't have to go through the airport alone. Because of his line of work – international development – he also has a passport that allows him to use the diplomat's line. He says he'll take me with him through the diplomats' passport line. Since he's German, he says, he's confident the Egyptians aren't going to mess with him. It sounds arrogant, but he's right.

Only recently, two German-Egyptian students were arrested upon entering Egypt. Like Dad, and many others, they were disappeared, surfaced in Tora prison and accused of supporting terrorism. The families immediately go to the media. As coverage spreads, a friend of mine in Berlin connects me to a journalist from *Der Spiegel*, who speaks to me over the phone and references Dad in the coverage of the case of these two students.

Within three weeks, these two young men are ferried out of the country and sent back to Germany. I am shocked at how quickly they are removed and sent home. Eager to find out if there's something I could take from this, Thomas connects me to a person he knows from the German Embassy. While the person is a consummate professional and cannot reveal much about the case, he hints at something important: Germany invests too much money for Egypt to ignore them. This is politics, this is international relations. This is money and power.

I wonder if the Australian government has ever flexed such muscle, or if they are hoping this will pass without needing much effort. Maybe I shouldn't overthink it, maybe it's that the Aussies are simply not on the same level as Germany on the international stage.

All I know for sure is that these two men were sent home after three weeks, but my dad has now been in prison for 11 months.

It is proof that it doesn't need to drag on this long: fast intervention is possible.

*

Before I fly out of Cairo, Dad has one last request.

Chicken.

He asks me to bring in roast chicken – enough roast chicken to share with his cellmates. He tells me that there are 13 men in his current cell, but that I should get six to seven chickens to share.

Between leaving prison and ordering the chicken a week later, I get jumbled.

I come to think that the order has been for 15 chickens. My rationale is that there are 13 men, so they should have one chicken each. I round it up to 15, because, well, why not throw in a couple extra?

Unsure of where to make such an order, I ask Thomas what he thinks. He suggests we place the order with ChickShack, a popular rotisserie around the corner from his flat. He also pays for it. When I protest, he insists that he wants to make a contribution to Dad's food bill.

When the chickens arrive on Wednesday, there are too many to refrigerate so we arrange the bagged chickens along the hallway – the coolest part of Thomas's flat. Luckily, it's almost winter. Thomas's cat goes wild from the smell and ends up locked out on the balcony.

In the morning, I get up early, bag all the chickens in the regulation white garbage bags, and then scrawl Dad's name across the front of each one. The flimsy branded boxes are disintegrating from soaking in chicken juice all night.

I go through the usual process at the prison. When I'm at the first bag check, the guard laughs. 'Kolo fereekh?'

'Aywa.' I nod. I've bought no other supplies, just three bags of rotisserie chicken.

Next comes the long wait in the corridor, and then it's through the iron gates. I approach the wooden tables where the crusty wooden spoons and grotty fingernails are used to dig through food.

After inspecting the chicken, the guard wants to know if that's it. I say yes. Then he asks where I got the chicken. ChickShack, I tell him. He asks where that is. I say Zemalek. He raises an eyebrow, amused. The bags of chicken are then carried off by the men in the green.

At the following week's visit, Dad stumbles out of the door into the cafeteria and sweeps me into a huge hug.

'FIFTEEN CHICKENS!' His laughter booms out. 'Why on earth did you buy fifteen chickens?'

'Isn't that what you said?' I ask, confused.

'No! I said six to seven chickens! I thought it would have been a quarter of a chicken each for the men. But you got them one chicken each, and then more! We shared the chicken with the men in the other cells … It's been the talk of the prison all week. It was delicious too …'

Sometimes, mistakes are good.

*

Mid-November has arrived.

Dad and I hold each other tightly. I quietly cry into his chest. I can't believe I'm leaving and leaving him behind.

I'm always afraid he'll die here. I fear this could be the last moment I hug him, and that if anything happens, I won't make it back in time.

While I don't have a clear plan for what to do once I'm back home, I know I need to do something different: I need new grounds to explore and new people to talk to. The change might mean new pathways open up, paths that will remain unseen if I stay here. Plus, I'm exhausted from the dystopic merry-go-round of prison visits and court hearings. Being home will be rejuvenating, a place to breathe, be safe and regather my energy. Like an army in battle, I must retreat, regroup and reassess. I hate military analogies, but this is how it feels.

I hope Dad can hang on without me.

PART THREE

'To be pre-suspect means one is *never not suspect*'

Randa Abdel-Fattah

Labour

Brisbane, November 2018

My sister, Jasmine, picks me up from the airport. Once home, I walk into the open-plan dining room and kitchen. The table is filled with food. There's even cake. Mum is sitting at the table with my other siblings: Amira, Harun, Kareem and Saja. Nana comes out of her room with her walking frame and I give her a hug. Amid the outpouring of happiness is an air of apprehension.

Jasmine tells me to close my eyes. I shut them, and she shoves a warm and squirmy thing into my arms. It's my niece, only four months old. Holding her, I splutter through my tears. 'She's … sooo … cute.' Nuzzling my face into her soft cap of skin and hair, I inhale her gentle, milky smell. A baby, the most mundane and magical of all miracles; a stubborn shoot of hope pushing into our lives with a cry.

Later that evening, Mum and I have taken over the couches in the living room; I've sprawled out, while she's slouched into the cushions, looking at her phone. Bound to the kid's bedtime routine, Jasmine left a few hours ago. Nana is watching an Egyptian soapie, while Saja, Amira, Harun and Kareem are all in their rooms upstairs. It's quiet, food and dirty dishes lying ignored on the dining table. Mum puts down her phone and looks at me. 'You look like shit … Dark circles under your eyes … Your skin, it looks a bit grey. And you've lost so much weight.'

'Thanks, Mum,' I offer with tired sarcasm. 'I'm exhausted.'

Irrespective of what I know about my mum's abrasive style of communication, it still stings. *Just say you're worried about me*, I think.

Irritated by this exchange, I want to go outside and have a cigarette. Right now, the only thing Mum probably loathes more than the Egyptian government is cigarettes. When I announce I'm going to have a smoke, she looks upset. But the packet isn't in my bag. It's not in my suitcase either. I realise I left my cigarettes at my cousin's house.

My cousin's house.

The kitchen, the black coffee, my cousin and I leaning against the counter as we talk and smoke. How was I in Cairo only 24 hours ago? How was I in Tora Prison 48 hours ago? The flight appears as a wormhole through space and I've emerged in a parallel universe where nothing has changed. I'm still bickering with Mum, Nana's still watching her soapies and the table is still waiting to be cleared.

'Don't worry, Mum. Seems I forgot them in Cairo. Guess I'll quit.'

'Alhamdullilah. See, Allah knows. He made you forget.' She smiles knowingly, satisfied with God's will.

She has no idea how much I've been forgetting; how my memory is full of burn holes. I used to take pride in my capacity for remembering people's faces, names and places. Now, when I see people I somewhat know, I struggle to recall how we met or what memories bind us. This affects my relationship, too. Thomas does all the remembering for us; where I have fragments, he has a full-length feature film with a narrative arc. He tells the story of how we met, tracking events that led us into each other's lives. It's a lot to trust someone with your remembering. Not having a solid grip on my mind and memory leaves me feeling vulnerable; I fear how easy it could be to manipulate or gaslight me. When I mention this fear to him, Thomas is upset that I would harbour such distrust, that I would believe him capable of such a thing. I tell him that I believe everyone is capable, and I'm glad he chooses not to. He insists it's not a choice he needs to make because it's just what everyone should do. He's right. It is what everyone should do, yet his verbal assurances don't spontaneously thaw out my fears. Rather, years of accumulative experiences of his relentless, earnest consistency alchemise my fears into trust.

Back in the living room, it's clear that my mother and I are unsure of how to talk about Egypt, about Dad. We're skirting around our emotions. Mum says she's waiting for me to open up, says that I scare her sometimes and she doesn't know how to approach me, because I seem walled up and fierce. I acknowledge that I pushed her away a lot during the past year, that there were many times I told her I didn't have space for her.

Now that I'm back, I need to let her back in. We need to support each other to get through this. But tonight, I'm tired and overwhelmed. I end our awkward chat by announcing I'm going to bed.

I make my way to the prayer room. With seven people already under the one roof, I'm given the daybed in the prayer room. Mum's tried to make it nice; a warm lamp by the bed and a soft, woolly throw over it. In a baroque frame on the wall hangs a piece of fabric from the Ka'aba, the black fabric with Arabic calligraphy woven in gold thread. There's a bookshelf lined with multiple Qurans and religious books. Beside it, a box overflowing with prayer skirts and long pull-on hijabs.

Next to the daybed is a basket with organic soap, chocolate, candles and incense. An envelope with my name on it is sitting on top of the goodies; I recognise Mum's handwriting. On the card inside, she's written down everything that I know she finds hard to say. Not everyone is verbally expressive, especially if they've grown up being constantly silenced. Mum's traumatic childhood inflicted damage on her ability to express herself, but despite her prickles, a huge, vibrant and sensitive emotional world exists within her, flowing through her art.

I go looking for Mum, finding her heading up the stairs to bed. 'Mum, wait.' She stops. I hold up the card then hug her. 'Thanks, Mum. I love you.'

'I love you too,' she says stiffly.

Later, Mum tells me she wanted to make me feel safe, that she could see my fragility and wanted me to rest. She also wanted to pounce, demanding I offer up every micro-detail I'd withheld over the past year. Most of all, my presence here meant my absence there, exacerbating her fears for Dad's life.

*

The first week home passes in a blur. I mostly sleep. I call it jetlag, but it's more than that. It's like I can't stay awake. I fall asleep in all sorts of places: on the floor, on the couch, in one of my sibling's beds. I feel like a piece of paper that's gone soggy after sweaty hands have folded it too many times.

Though I'd love to keep sleeping, one week of rest must be enough. I book flights to Sydney and Melbourne.

*

In Sydney, I stay with a friend who is a lawyer. Samia is not only in possession of immense compassion and kindness, she is politically astute and an incredibly dedicated lawyer. As she sweeps me under her wing for the three days that I am in Sydney, her solidarity is unwavering. She makes calls on my behalf to prominent human rights lawyers and barristers, doing all she can to find information that could help, but not much comes through.

Samia also takes me along to the Legal Aid Christmas Party. To be among the everydayness of an office party is a pleasant immersion in the mundane rhythm of work: people complaining about their workloads over full plates of food, teasing their colleagues, discussing cases and meandering back to their desks to 'check something'. I wonder if I'll go back to work after this is all over. I wonder if Dad will? *Wait, will we even want to?*

I meet two human rights lawyers and activists in Sydney: Zaahir Edries and Sara Saleh. Zaahir is the President of the Muslim Legal Network, while Sara is known for her work with GetUp! and APAN (Australian Palestine Advocacy Network). Zaahir and Sara are two people I admire: they both possess an unwavering commitment to justice, evident in their work and activism. As a result, they both also have an understanding of anti-terror legislation, lobbying and navigating the media. Over burgers in Newtown, we discuss Dad's case and how to properly launch a public human rights campaign.

Conversing with them reminds me of another conversation I had with the American-Egyptian activist, and former prisoner himself, Mohammed Soltan; he was released from Tora and returned to America after a hunger strike in 2015. I spoke with Soltan back in March 2018, only a few months after Dad's imprisonment. Soltan informed me that he'd had a team of 60 people working on the #FreeSoltan campaign. They did everything from daily tweets to writing letters to local representatives and meeting politicians. At the time of receiving his advice, it was all too fresh. I was too afraid to 'go big, go loud', as he had urged. Reflecting back on that conversation after burgers, I see that he was right all along.

It is time to yell.

Though I don't have a team, I'm grateful for the insights from Sara and Zaahir. It helps me map out what's possible, thereby having clarity over deciding what I can and can't do. Most of all, I'm motivated by their care, encouraged by the fact they're people who put their actions where their words are.

In Melbourne, I meet another Egyptian lawyer. Over coffee on Lygon Street, I ask him what he thinks of the regime arresting Egyptians from the diaspora. He says that the community is spooked, that people in the the Egyptian community he's surrounded by expressed fear over returning to Egypt – the feeling that 'if it happened to him, it could happen to me'. Some believe it's likely Dad is innocent; faithful regime supporters say he must be guilty.

The binary of guilt versus innocence grates on me. I want people to know Dad doesn't have to deny his opinions to obtain the ephemerality of innocence – there should be nothing wrong with criticising a government or empathising with political or religious groups who experience persecution, irrespective of whether you agree with their beliefs or not. Dad's opinions are allowed to exist: they do not need to be denied for him to be freed. Why must we mutilate ourselves to be made acceptable, to be made innocent? To strip ourselves of 'radicalism' – which is what? Attending the mosque? Leading group prayer? Posting a du'a on your Facebook? Wearing a beard? All so that we may no longer be feared or fear for ourselves? I refuse to acknowledge the violent binary of innocence and guilt, and the law that polices it. I refuse to mutilate myself, or my father, any further to earn the right to safety. The real violence here is the singular narrative; the singular narrative is what the state seeks monopoly over. A narrative that denies nuance and plurality, and centres its own interests. This singular narrative is peddled as unifying, as truth and history; those that challenge it are called radical, counter- and marginal. They're called criminals, terrorists and political prisoners. This is what the Egyptian state has spent the last decade trying to achieve, and what the colony continues to need. There are multiple narratives that tell the story of the Arab Spring, of the 2011 Revolution and all that happened since: the plot is still built on facts. Who weaves the facts, how they've woven them and which are 'forgotten' is what becomes (hi)story.

*

I only have 10 days left in Australia before I leave for Vienna to meet Thomas. I thought Dad might have made a call while I'm here, but we haven't heard from him and it's still going to be another two weeks until I see him.

Leads

I find out that Peter Greste lives in Brisbane, and currently works at the University of Queensland. His email is publicly listed on the university website, so I contact him.

His response arrives quickly. He writes that he's glad I contacted him, that he's familiar with Dad's case, and offers to meet Mum and me to talk. Anticipating it'll be insightful to talk to him, his interest also gives me a boost of optimism; he's the only Australian that I know of with a similar experience. Though, when our campaign builds, the publicity means that people in similar circumstances start reaching out to me.

Our meeting place is a small cafe in Brisbane's inner north. I'd seen interviews with Peter online where he'd come across as quite fierce and decisive. Yet, upon meeting him, I find Peter to be gentler than I expected. He's soft-spoken, thoughtful and deliberate with his words.

Hungry for all the information he could offer, I waste little time getting to the point of why we were meeting. Sharing my distress over how confusing and hopeless the system in Egypt seemed to be, Peter offers his own understanding of it. What I understand from his explanations is that what I label 'government' is made up of disconnected bodies – intelligence, courts, police, military – that don't speak to each other. The state struggle to maintain oversight across the different arms of government means that there is plenty of internal conflict, mystery processes and a challenge of who is supposed to be accountable to what. Within all this, appointments to high-ranking positions unsurprisingly go toward individuals sympathetic to the regime.

During this conversation, what had seemed opaque for so long starts to clearly come together. It helps to speak to Peter as it feels as though he understands how to communicate across the same gap I face within myself, and with others – such as politicians and journalists – when I'm talking to them about Dad's case. He's able to take what he knows about Egypt and re-articulate it in a way that makes sense to someone who has no idea about Egypt.

Our conversation solidifies an idea I've been mulling over for a while: there isn't anything inherently evil in the world. There are no special individuals or groups carrying out nefarious plots. There are just entanglements of self-interest, personal beliefs, power plays and opportunism, and the violences that fuel, and sustain, them. There is a multitude of individual choices, all interacting within an oversized, centralised framework within a state that functions poorly, slowly, extractively and oppressively. There are so many policy challenges in Egypt; the prison system is just the crystallised tip of the iceberg, a compressed microcosm of all the wider issues facing the Egyptian state – an unsustainable solution to a host of political, social and economic challenges.

Reflecting on this, I decide I no longer care what label is placed upon a country: a dictatorship, democracy or whatever. What I'm interested in is what it *does*, what outcomes it *produces*. The Arab Republic of Egypt is a state that produces oppression and poverty for many, many Egyptians. It is not much different to its funders and supporters in its outcomes: an expanding carceral system, increasing inflation, social services and subsidies lost by cuts, and a minimum wage that barely covers basic needs.

I no longer need to provide caveats that there is more to Egypt than its traumas; the state is an entity separate from people and land.

As we grow more comfortable with each other, we move away from politics. Peter asks about our emotional state, expressing empathy for the impact this must be having on Dad's mental health. He then speaks about his parents and their efforts to support him during his incarceration. At this, Mum bubbles over; she speaks about how hard it's been for her, my grandmother and my siblings. I bristle: *Put a lid on it*, I think. She soon senses my discomfort and goes quiet. I feel guilty for bristling at Mum's disclosures, I know I've wronged her by shutting her down, but I want to power ahead: once again, I'm obsessed with facts. No emotions.

We return to discussing the importance of launching a public campaign as Peter details the relationship between media and politics. My scribbly notes read: *need to go public, need the public accountability. Lights a fire under politicians and compels them to act.*

Then Peter gives me a tip: look up Doughty Street Chambers and Foreign Prisoner Support Services.

This tip would prove to be life changing.

It's been meaningful to have this conversation with Peter: we've not had to describe or over-explain anything, he just gets it. He candidly shares not only his knowledge of media and politics, but the personal insights he gathered from coming to terms with the trauma he faced in Tora prison. All the while, he acknowledges the difference in treatment between him – a man categorised as a professional journalist, as white – and my father.

He insists that we have more rights than we think, that we can demand the government do more to bring Dad home. One day, I hope, that it'll be Dad with the insights; that he'll have a second chance at life, that he'll be able to reflect with wisdom upon what he's been through too. Most healing of all is the deep understanding and empathy that flow like an undercurrent through the conversation, allowing Mum and I to feel held, seen and understood.

Before we leave, Peter suggests I read Victor Frankl's book, *Man's Search for Meaning*. Despite it being such a famous text, it's the first time I've heard of this book. I later pick up a copy at Avid Reader and take that copy to the prison for Dad. Over the year, I'd managed to take plenty of books to the prison. His favourite would be one I picked up at the American University of Cairo book fair: a 12th century Sufi text, *The Shape of Light* by Al-Suhrawardi. It is a philosophical meditation on the soul, the limits of the human, and what Al-Suhrawardi posits is our theomorphic essence – the divinity within us. It would provide the inspiration for the title of this book. Exchanging the divine for the earthly, the light for dust: the element that was used, according to Islamic theology, to craft the human. Along with Frankl's book, Al-Suhrawardi's text would be one of the few he'd take with him out of the prison, dog-eared with notes scribbled in the margins. He left the rest for the makeshift library he had set up with his cellmate.

We say our goodbyes to Peter, then walk back to the car.

Lost in thought, I go to cross the road without looking. Mum grabs my arm, aggressively yanking me back. A car whizzes past.

'Lamisse! Did you see that car?'

'No?' I answer vaguely and continue walking, still chewing over Peter's words in my head.

Mum's shaken. 'Let's get outta here and go home,' she says.

On the drive home, I apologise to Mum for shutting her down.

Accepting my apology, she reminds me that, if we are to go to any more meetings together, I must step back and allow her to express herself in her own way.

I agree.

My sense is that I've now gathered as much as I need from this trip. I have a notebook full of advice and conversations to contemplate. I've reacquainted myself with home and reminded myself of the options I can access here.

Next stop: Vienna.

Vienna, December 2018

From hot, humid Brisbane, I fly to sleeting, freezing Vienna. I'm wholly unprepared for the cold. Even in bed, I shiver. The foggy, bone-weariness has followed me from Australia, depleting my will to move and engage with the world around me.

Thomas's parents lend me a jacket and fur-lined boots. We venture out with his father to explore the First District. Realising I know very little about the Austro-Hungarian Empire, I make a note to find out more about the bloodier sides of the opulence around me. When I express my more critical thoughts, Thomas sighs and says 'just enjoy it, Lamisse.' I want to, I do. Apfelstrudel is my favorite dessert, Gustav Klimt my favorite over-hyped artist and the architecture of the city is captivating. But every piece of glitter has a corresponding speck of dust. In the end, I push aside my critical pondering and allow myself to enjoy the sumptuousness of Vienna. The whole trip is a gilded respite – a surreal, beautiful dream. Life here appears so comfortable and safe that I could so easily forget that there's anything terrible about the world.

Thomas and I see out the new year in a ski cabin on a mountain a couple of hours outside of Vienna. It snows – cinematic snow that falls gently and wraps the forest in a glittery, soft white glow.

Before we leave Vienna, I decide to give myself three weeks in Cairo and book my flight back to Brisbane. I'm done; it's time to go home and fight.

Broken

On the flight to Cairo my paranoia has a dramatic resurgence.

Surely it's only a matter of time before I end up in prison too. Though I've been told multiple times it's not possible, the seemingly impossible has already happened. So, as far as I'm concerned, anything is possible. Thomas outlines what we're going to do when we land: 'So, you're my partner. We'll go through the diplomatic passport line. Because you're with me, you shouldn't worry about having any trouble with passport control.'

I would usually enter the country using my Egyptian birth certificate to skip the need to purchase a tourist visa. Prior to taking this flight, I'd already decided against doing this. Though, the question still niggles: am I or aren't I a citizen? While I used to hope I was, I now hope I'm not.

We land at the airport in the afternoon; the sun bright, the wind cold. Inside the Arrival terminal, I need to withdraw some cash to pay for the tourist visa. Hands shaking, I rummage for my bank card.

With the money I've withdrawn, I purchase my visa and stick it into my passport. Then Thomas and I walk to the passport desk, burgundy ropes delineating the passage between those with special passports and those without. We coast through, no issue.

At the taxi stand, I do the usual double-check: wallet, phone and passport. I open my wallet to make sure everything is in there.

There's no bank card.

I go through my pockets, my bag. It's nowhere to be found.

I ask Thomas, 'What did I do with my card?'

'You withdrew money at the airport, remember?'

I tell him I don't remember doing that.

'You had to buy a visa, Lamisse.'

This jogs my memory: yes, I did buy a visa! Retracing my steps in my mind, all I recall is a fuzzy image of an ATM. Thomas halts my spiral into distress: 'We'll work it out. The card is gone and right now, we just need to get home.'

*

The following day, I show up to the prison carrying two large, full bags that strain my forearms. I've got to break the news to Dad that I'm leaving, that I'm taking this fight back home.

Dad comes out looking skinnier and sadder than when I left. He insists he's fine, but it's obvious he's not. My guilt for putting him through six weeks with no visitors is hard to bear.

Taking a deep breath, I tell him I'm going home for good. We need to campaign now, we need a change in strategy. Out of us all, I have always had an interest in things like politics, human rights and media. I've got the lived experience in Egypt, with Dad and the prison. So, I've got to be the spokesperson. I tell Dad that the family are all willing to support the campaign, to get past their media-shyness. However, we haven't discussed if anyone will replace me in Egypt – the same reasoning had come up in the conversations we'd had about what to do. Once again, I've got the experience. I'm the one who 'knows'. Internally, I wish I wasn't the one who knew anymore: I would like to hand in my resignation as eldest daughter, please. Instead, I earnestly explain to Dad, trying to convince him that by leaving him here alone, I can take action back home. With the family, we can campaign, we can find ways to put pressure on the Australian government to act. *Egypt is dead soil*, I tell him; *I can't cultivate anything here.* Being dual citizens, we have choices. It's insanity for me to stay and keep suffering through this senseless process.

Dad understands, but understanding does little to assuage his fear of being left alone. And I'm afraid for him too. I point out he'll still have the Embassy visiting once a month, and I'll see if they can maybe bring him money for the canteen. I have no idea if they will bring him money, but I don't know what else I can do – I can't be in Egypt looking after Dad *and* be in Australia to advocate for his freedom.

Something has to give.

*

The days pass in a blur. I host a goodbye party, masking grief in joy. I flit from person to person, making small talk, all while wondering if I'll ever see any of my friends here again. Trying to take in everyone's faces, to absorb their energy, I photograph the moments in my mind because I don't want to forget all the love I also found here. My obsessive love for Cairo consumed a decade of my life, encompassing most of my 20s and undoubtedly shaping who I am. Despite the barriers, the sense of belonging I had in Egypt was always beneath language, beneath logic; it was just the feeling of being home.

*

On my last visit to the prison, I haul in bags I can barely lift and dump them on tables for inspection. Over the last two weeks, I've been bringing in as much non-perishable food as I can carry. I can at least stock Dad up with extra food before I go.

I rattle off the list of the things I've brought to Dad, as though giving him an inventory of the supplies will prove there's enough to last until … well, we don't know when. But there will be a next visit. Realistically, I can't claim I'll be gone for good – if we don't find a resolution to visitation, either through getting an exemption for extended family to visit or the Embassy taking in supplies, I will have to come back. The Embassy are aware I'm leaving and that Dad will be without visitors for an unforeseeable amount of time. They express their concern about this – both because it impacts on Dad's welfare, and because I won't be able to share information with them anymore. In the meantime, our new lawyer, Mansour, is working on getting my cousin permission to visit the prison.

It's been said before, but lack of family visits is no small thing. After all, denying visits is a common form of punishment. Yet, here I am, choosing to do this to Dad.

It's an enormous risk, but it's time to take it.

The whistle goes off, signalling the end of the visitation hour. Intense panic grips me. I look around the room, taking it all in one last time: the families, the children, the granite benches, the dusty damp smell, the men in white, the guards. *Is this the last time I'll stand here?* I hope to God it will be.

Then my eyes meet Dad's. We see it in each other: the paralysing fear, the trapped screams in our bodies.

Noooooooo! No! No! No! No! No! I'm not going without him! The words flood my head. I want to yell and hold onto Dad's leg, refusing to go without him.

Instead, we get to our feet, silent. Dad wraps me in a hug and I cry into his chest.

The same pain of separation has been there every time I've left the prison, even after a year of visiting almost every week, it still breaks me down into a scared, clingy child.

While I pray I won't have to see Tora Prison again, I pray I get to see my father again. I pray that the next time I see Dad, it'll be in Australia. I envision the moment he steps off the plane, the triumphant feeling of his return.

I hold onto this vision.

It's going to be worth it: it has to be.

Eventually, the guard with the whistle approaches and barks at us to hurry up. Dad and I step apart. I can't stop crying. I choke out a final goodbye to him, then turn and follow the other stragglers out. We file through the iron gate and walk up the steps. We're guided into a waiting area: a large cage that sits at the top of the steps above the iron gate, on the dirt road. For a reason I cannot discern, we have to wait before we're allowed to leave. But it doesn't matter why; there is never a 'why' in prison, only 'follow' and 'do'.

I stand facing the cage's wall, cover my face with my hands, and keep crying. A hand touches my arm. 'Ma'lesh, kefeyya.' It's a woman I've met a few times: she comes to visit her husband. Sometimes she brings their children with her, but today, she's alone. The other women in the waiting area glance over, watching us. She stays standing beside me. While she speaks in a kindly tone to me, she keeps a bit of distance. It's like she wants to comfort me, but doesn't want to get too close, as though my grief is infectious. Then she turns her head to peer out at the street and says, 'Mashy, il-baab maftooh.'

At the open gate, I avoid eye contact with the guards. I'm snotty and puffy-eyed and ashamed.

Once I'm out, I release a shaky sigh and survey the street, absorbing the post-visit stillness. No carts, no sellers. No families waiting under the tree. No tuk-tuks speeding past, no taxis honking. I'm struck with a strange nostalgia: I hate this place, yet I leave a piece of me here: a Lamisse that died in that prison, a Lamisse that is yet to be born from the rubble. I leave changed by what it means to still possess love, kindness, dignity and power amid crushing hardship.

It's just Umm Baha at the desk under the tree, waiting for her son – the guard, Haytham. He walks up to his mum, gives her a kiss on the cheek, grabs one of the plastic chairs and sits down next to her. Another tiring day is done; tomorrow, they'll do it all again. I feel a tenderness towards this mother-son duo. Umm Baha's patience with my misunderstandings, Haytham's strange ways of looking out for me: always letting me in even when I'm late, teasing me for arriving in taxis when I could take the train, but still fighting an aggressive taxi driver who'd chased me all the way to check-in. Was it cultural or was it care? Was it the rules or was it personal? I don't know.

I walk to the corniche. A cab pulls up in response to my wave. As usual, I sit in the back seat and lean my head against the window. As Tora Prison's walls recede, I make one last prayer: please, Dad, don't die.

Hazem

Dad reflects on being told I'm leaving.

Hazem: It felt like we'd had to swallow too much deception and injustice. In Lamisse's last visit, she tells me: 'Dad, I think I am done here. I've got to go back and run this campaign, talk to anyone who'll listen. I can't do anything more for you here.' I was quiet as I thought about how I am stuck here, how I will lose my only link to the outside world. I stay resilient and strong, even though I am devastated to lose her. 'I absolutely agree with you. I will be fine, don't worry about me.' I ensure that my facial expression and tone of voice reflect confidence in her, trust in her success.

Lamisse then explains more of what she will do back home. I agree, and comfort her with words of assurance that I will be fine, and that she's making the right decision. I hoped someone else might be able to visit me, but deep down, I knew I would be alone and would have to depend on myself. Over the weeks, my food supplies dwindle and my cellmates share what little they have with me. The days pass longer, heavier. With no visits to break up the week, time blurs. I feel myself tempted to give up, to surrender to this feeling of depression and resignation. I have nothing to look forward to except the next court date, and the hope that just maybe … maybe I'll get out.

Go Home, Go Big

12 January 2019

I look up the London-based firm, Doughty Street Chambers, and scroll through the profiles of lawyers and barristers. There are too many to look through. Clicking on the internal search function, I type: 'Australia'.

Jennifer Robinson is the second profile I click on.

I skim through her bio. What stands out to me is that it says she's worked on cases involving Bahrain and Iran. This seems as close as I'll get to an Australian human rights lawyer with experience in the so-called Middle East, so I compose an email and send it through.

After sending the email, I think that I should probably find out more about this person. Googling her, I immediately discover she's most famously known for representing Wikileaks co-founder, Julian Assange. It inflicts me with a moment of doubt: if that's the kind of level she's on, then was I totally naïve to have asked if she'll work with us?

I needn't have worried.

A few weeks later, Jen emails me saying she'd be interested in representing us, pro bono. She informs me that her QC, Caoilfhionn Gallagher, will be joining her in working on Dad's case.

Gobsmacked that this is working out, I'm afloat with tentative hope.

*

The campaign for Dad is called #BringHazemHome. We launched the name and hashtag before the first interview went live with *The Project*, back in July. Saja did all the design work for it, creating the logo, banner and profile picture. Saja and I also create a BringHazemHome website together. Given that Dad's in prison because of alleged social media posts, I no longer feel safe online. My campaign updates are sporadic as I increasingly come to hate interacting with social media.

Throughout January 2019, another case of wrongful imprisonment makes the headlines. It's in Thailand; the man's name is Hakeem Al-Araibi.

I wholeheartedly support Hakeem. I don't want him to be extradited; I want him to be freed and returned to Australia. I hate to witness yet another injustice happening against an individual who was just living their life, wanting to have a holiday. I hope the bungling of handling his case by the Australian government sets a precedent in the public's understanding, that they are seeing that government or consular help isn't a given.

As his case dominates the headlines, those in the know tell me the news cycle can't do multiple stories of Arab men imprisoned overseas, especially since their names are kind of similar too. I'm told that we need the attention on Hakeem to subside before we try to get any attention on Hazem. I guess viewers of mainstream Australian media can't handle too much colour; there's only enough empathy for one brown man at a time. Frustrated, I fall into the trap of comparison, haunted by the myth that empathy is a finite and scarce resource.

Since public advocacy is about considering things like optics, narrative and talking points, let's state it plainly: my father is a man in his mid-50s accused of terrorism; he lacks the glamour of a young, newly-wed elite athlete refugee fearing extradition. I resent how interacting with the media reduces human beings to categories; that this engagement asks us to see ourselves in this way too. As I contemplate how to manoeuvre through the terrorism tar, I also have to work out how to convert attention on Dad's case into quantifiable public support: signatures on a petition, Facebook likes, and clicks on the news outlets platforming our story. No one, and no story, can get by without these numbers. In the media landscape, it seems a life is only as valuable as the attention it will generate. It doesn't matter how much it frustrates me, one of the ways we've learnt to measure success is by how we translate attention into profit. In this case, success means signatures and views. The metrics that will keep a media interested because the story sells. Plummeting into cynicism, it seems humans are only valuable when profitable or dead.

While we wait for Hakeem to be freed and returned home, Jen, Caoilfhionn and I start to map out the plan for our advocacy and getting #BringHazemHome back into the media.

Crisis

Brisbane, 10 February 2019

Dad calls.

Across the echoing distance, he informs us that he's struggling without regular visits. It's now been about six weeks since I left, and he's running out of food. DFAT has also emailed us to say they've undertaken their monthly visit to Dad and reiterate what Dad's already told us: he needs money, food and medication. He needs visits. I've no doubt Dad is suffering.

In the email, the Embassy confirms that there's no way to send money electronically, noting that the visiting staff have checked this with the prison warden. *What a revelation,* I think sarcastically. You only need to set foot in the place to see that the prison is wholly a cash and barter economy. At least the Embassy asked.

In the email, the Embassy also notes that Dad has extended family in Cairo. Here, they seem to be insinuating that extended family members should be visiting him. Though I asked Mansour to try to get an exemption so my cousins could visit, I haven't heard back from him. It's either the tyranny of distance or that the request has been denied and I just don't know it yet.

It's a challenge working across multiple time zones and locations – Egypt, Australia and the UK. Out of all of them, Egypt is the hardest to keep track of. Most things have to be done in person, with paper and cash. With no proxy on the ground to work through, I'm effectively helpless to address any of the concerns Dad is raising.

I have to go back. There's no alternative.

Mum, Jasmine, Saja, Amira, Harun and I gather around the dinner table to discuss what to do. As soon as I say I'm considering going back to Egypt, my voice cracks.

'I'm so exhausted,' I confess through tears. 'I just don't think I can do it. I want to help Dad but I can't ... I don't know if I can go back.'

Saja pipes up: 'I can go.'

We all look at her, surprised by the determination in her voice.

'I'm serious. I've been thinking about it ... Lamisse needs to stay here. No one else can do the media and political stuff she's doing. I can go to Egypt.' She turns to me. 'You can just tell me everything that I need to know. I can get help from your friends, from Thomas ... I can do it.'

She's only 23, I think. *I can't send her into that chaos.* Then I remember: I was 23 when I first went to Cairo alone, in 2013. I'd glimpsed Saja's determination and strength in Cairo. She isn't a child I need to protect. However, I can see Mum is petrified: 'Not another daughter,' she says. 'Does it have to be Saja? Can Harun go?' It's a gendered request: one that assumes that Harun, as a man, should go. But he can't. Harun is needed in other ways; his financial support is the only thing allowing us to cover all these extra expenses. I couldn't work so long as I was working on the campaign. I knew Saja was the best person to send; where Harun was overwhelmed in Cairo, Saja was open and determined.

In the end, we agree: Saja will go to Egypt. She'll stay for six weeks, visit Dad and assess the situation. If she needs to stay on, we'll change the return flight and extend her stay.

I book the flights. She's leaving in six days.

11 February 2019

Hakeem Al-Araibi is released and he'll be returned to Australia the following day. I'm elated! This is great news both for Hakeem and his wife – and for us. This again shows that a campaign can work, that it is possible to advocate and get a loved one home.

Jen says we can now prepare for our media campaign. We make the tentative commitment to launch in ten days' time.

First, we need Saja to get to Egypt, and for her to let us know what the situation is on the ground.

14 February 2019

Though I'm staying with Jasmine at her apartment, I'm at Mum's house almost daily. Today, I've come over to prep Saja for her the trip. I draw her a map of the visitor's section of the prison, talking her through my questionable scribbles.

We look at the Tora Complex on Google Maps together and I point out the streets where she should get a cab to drop her off, where the train station is, where the sign-in area is and which iron door to wait at. Looking at the bird's eye view of the prison with Saja, I notice that the visitor sections are such a small part of the prison.

I show her how to write Dad's name in Arabic, and she practises it a few times. Then, I write out the grocery list, as well as the medications she'll need to purchase for Dad. She's taking some supplies from Australia too. Mum's bought him creams for his rashes, a couple of blocks of Cadbury chocolate and a 1.2 kg box of Weetbix.

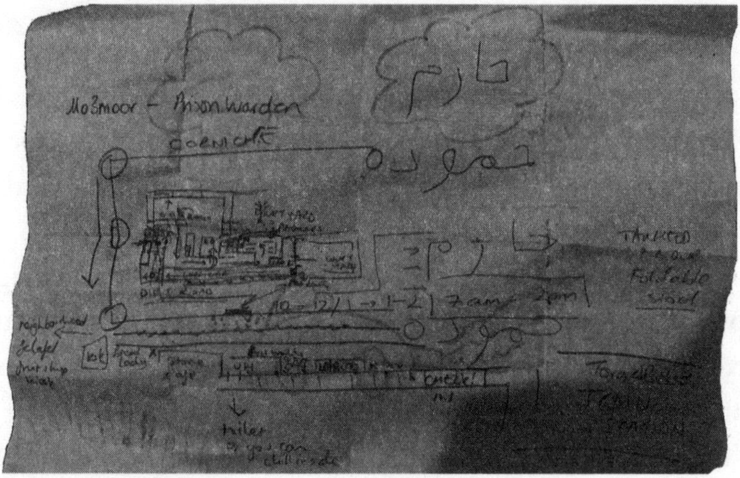

Photo Credit: Saja Hamouda, February 2019.

Thomas has offered to host Saja while she's Egypt; he's set up the spare bedroom for her. Before I'd left, I'd taken Thomas to the prison with me. I tell Saja, 'If you need help, ask Thomas. I took him to the prison before I left because I felt I needed to show someone what to do. He couldn't come inside with me, but he at least knows where the prison is, the sign-in process and where to wait to be called.'

I've given Saja as much information as she needs right now. 'And remember, call me if you're unsure of anything.' She nods, quietly folding up the piece of paper and slipping it into her journal. 'I'll visit the day after I arrive,' she says.

16 February 2019

Saja flies to Cairo.

I don't remember anything else about this day.

17 February 2019

Saja arrives in Cairo and takes a cab to Thomas's flat.

Sometimes, I think Thomas must be a little bit mad to be so accommodating of a family he doesn't know, but I'm grateful of how willing he is to keep extending himself to support us.

My contact at The Embassy informed me that I was no longer allowed to directly contact them. Now I'm in Australia, the correct procedure is to first contact a staffer in Canberra who'll pass on any message to the Embassy in Cairo.

The extra step seems like it'll waste precious time, especially when working across an eight-hour time difference.

So, when Saja sends me her Egyptian number, it's late evening in Canberra, well outside office hours. However, I know the workday in Cairo has just started. Ignoring procedure, I directly email one of the Embassy staffers in Cairo with Saja's number.

The staffer writes that, for this time only, it's okay that I didn't follow the rules.

Breakthrough

18 February 2019

Woken by persistent ringing, I roll over to check my phone: it's Mum. Still groggy from sleep, I answer. She speaks fast, excitedly. I can't get my head around what she's saying. She got a call from DFAT saying Dad will be released! The charges have been dropped! I don't believe it.

She forwards me the email she's just received from DFAT.

From: Centre Conops

Date: 18 February 2019 at 9:36:01 am AEST

Subject: Consular: HAMOUDA, Hazem: Update [SEC=UNCLASSIFIED]

Dear Evelyn,

Thank you for speaking with us earlier. I am glad we could relay such a positive outcome. The report that was provided by the Embassy and read out to you is below.

Report begins

At approximately 17:30 local time, the Ambassador was contacted by Nabil Sadek (Egyptian Prosecutor General) who

> advised that Mr Hazem Hamouda would not face any charges and that he had issued an order for Mr Hamouda's release. He expected that this would occur either later today (17/02/19), or tomorrow morning (18/02/19). Sadek had no further details to provide ...

I scan the text of the email, baffled. Saja hasn't even been in Cairo for 24 hours and now Dad is going to be freed! This is HUGE.

I call Mum back. Now I'm the one speaking fast. She urges me to slow down, get off the phone and come over as soon as possible. We need to contact Jen, discuss what the next steps will be. I ask her if she's told Nana. She says she has, that Nana cried and prayed in thanks to Allah.

After we end the call, I lie back on my niece's pink sheets and let the tears flow. I hadn't been expecting Dad's incarceration to end so suddenly. Saja and I have been gearing ourselves up for a long public fight. Sometimes, even good news can feel like a rug being pulled out from under your feet.

I take a photo of myself crying, hoping to make this real by witnessing myself. I've taken many selfies over the past year, using them as a way to tackle the depersonalisation of disassociation: they've become a way to remember I'm a person, and that what I experience continues to be real. In the photo, I see relief, grief and disbelief mingled into one contorted, mascara-smudged face.

Part of the disbelief is that the clinical tone of the email does not reflect the enormity of this moment, making it feel impersonal. They're notifying me and then will stamp and put the file away. Shot with a spark of jealousy, I wish I were in Egypt to celebrate with my friends and family in Cairo, to greet Dad when he walks out of the prison. I want that moment, I want that closure.

Leaving the room to find Jasmine, I share the news. We hug, both of us crying. She expresses disbelief, 'I can't believe I haven't seen Dad in over a year, that I had a baby during that time … he's coming home to a bigger family than when he left.' Next, I phone Saja, waking her up. It's just after midnight; she'd gone to bed early given she'd be going to the prison in the morning.

She's shocked, but ecstatic to know that Dad will be released.

'So, what's next?' she asks eagerly. 'What do I have to do now? I went shopping for Dad, should I still go to the prison in the morning?'

'I don't know. We need to find out,' I say.

I can't advise her what to do. I only know what a prison release looks like in the movies: the guy who gets his old clothes back and is waved out through the gates.

Cue credits.

It becomes quickly apparent that being released from prison isn't simple. I go back to review the rest of the email from the Embassy. It confirms that this is not a quick or easy process. Dad will first be released into police custody. He'll be taken to a transfer point for released prisoners. Our understanding is that Dad will be sent to the central police station, Khalifa Police Station. Once the transfer paperwork is finished, he'll be moved to another police station – one that corresponds to his area of residence. Apparently, this is where his release paperwork is finalised. This whole process can take weeks, however, one positive is that Mansour, our new lawyer, and Saja will be allowed to visit him at the station every day he's held there.

Saja and I agree that it'll be better for her to talk to Mansour and arrange to go to the police station with him, rather than going to the prison tomorrow.

There's concern over which police station Dad will be transferred to for his release: he has no registered area of residence. The address on his identity card simply reads: 'Living abroad'.

Quite a few friends have stepped forward to support Saja, offering lifts and translation help. Suleiman helps Saja translate the conversation with Mansour. Mansour hypothesises that our father could be transferred to a police station near the airport, the rationale being that he'd arrived as a tourist and was taken from the airport. Or maybe he'll be taken to the main police station in my former area of residence, Dokki. But this is all speculation. For now, the plan is for Mansour and Saja to meet Dad at Khalifa Police Station. He's due to arrive the following day.

The following day is Nana's birthday. What better gift could our grandmother have than for her son to be freed?

The next day, Saja and Mansour arrive at the Khalifa Police Station. It's the middle of the night for me, but I stay awake, nervously waiting for the news that they've seen Dad, that this is *really really really* real.

After a couple of hours of waiting for an update, Saja phones in tears: 'I think Dad's missing again.'

Setback

Saja and Mansour spend several hours waiting at the police station, but no Hazem Hamouda is delivered. Station personnel said that no one of that name had arrived; neither had they been informed to expect someone of that name. Mansour makes some calls to find out if Dad might still be in Tora or if he'd been taken elsewhere … but no one can tell him where he is.

Over the next two days, the Australian Embassy do their own checks. Saja meets with Embassy officials and she's told that Dad might be with National Security. When she queries further, they state that they have no further information about his whereabouts.

Then, we're informed by Mansour that it's usual for National Security to do 'checks' on prisoners due to be released, so it's possible Dad's been taken again.

Checks? So, Dad's been disappeared? Again?

It's déjà vu, a gut punch.

Jen suggests we file a complaint to WGAD.

There are two United Nations working groups dedicated to state-related disappearances and arbitrary arrests: the Working Group on Arbitrary Detention (WGAD) and the Working Group on Enforced or Involuntary Disappearances (WGEID).

WGAD has the role of investigating cases involving the deprivation of liberty under guidance of standards set within the Universal Declaration of Human Rights or any other international legal instructions that a state may have signed onto. Through this, independent human rights experts conduct investigations and send appeals and communications for clarity and/or to bring attention to cases. In other words, the best thing they can do is have a firm word with the governments concerned.

Tapping people politely on the shoulder to have a stern talk to them, once again, appears absurd. That being said, at least it's something we can do.

Wednesday 20 February 2019

Before she submits to WGAD, Jen emails me the draft complaint to review. We still have the option of going to the media; I'm raring to go. I don't want to make the mistake of staying silent again.

Jen mentions how she's spoken about going to media with the Australian Embassy in Cairo, but they have advised us to wait until Sunday 'before shaking the tree'. By Sunday, Dad will have been missing for four days! Back in January, we followed the advice to wait forty-eight hours. Within that time, Dad was interrogated, tortured and dumped at Tora. In my reply email to Jen, I refer to this as a 'less than inspiring response' – mild terms for the rage I'm feeling at being told to wait, yet again.

I struggle to understand how the perpetration of state violence can be allowed to continue, even pick up speed, as a handbrake is applied to the actions that could stop it. The response is to wait, to follow the law, to get in line. It's infuriating, yet I'm resigned to the injustice that victims must follow the rules while states can bypass the law.

To rage, to scream and burn it all down – that's what I'd really love to do. To experience this rage, and the forced repression of it, is incredibly taxing on my body and mind. I cannot burn bridges. I have to trust the Embassy when they say they're 'making representations' to the Egyptian, even though I don't know what that tangibly means and I can't ask. Is it an email? A phone call? An in-person meeting? What do they say to each other?

Jen makes the submission to WGAD then emails The Department of Foreign Affairs and Trade to inform them. The following day, a DFAT secretary responds, restating the Embassy is 'making extensive efforts to locate his current whereabouts' and that they've offered for me to speak to their media liaison. It's true, they have but I'm not particularly trustful of taking advice from the DFAT media liaison when the recommendation has consistently been to 'not go public.'

Now the WGAD complaint has now been submitted, I'm under no illusions the Egyptian government will frantically respond and thrust Hazem into our hands.

Yet, submitting to WGAD has benefits beyond the soft power exercises of direct communication and appeals to government. The UN has a kind of halo effect. These institutional stamps of either association or approval are important when advocating, lending us a little more legitmacy and weight.

On a personal level, I feel disillusioned by these bodies and concepts built around human rights: disappearances and arbitrary detention haven't stopped, in spite of all these efforts. Furthermore, while we lodge this complaint against Egypt, Australia continues to practise arbitrary detention too: from asylum-seeker detention centres to the high incarceration rates of First Nations people. I'm not fooling myself into thinking I stand on any kind of moral high ground as an Australian.

Arbitrary detention and disappearances inflict a deep psychological wound, both to the individual and within the collective consciousness. On the one hand, when something is arbitrary, there's no predicting who'll be targeted. It is the reverberating fear that it could be you. This acute fear makes us desperate to separate ourselves from the violence: we blame the victim, looking for reasons why they deserve it. We lump targeted people into a group and criminalise them, pathologise them and surveil them. We imagine ourselves as different from the people being harmed. This imagining almost always involves a process of dehumanisation. We moralise this process; we call ourselves 'good people' who have 'nothing to hide'. Or we denounce, we enforce distance through binaries so that we can say we are 'not like them'. In doing so, we can convince ourselves we are secure, that we will not be harmed. By seeking to ease our anxieties by blaming the individual, we avoid facing the violence of the structures we inhabit.

We should be turning towards violence, towards the victim, as witness, as listener and believe their testimony. Because yes, it could be you.

People with Heart

I'm annoying and I know it but I can't stop myself. Saja is growing tired of my efforts to dictate her actions from abroad: I still want to lead things in Egypt and I'm treating Saja as my soldier, not my sister. Finally, she ferociously tells me to back off. She reminds me that I'm not the one in Cairo, she is. 'Focus on what you've got to do in Australia, Lamisse.'

Knowing Saja is right, I apologise and turn my attention back to what I came home to do: advocacy and the campaign. It's hard to stay focused and believe we're going to get somewhere with campaigning for Dad: every email and social media post feels like a howl into the abyss. But there is momentum: our Change.org petition is up and getting signatures. A journalist from the Associated Press interviewed me, and a couple of other articles have been published about Dad.

Earlier in the week, our local representative, Member for Stretton Duncan Pegg, reaches out. With reluctance, I speak to him on the phone. I know I'm supposed to be re-engaging in political advocacy, but speaking with politicians leaves me feeling hopeless. They don't care, why would they? And what power do they have anyway? However, Duncan is warm and genuine on the phone. It's obvious he's been emotionally affected by our case and wants to help. He emphasises how keen he is to explore the possibilities of supporting us, so I arrange to meet him at his office in Sunnybank Hills.

During the meeting, Duncan reminds me that we're his constituents and it's his responsibility to help the families in his constituency. Helping people is the reason he got into politics. He offers to make a speech in the Queensland Parliament, saying the least he could do is use his position to publicly advocate for us and put the case on record. 'We can print T-shirts, organise a rally or a barbecue to gather people together and raise awareness for what's happening to your dad,' he says, excitement building. This, he adds, would come at no extra cost to us.

Is he really this earnest? So many politicians I've spoken with have shied away from supporting a case involving terrorism. Perhaps we've reached a tipping point: the injustice of Dad's imprisonment now has more traction than the threat of a bogeyman terrorist.

Duncan begins making arrangements for the speech: he gets back in touch with me to check names, dates and facts around the case, and he organises 'Bring Hazem Home' T-shirts to be printed. Later that month, when Duncan gives his first speech about Dad's case, he tears up. We're watching from the wings as Duncan chokes through the rest of his speech. Mum wipes away tears with the tail of her hijab. When he finishes his speech, there's a loud round of applause as politicians look up at us, waving and giving thumbs-ups of encouragement.

*

Around the same time that I began talking to Duncan, I remember that Peter had given me another tip: get in touch with the Foreign Prisoner Support Service. He'd mentioned that I should ask for Martin Hodgson.

Martin is a senior advocate with the Foreign Prisoner Support Service. After a short email exchange, Martin sends me a number to contact him. I give him a call and within a few minutes of chatting, his fiery commitment to supporting people facing injustice and oppression is undeniably clear. His approach is fearless and radical. He straddles the tension of working with the law while refusing its assumed power – all his efforts are to centre the people he advocates for. Furthermore, he has experience with cases involving terrorism, including cases with people imprisoned in Egypt.

During our phone conversations, he veers between lawyer and therapist. He explains precedents in relevant cases of people imprisoned overseas, while also holding space for me to talk through some of my messy emotions. I appreciate Martin's warmth and empathy as he talks me through the pain of injustice, especially its legacy. Gently, he warns me, 'Getting through this is not the hard part. The hardest part is the aftermath.'

This is incomprehensible. *How is that possible? This is the toughest thing we've ever faced!* Yet Martin's advice is a nod towards the shattering impacts of post-traumatic stress disorder – a pain that comes to last far longer than the time Dad spent in prison.

Teamwork

Jen and I decide not to wait, but to shake the tree as hard as we can. She suggests that we release the press statement on Friday 22 February.

She brings in Holly, a public relations expert based in Sydney. Holly's going to help us navigate the media landscape, starting with the preparation and release of a press statement. I reach out to the Country Director of Change.org, Nic Holas. Nic is quick to respond, his emails infused with warmth: he offers to promote the petition to the front page and edit any copy I write for our updates.

It dawns on me that we've informally built a team. In Egypt, there's Saja, Mansour, Thomas and friends – particularly Drew, Salma and Suleiman – all of whom help with errands, translating and driving Saja around Cairo. There's our international counsel, Jen and Caoilfhionn, who are leading the advocacy and legal work of Dad's case. Jen's in Sydney, while Caoilfhionn continues working from London. In Brisbane, there's Duncan repping us in Parliament, and Peter has made himself available to support us from the personal struggle to the political struggle of publicly advocating for Dad. Then there are Martin, Nic and Holly, all of whom give support to our various channels of advocacy: from PR to the petition and pestering politicians. Help from our community also flows in: both the National Zakat Foundation and the Muslim Charity Foundation offer financial support to our family, offering everything from Coles vouchers to help paying our bills. To be surrounded is transformative: it seeds a conviction in the necessity of community, as I both feel – and witness – the impact. I wish I could show this to Dad. I want him to see the team that's rallied behind him.

The night before we issue the press release, I stay up to talk to Saja. After we finish talking, I lie in bed, unable to sleep.

I stay awake until dawn.

At 8.30 am, Holly sends out the press release.

Thousands Call Foreign Minister's Office Demanding Freedom for Hazem

22 February 2019

Australian man, Hazem Hamouda, has been held in an Egyptian prison without charge for over a year. His lawyers had just secured his release from one of Egypt's most notorious prisons, Tora in Cairo, only to learn that he has disappeared.

Thousands of Australians, who had signed a Change.org petition calling for the Foreign Minister to intervene with the Egyptian government, called the Department of Foreign Affairs and Trade (DFAT) today asking them to do something.

Over 18,000 people have signed the Change.org petition, with many more signing since Hazem's disappearance.

'We were overjoyed to learn that the Prosecutor General of Egypt ordered Dad's release from prison. But now, Hazem has disappeared. Our dad was never brought to the appointed police station for his release. We are so worried for his safety,' said Lamisse Hamouda, 29-year-old daughter of Hazem.

'The Australian Embassy must intervene with the Egyptian government. We need them to urgently act before it is too late. Once someone disappears inside Egypt's prisons, you may never see them again.

'We are calling on Minister Marise Payne to do everything she, and the Australian government, can to find and free one of its citizens,' said Ms Hamouda.

'Mr Hamouda is an Australian citizen who has already been unjustly and arbitrarily detained in Egypt for over a year. There is no lawful basis for his continued detention,' said Australian human rights lawyer, Jennifer Robinson, of Doughty Street Chambers and international legal counsel for Mr Hamouda's family.

'We have grave concerns for his safety and security after his disappearance. We have filed an urgent appeal with the UN, calling upon Egypt to provide information about his whereabouts and to ensure his immediate release to end this horrific ordeal for him and his family. We call upon the UN and international community to raise their concern with the Egyptian authorities' said Ms Robinson.

*

A producer at SBS reaches out to cover Dad's case for SBS Arabic; a friend at ABC in Melbourne connects to me to a journalist at the ABC office in Brisbane. *The Project* gets back in touch with me, as does a journalist from Agence France-Presse. ABC Brisbane invite me to talk on the afternoon drive-home show with Steve Austin. Another show on ABC Radio also seeks an interview, as does a producer from the late-night news show, *ABC World*. I want *The Guardian* to cover the story too, but the reply I get says they're not yet interested. I get an offer to go on *Sunrise*, but I'm too nervous to enter into breakfast television territory so I turn it down.

The next day, I drive down to the ABC studio in Brisbane's Southbank for my interview with Steve Austin. February in Brisbane is heavy with humidity and heat; entering the large foyer is cool relief after the short, sweaty walk from the carpark. I check in at the reception desk where my photo is taken and I'm issued a visitor's pass on a lanyard.

I'm directed to head upstairs, where a producers greets me. She and I sit on a couch, waiting for Steve to wrap up his current segment so I can enter the booth during the song break. The song comes on and I go in. Steve smiles, shakes my hand then directs me to one of the microphone and headphone sets.

The song fades out. Steve does his opening, then introduces me and summarises Dad's case. Then he asks, 'So, what's the scuttlebutt on the street in Egypt?'

I lean forwards to speak into the microphone. 'Umm ... I don't know what a scuttlebutt is?'

It's a small, easily fixed misunderstanding. Yet, in my heightened emotional state, it rattles me. I want the gravity of the situation to be present, not to be lightened with silly slang. Doubting myself, I start wondering if drive-home radio is the right place to have a serious conversation. But we move through the gaffe. The interview ends up going well; Steve is quite kind, as is the producer. As I leave, they both wish me luck and say they're interested to have me back if there are any updates.

Though I've driven home from Southbank countless times, I get lost. Sleep-deprived, hungry and consumed by my thoughts,

I'm not concentrating on the road. I swing into a random McDonald's to pick up a Filet-O-Fish meal. I need to sort out my thoughts, but I'm eating so, instead of writing, I talk while filming myself. The video diary helps, but it's not as helpful as my journal.

By the way, scuttlebutt just means rumour.

*

That same evening, *The Project* airs a piece we'd filmed just before Saja left. My siblings, Mum and I crowd around the television to watch it. When we were first in discussions about having *The Project* come, Mum had asked me if she should take off her hijab. 'Maybe it's better if I look more Australian,' she said.

More Australian. I can't describe how much I hated that she asked this: that the fear of judgement made her doubt herself, that she thought removing her hijab to reveal her white-Australian appearance would make us more deserving of empathy. I hated it because, on one hand, she's not wrong to think this. On the other hand, what kind of society are we living in that would make people feel this way? Proud of my mother, I told her no, that we should be seen for who we are. I emphasise that we don't need to distance ourselves from Islam in order to pursue the conditional compassion of the prejudiced. It is possible to ask for empathy without needing anyone to understand; that's what we're asking for when we ask to be believed. To me, it is a request that the listener feels. You don't need to understand with your mind, but your heart. Already, in this relationship with the media, we are surrendering to the violence of concession: that, to be heard, our voice is handed over to someone else to speak for us. Yes, we may be interviewed but who does the interviewing? Who does the editing? Am I invited into the room where questions are prepared? The music is selected? The voice-over text written? The answer is still no.

The Project has pulled together various excerpts from the interviews. They've cut in dramatic scenes from the 2011 revolution and added some of that generic 'oriental' string music. There's a snippet of Peter Greste offering his political analysis of Egypt. The framing of it makes me cringe; it feels like he's been called in by the producers to take the place of 'expert' rather a formerly incarcerated person in solidarity with us. Are we not expert enough on our own lives? Can't I also offer a political analysis? The segment finishes with a close-up of Saja saying, 'Dad is just a little guy: like he's just a little man, a little family man. He's just … my dad.'

Traffic on the petition spikes. Multiple signatures arrive with comments that they're there because of Saja, because of her earnestness, because her dad is just a 'little family man'.

Not everyone understands politics, but everyone understands family.

Lost and Found

25 February 2019

Mum and I are lounging on the couch, listless. Her phone rings.

She's not wearing her glasses so she squints at the screen. Then she sits bolt upright and shoves the phone in my face. I see an unknown Egyptian number.

'It could be your dad!' she cries.

But before she can answer, the phone goes silent. Determined, Mum calls the number back and puts the phone on loudspeaker.

'Hello?' comes the voice of Dad.

Mum and I scream – a combination of a cheer and a wail.

'Hazem, Hazem,' Mum says breathlessly. Then she hurriedly hands the phone to me. 'I can't talk, I can't do it …' she says and bursts into tears. I take the phone from her.

'Hey, Dad,' I manage to say, despite a lump in my throat. 'We thought you had disappeared …'

'I'm fine,' he says nonchalantly. 'I'm still here in Tora. Nothing has changed.'

My mind is spinning, I try to compute all this: *Dad is in Tora. He says nothing has changed. Does that mean he doesn't know?*

'Dad,' I say tentatively. 'You've been released.'

'I have?' he replies.

'Yes, you have!' I explode. 'Saja is in Egypt. She was supposed to get you!'

'What? Saja? What? I'm getting out?' I hear shock and bewilderment in his voice.

Now, I can't hold back my own tears. It's beyond belief he's been in Tora this whole time with no idea he's been freed. And this whole time, we thought he'd been missing! And he was right where we left him! Did no one check? Do they not even know who's in the prison? Did the Egyptian authorities deliberately not disclose this information? Who were the Embassy contacting when they were making their 'extensive efforts' to locate him? How could such a serious miscommunication occur?

'Sorry, Dad … I … I can't.' I wave the phone at Mum. It's my turn to cry; it's all too overwhelming.

Mum's recomposed herself. She takes the phone and turns off the loudspeaker. I faintly hear Dad's voice rising and falling as Mum replies in soothing tones. 'Yes, it's true. Alhamdullilah. Yes, Saja is actually in Cairo …'

By now, Amira and Harun have entered the room, both of them wide-eyed and watchful. They're only 13 months apart, in moments like this, I forget they're not twins.

'You should tell Saja,' urges Amira.

'Maybe get her to go to the prison,' says Harun, 'and check on Dad …'

I take a big sniff and wipe my nose on my sleeve. 'Yeah, you're right. I'll call her. I'll let her know we've found Dad.'

*

I find it awkward telling Jen and Caoilfhionn that Dad is still in Tora, that all the high drama has been because of a complete failure in communication. They empathise with my sense of frustration and embarrassment.

I still haven't informed the Embassy that we know where Dad is. When I inform Saja that Dad called us from Tora, we agree that she needs to go for a prison visit and confirm he is definitely there. Then, we can tell the Embassy.

It's a hard moment to reconcile with; it goes to show that we truly have no idea what's going on, whether we're in Australia or Egypt. It highlights just how many of our decisions have been based on speculation – that we're always playing a guessing game, weighing up possibilities while hoping the information we have is true. This incident is another nail in the coffin for our trust in the authorities, both Egyptian and Australian. Are we dealing with obstruction or gross incompetence? Ignorance or crushing carelessness? Poor communication?

If I were to brush it away as a communication breakdown, does that obscure the violence of neglect that this breakdown represents? The *intent* to harm is also contained in the choice not to do or to do poorly. Neglect is harm. Ignoring is harm. Carelessness is harm. In the responsibility that is governance, to not act – or to do something poorly – can be as harmful as a direct and conscious act of violence.

No matter how I turn these things over in my mind, there's no satisfying reason I can give for this miscommunication. Yet, to move forwards, I have to forget about it. Now that we know where Dad is, we need to get him out of Tora and onto a goddamn plane.

The Masr Gadeda Cop Shop

Tuesday 26 February 2019

In the morning, Saja goes straight to the prison to see Dad. She's not obliged to follow my prison routine of primarily visiting on a Thursday.

After the visit, she calls saying that Dad is still finding it hard to believe what's been happening. Or more specifically, he won't believe he's free until he's out. 'Even though he's skinny,' Saja tells us, 'he still looks good, like he's okay.' When I ask her if she's okay, she says, 'It was such a whirlwind that I didn't have time to take anything in … I just can't believe you did this for a year.'

'Some people do it for longer … You're doing so well in Egypt already, Saj. I'm so proud of you.'

She brushes over my comment. 'So, what now? Should I speak to the Embassy?' she asks.

'Yeah, tell them you went down to the prison to check if Dad was there and he was … Then urge them to get him out.' I pause, sighing heavily. 'I still can't believe no one checked the prison.'

'Neither can I.' Saja sighs too. 'I can't believe Dad was there the whole time with no idea about anything.'

27 February 2019

It's late at night, Cairo time. Saja, Thomas, Mansour and Mohamed – a friend of mine who is helping Saja out with translating – head to Khalifa Police Station.

For me, it's the early morning. I'm already up, sitting at my laptop with my coffee.

My WhatsApp pings.

It's a photo of Dad's back as he walks along the street in his white prison tracksuit. His black sneakers, the only shoes he was allowed to keep from his suitcase, are on his feet. In his hand is a large white garbage bag containing the few possessions he's taken with him from prison. His head is slightly bowed and his small bald spot is visible through his cropped salt-and-pepper hair.

It's real.

I explode with a scream: 'YES. YES!'

Abandoning the email I'd been writing to Jen, I leap up and dance around the lounge room. I need music. Dad's an Aquarius, so I put on 'The Age of Aquarius'. It's cheesy but the soaring vocals of this psychedelic soul classic match my giddy relief. Spotify flips through soul song after song, and I dance, losing track of time.

Feeling a blister forming on the sole of my right foot, I flop onto the couch.

Then I reach for my phone and open up the Quran app as I want to read the surah Saja is named after. Like most Arabic names, Saja's name is loaded with meaning. It refers to the darkest point of the night, a time that is just before the dawn breaks. It's fitting for her to be in Cairo right now: to be there when the darkness begins to end. Reading the surah, I'm overcome with gratitude and grief: a bittersweet mix of relief and heaviness. I'm celebrating our survival while mourning those I know are still stuck inside. Dad's liberation is our personal victory, but I still feel chained so long as I know liberation is denied to so many other people.

*

I should have predicted that the joy would be short-lived.

'It's not over,' says Saja in a text message. 'Remember, he still has to go to another police station for processing and stay there.'

'For how long?' I text back.

'Don't know …' comes her reply.

From Khalifa Police Station, Dad is taken to a police station in the suburb of Masr Gededa.

Dad hates the holding cell in Masr Gededa police station: the fluorescent bulb is kept on 24/7. There's no ventilation, no windows. There's not even watery beans or bread being dished out. He reckons Tora was better. Saja visits Dad every day, bringing food and supplies. She gets him a phone so he can talk to Mum whenever he wants. At least this part is better than Tora.

Saja tries to carve out some fun in Egypt. When she goes out and meets people, they always ask, 'So, what are you doing in Egypt?' It's an innocuous question, but she can't respond to it with the usual answers – work, travel, study, family. Saja says she would rather tell the truth than lie to deflect the question, but it brings Dad into every room and sours the mood. I suggest that maybe sometimes people don't need to know; it's not lying, it's just … self-protection? Regardless, she stops socialising and sticks to hanging out with people she knows and trusts: Thomas, Suleiman and our cousins.

Despite all the pressures she's under, she's upbeat. She says it's all bit easier now because 'it's close to the end and there's hope.'

el-Asfaalt

Wednesday 6 March 2019

'We're going to pick him up at midnight,' says Saja. That's 8 am Australian Eastern Standard Time.

The day has arrived! This is the last and final step out of the prison system. Dad will now be able to physically experience the freedom he's been promised.

I can't sleep from the amount of anticipation, nerves and excitement pumping through me. Knowing I won't be able to switch off, I simply stay up all night.

Throughout the night, Saja texts me with periodic updates:

We're leaving the flat now.

Driving with Suleiman to the police station.

Just got to the police station.

Then it's quiet. We wait for a call, for a text.

Then Saja sends us a photo. No words. Just one single image.

It's Dad standing between Saja, Yacoub and Amgad. They all have their arms draped over each other and they're smiling wildly into the camera. It's the best photo I've ever seen.

I know I must have shown this photo to Mum, Nana and my siblings, but beyond receiving the photo, I don't remember anything about that day. It saddens me to know that some of the devastating memories are so sharp, but the better ones are lost or blurry.

An hour later, I get another photo: it's of Dad lying in bed, a blissful smile on his face. After 403 days of sleeping on a concrete floor, sleeping on a mattress must feel amazing.

I book their flights for the following day. We have to bring them home. No hesitation, no delay.

Retraumatised

Thursday 7 March 2019

Saja and Dad have less than 22 hours to pack up and get to the airport. I didn't wait a second to book them their flight out, but Saja is stressing about the turnaround.

In Brisbane, we're all eagerly waiting for the relief of Dad being home and a day seems like more than enough time to sleep, pack and say goodbye.

The flight route out of Egypt will take them through Istanbul and Singapore, then on to Brisbane. It's carefully planned: we've been advised to avoid countries that have extradition treaties, or any other agreements that could result in Dad being handed back over to Egyptian authorities. Sounds extreme, but it's not. Malaysia has recently been making headlines for extraditing Egyptian citizens to Cairo. One of the men deported (and disappeared) is the husband of an Australian woman, who, coincidentally, is also from Brisbane. It's a few weeks later that we are put in touch; however, her husband is not a dual national and with that, I feel at a loss over what to advise her. In the coming years, she's not the only person I am put in touch with. Once your eyes are opened, you realise you are neither alone nor unique. Similar to being in the prison cafeteria, this sense of shared suffering overlaps between being comforting and deeply distressing.

Yet, in this present moment of trying to get Dad and Saja out of Cairo, the pressure to risk assess every move is further fuel for my ever-present and always-growing paranoia. Inside me, a voice keeps screaming with increasing urgency, 'There is no safety except at home!' We ask the Embassy if the Ambassador can escort Dad and Saja through the airport. This is a safety measure: we fear that, unless there's visible support from Australian authorities, Dad could easily be taken again, and Saja would be helpless to stop it. On the flip side, we also make the request to assuage Dad's fears. After all, he doesn't see the airport as a safe place. For Dad, he's going back to where his nightmare started. Or, to use Dad's words, 'the place where I was kidnapped.'

I ask for text updates at each step: the packing, the goodbyes, the taxi ride, the arrival at Cairo Airport and at every checkpoint in the terminal. I wake up around 4 am ready to follow their journey.

When they get to Cairo Airport, Saja texts me: *So far, so good.* I picture the route they're taking: luggage check at the entrance, the check-in desk …

Saja phones.

'Dad's been stopped!' she says frantically. 'Dad got stopped by security and told he wouldn't be able to go through. Then he freaked out and started screaming, "NO. NO. I'M NOT GOING BACK. I'M NOT GOING BACK." and tried to run away. But because of his broken leg, his damaged leg, he fell. He couldn't run!' She starts crying.

'What? So you can't board the flight?'

'No, we can't! They won't let him!' When she says 'they', she means National Security.

My brain turns to static. I hold the phone away and scream. Then I pull myself together. 'Just get out of the airport. Go back to Thomas's apartment, okay?'

We end the call. I'm shaking. *Why does this shit keep happening? Hasn't it been enough? What's the purpose of dragging it out?*

Mum is standing at my doorway.

'What happened?' Her eyes – weary and scared – search mine.

I can't answer her. I look away and rest my gaze on the wall beside me. I visualise it, like a film projected onto the white wall: Dad running, falling, the desperation and fear on his face.

I explode. 'It's so cruel! Why? Why can't they just let him leave?'

*

Once Saja and Dad are back at the flat, Saja asks that we give them some space to calm down and rest. Respecting their wishes, Mum and I also take some time out. Yet, my brain never quite shuts off. As I drift off into a nap, I'm thinking about what the hell we're going to do now.

*

In the following section, I relay Dad's experience that day. For the purpose of clarity, I've re-written the interview into prose, interspersed with verbatim excerpts from Dad.

Taken to an office in the basement, again, the air was full of cigarette smoke. Several plain-clothes security offers are sitting around with their feet on the desks. Scared he was about to repeat the horrors of his first arrival, Dad's already triggered.

He is told he'd 'overstayed' his visa. To make everything right – and in order to leave the country – he needed paperwork to show he'd been 'staying' in Egypt for all this time as a citizen. To do that, he was obliged to present his identity card.

Bamboozled, Dad explained that he'd been in prison for 14 months and he no longer had his identity card. He states that it had been lost when he was transferred from Tora to Khalifa Police Station. The last people to have had his identity card were National Security. One of them had taken it to fill out some paperwork. While Dad was fielding these questions, the Embassy staffer sent to accompany him through the airport was making calls.

Unswayed, the National Security officers informed Dad that he must sort out his identity documents. As if the goalposts hadn't moved enough, they gave him one more instruction: he needed his military exemption certificate.

Given Egypt has a system of conscription, every man under the age of 30 must serve. There are a few ways out of this: one is to leave the country and not come back until you're over 30. Having emigrated from Egypt in his 20s and settled down in Australia with Mum, Dad didn't serve. In 30 years of visiting Egypt, he'd never been asked for an exemption certificate.

At this point, Dad says his fears were sky-rocketing. Even though they'd let him go, he was still terrified he could be taken. Perhaps it was a trap. Perhaps they were waiting for him outside the airport.

Back in the waiting area, he stood with Saja and the staffer. In the distance, two plain-clothes officers started walking towards them. Positive they were coming to arrest him, Dad leapt out of his chair and started running.

Dad says:

As I get up to run, I am filled with adrenaline. But my injured leg is not working properly, so it collapses under me and I fall to the ground. Then I just go into a complete rage. I rage: 'I'm not going back there!' I threaten that no one should come near me. But with all this rage, I don't know where to go. Those two men kept walking, walking past me […] but in that moment of time, I really thought they were going to be chasing after me.

Then Saja approaches me, and she's trying to comfort me. I break down and cry. It feels like a complete nervous breakdown. I cry and tell her I don't know what to do.

The staffer managed to ascertain that it was safe for Dad to leave the airport. On the phone, Thomas assured my sister that she and Dad were welcome to stay at his flat for longer. All that remained was to convince Dad it was safe to leave the airport. At first, he insisted that the only places he'd stay was the Australian Embassy or with the Ambassador, but that wasn't possible. The other option was a big, secure hotel, but it was no surprise Dad said he wouldn't feel safe around Egyptian security guards. Thomas then sought to further reassure Dad by saying that, as a government-employed German international development worker, he was fairly confident his flat was safe from being raided. Reassured by this logic, though a logic only backed by assumption and not evidence, Dad acquiesced. Saja and Dad then left, escorted by the staffer.

The day after Dad was turned away from the airport, he received a visit at Thomas's apartment from the Ambassador, Glenn Milne. Dad relays: 'At that point, I accepted that I'm an Egyptian on Egyptian territory and that I am going to have to comply with Egyptian rules.' He agreed to go through the motions and do what was being asked of him. Before the meeting ended, he asked the Ambassador: 'Please, at least stay in touch with me.' The Ambassador agreed.

For the rest of their time in Cairo, Dad and Saja were allowed to directly contact the staffer and the Ambassador as needed.

*

Jen and Caoilfhionn look to the law for a solution to Dad being denied exit from Egypt. They draft a legal opinion based on the primacy of Dad's Australian citizenship over his Egyptian citizenship. It wasn't enough to have a staffer accompany Dad through the airport, they say: the Ambassador needed to have accompanied him.

It's generous of Thomas to host Saja and Dad in his apartment. We want Dad to agree that he shouldn't leave the flat alone. Dad disagrees. The last thing he wants is to feel trapped, so we reach some compromises:

1. He must always have his phone on loud, and on him.
2. He must keep his daily walk to a small radius in Zemalek.
3. He has to tell someone when he's going out.

In climates of paranoia and unpredictability, we bargain with uncertainties by wilfully deluding ourselves into certainty. The truth is, we have no idea if any of what we're doing protects Dad, or if our efforts are more about our need to believe we still have the power to secure our own safety. In hindsight, I think the latter.

Dad wastes no time sorting out his documents. Within 48 hours of leaving the airport, he secures a new identity card. He hints that the skills of 'negotiation' he's picked up in Tora account for the speediness of this feat.

No such luck with the military exemption certificate. He has to go to the military court to get it. The date of his military hearing is set for three weeks' time.

Who Gets to Be Safe

March drags on.

Dad seems to be doing mostly well: he's going on his daily walks, keeping Thomas up with philosophical chats, and has Yacoub and Amgad coming to visit. He expresses that he feels claustrophobia if there are a lot of people around him. Saja informs us that she can also tell Dad is in a heightened state as he keeps being triggered by loud noises and sudden movements. On one disastrous evening, they discover that these triggers make going to busy restaurants an absolute no-go.

All of us are counting down the days till Dad attends the military court. We're plagued by the uncertainty as to whether this is genuinely a bureaucratic delay or if it's giving authorities more time to trump up new charges; that is, to find another reason to delay – or detain – Dad. Paranoia is exhausting.

In the meantime, we turn our focus to what we can do: pressuring the Australian authorities to give Hazem diplomatic protection. Really, all we actually want is assurance that the Ambassador will accompany Dad and Saja through the airport and ensure they get on their flight out of Egypt.

We wouldn't be demanding this if it wasn't for Peter. He informs us he'd been transported directly from prison to the airport, and that the Ambassador shepherded him onto the plane. He outlines this moment in his book, *The First Casualty*, so it's not a secret. Meanwhile, Martin doesn't hold back in his criticisms, describing how Australia has a reputation for dragging its feet. In the end, Peter, Jen and Martin all offer the same advice, each in their own way: since consular support is always a matter of 'discretion', remember that the Embassy can always do more than what they let on. To get it, you've got to push.

Demand. Demand. Demand. I'm tired of fighting. *Why is it always up to us to ask? Why is it always up to us to insist? What is the point of rights if they're not a given?*

Caoilfhionn and Jen start work on a legal opinion on Dad's case for submission to the Department of Foreign Affairs. Knowing they're doing this provides me with a sense of reassurance. While I can know that what is happening is wrong, I can't point to the laws and legal frameworks that would help me argue my case. As such, I eagerly await this legal opinion: I want to know how the lawyers do it – that is, the Barrister and the QC; I want to read how they tell this story through the lens of the law.

13 March 2019

Holly, the publicist, arranges a meeting with Greens Senator, Larissa Waters, and former Greens party leader, Richard Di Natale. Jen sends through talking points to prep me. She summarises some of the legal specifics relating to dual-citizenship; specifically how Dad does not need to renounce his Egyptian citizenship for Australia to exercise full diplomatic protection over him, and that they ought to ensure he has equal access to rights as any other Australian arrested abroad. She adds that, 'At minimum, he deserves treatment equal to that offered to Peter Greste – and it is clear he is not receiving this level of support.' I feel bad that we have to keep drawing on Peter's case to make our point. I don't like playing the game of comparison; Peter had a rough time too. His family advocated hard, and he spent more days in prison than Dad. I shouldn't need to make any comparisons to make my point: every Australian, regardless of whatever other citizenship they hold, deserves recognition and protection.

I park down the road from Larissa's office in Paddington, a gentrified inner-city borough of Brisbane. I'm ushered into a meeting room and greeted by Larissa, Richard and a staffer. We sit at a large square table: I'm at one end and they sit side by side at the other.

The meeting lasts just over an hour without a pause in the conversation. They seem curious, and while I'm there, I hope it's accurate for me to interpret their interest as care.

Turns out I'm not mistaken. Jen later notifies me that Richard and Larissa both personally reach out to Marise Payne, the Minister of Foreign Affairs and Trade. Jen also informs me that Richard is planning to 'bail [Marise Payne] up in the chamber' when he's in Canberra, intending to press her about the assurances we're seeking. The last thing she mentions is that she's been in contact with a good friend of hers, Labour MP Anthony Albanese, to do the same thing.

After this, we send out an ask through the petition: call or email Marise Payne and let her know we need to bring Hazem home. After a while, our consular representative at DFAT asks me to stop people from contacting them. They get the point, he says, and we're doing our best. I couldn't be more pleased by this call: if they're annoyed, then good.

I don't tell anyone to stop. We've got to keep pushing.

16 March 2019

Thomas is in Australia; he's taken two weeks off work. He says it was all getting a bit much in Cairo, with Dad and Saja and all the tension, that he needed a break and wanted to see me. While it's been nice having him here, it's also been challenging. I have so much on my plate with Dad's case that I don't have as much time for him as either he or I would like. A weekend away in Coolum is interrupted by the need for me to get back to Brisbane. I leave Thomas up on the Sunshine Coast for a night, alone with just the tiny Airbnb house and the surf.

*

I jolt awake in the middle of the night. Burning fear has my skin buzzing. I tense up, my ears straining for sounds of danger. Beside me, Thomas is fast asleep. I lie back down, bring my legs to my chest and hold my breath. That way, I can hear better. I'm convinced someone's coming to kill me, and everyone I know is going to be killed too.

I start hyperventilating. Thomas stirs, and puts his arm over me. Sleepily, he says, 'Lamisse, you're safe.'

I'm not. He doesn't understand how much danger we're all in, that we're all about to be murdered.

The panic attack throttles me. I choke, shaking and struggling to breathe.

Thomas is now completely awake. He sits up and puts his hand on my upper arm. 'Lamisse,' I hear him say firmly. 'Lamisse. Breathe. You're safe.'

Yesterday, 55 people were gunned down across two mosques in Christchurch, New Zealand.

Safe? Who gets to be safe?

On the morning of the funeral prayer at the Islamic College of Brisbane for the victims of the Christchurch shooting, the draft legal opinion for Dad's case lands in my inbox. I leave it unopened, with the plan to read it after the service. The school where the memorial is held is overflowing with people; shock, fear and grief are visible among all of us. The Maori community makes a show of force, expressing their solidarity with the local Muslim community. Being at the service reminds me of the beautiful shards embedded in a tragedy; the shards I always wished would last beyond the shattering, uninhibited expressions of love, solidarity and care.

After the service, I head home, take out my laptop and start reading. To this day, it remains the only document I have that itemises the human rights Dad's been denied: his right to freedom from arbitrary arrest or detention, his right to a fair trial, and his right to freedom of expression and assembly.

The opinion states:

> *In our firm view, there is evidence of multiple breaches of Mr Hamouda's rights under international law and multiple breaches by Egypt of its international legal obligations, which entitles Australia to take action.*

The document continues:

> *The critical point is that, given the length of Mr Hamouda's detention and the exceptional urgency arising from his abhorrent current conditions of unlawful detention and the arbitrary circumstances in which he has been prevented from leaving the country, all available diplomatic lobbying channels must be pursued as expeditiously as possible to ensure he can return home. At the very least, he deserves the same protection and support as that offered to Peter Greste.*

Further on, the opinion outlines Australia's policies on dual nationals, explaining how, and why, diplomatic protection is justified in Dad's case. For this protection, three conditions must be met: proof of predominant Australian nationality, the commission of an intentionally wrongful act by Egypt, and the exhaustion of local remedies. The first listed – proof of predominant Australian nationality – is, as far as I can tell, easily proven. They require one's nationality to be 'real and effective', which is clearly evidenced by his 30 years living here, his naturalisation, his career, his taxes, his wife and us: the six children all born here and in possession of Australian nationality.

The legal opinion expands on this further, stating how 'States are not prohibited from excising diplomatic protection in cases where dual nationals are subject to injury by the other state of nationality.' In other words, if you're a dual citizen and find yourself harmed by a state you hold citizenship of, then the other state can legally step in.

The legal opinion then clearly states: 'In these circumstances, it is clear that his dominant and effective nationality is Australian. This means that Australia was *always entitled to act* [italics are mine], as a matter of international law.'

'Aways entitled to act': this phrase sticks with me. So, if that's the case, then what took so long? Was it simply a matter of preferring to focus on the remit to 'exhaust local remedies' rather than undertaking actions made permissible through recognising his 'predominant nationality' and the 'intentionally wrongful act' by Egypt? Is this proof my suspicions were not wrong, that they could have – and should have – done more?

The last part of the document addresses the necessity to exhaust legal remedies. From the start, we were repeatedly told we had to go through the Egyptian legal system because Egypt has its own processes that must be respected, that these cannot be interfered with. As I read the legal opinion, I find myself seeing that this was not necessarily the case. The opinion reads: 'Local remedies need not be exhausted where local courts are notoriously lacking in independence; where there is a consistent and well-established line of precedents adverse to the victim's position; or where the respondent State does not have an adequate system of judicial protection …'

It's no secret that the courts in Egypt are notoriously lacking in independence. The international organisation, Human Rights Watch, has extensive documentation of the dwindling independence of Egypt's courts: evidence that there is a 'consistent and well-established line of precedents', outcomes which aren't in favour of those captured, is seen in the increase in the issuances of death penalties, the lengthy stays in pre-trial detention and the heavy-handed sentencing of political prisoners.

In March 2021, a joint statement was issued (on behalf of 31 countries, of which Australia was not one) at the 46th United Nations Human Rights Council, expressing concern over the trajectory of human rights in Egypt. The statement explicitly references Egypt's abuse of terrorism charges, urging Egypt to 'end the use of terrorism charges to hold human rights defenders and civil society activists in extended pre-trial detention … we also ask Egypt to cease the use of terrorism entities list[1] to punish individuals for exercising their right to freedom of expression.'

The concluding statement in the legal opinion summarises what Dad's been through, including the refusal to allow him to travel, while reiterating that there have been 'multiple and grave breaches of Mr Hamouda's rights under international law.' It ends by insisting: 'This is a situation of the utmost urgency, concerning an Australian citizen who has been detained abroad for over a year. These fundamental breaches of his rights are sufficient to enable Australia to exercise diplomatic protection over Mr Hamouda.'

Reading this legal opinion is both enraging and vindicating. As much as I'm deeply saddened by seeing these abuses listed so explicitly, I feel empowered.

We're not wrong to ask for our rights.

1 The terrorism entities list is a list of entities (groups, orgs, people) that have been declared terrorist (thus illegal). Keeping this list allows the government to keep track of people on the list.

Camp Huckstep

While I'm not actually thrilled that Dad's having to go to a military court, I am hopeful that this final hurdle will be overcome. We're all on edge. Dad will have to leave his mobile behind. There are no phones allowed inside.

The court where Dad is going today is is located in the Hikesteb Military Area. If Dad can get the military exemption certificate today, then he can leave. Whenever we talk about Dad leaving, I imagine an asterisk on top of the word leave, reminding me that there's always the possibility he'll be stopped, again.

When Dad first talked to me about Hikesteb, I was a little confused. It didn't sound like an Arabic word. Looking it up, I found out it was a US military base established in 1943 as a supply depot – complete with a hospital, air base and radio station – named Camp Huckstep. The site was then passed to the Egyptian Armed Forces after the war. In line with principles of Egyptian Arabic, Huckstep turned into Hikesteb (pronounced: Hi-Ka-Steb) and a military court and prison were set up. Since the 1940s, the rollcall of those imprisoned there has included: communists, the Muslim Brotherhood, defectors and activists.

Dad told me that, in his youth, Hikesteb had a reputation for being above the law: the place symbolised a kind of fearsome darkness. Dad reveals to me, during our interview about this day, that he was already familiar with Hikesteb due to his father. Growing up, his father had been in the Egyptian army and was reasonably high-ranking. Dad grew up accustomed to the power and access that his father's status afforded.

As he enters Hikesteb, Dad summons the entitled energy of his youth. In an interview, he tells me how events unfolded.

When I went back to get my papers, I summoned the energy to walk directly into an officer's area. Usually, there is a soldier sitting on a desk and he doesn't allow anyone in, but he wasn't there. The only reason that you would step inside these places is if you are ranked. So, I just moved the desk and walked in. I remember going to the first office, and I said, 'My name is Hazem Hamouda and I have this application for the certificate of exemption and it needs to be completed.' The guy gave me this look of 'Who the hell are you? And why are you talking to me?' But then, he gave me the name of another officer.

Officers and such were walking past me in the corridors, but no one challenged me about why I was there. Which, for me, was awesome. It was like the young me coming out ...'

Dad's voice trails off as he seemingly loses himself in his thoughts, then he continues:

So, I found the office for this guy, and I called his name. He gave me a confused look because you don't call their names; you are supposed to call them by their rank. But I ignored his look and said, 'I'm Hazem Hamouda and I have this form.' And he replies, 'Oh, yeah, I've seen your paperwork.' Then he shuffles his papers, finds mine and signs it. Stamped and everything! Then he gives me the receipt for my case. So, I take it all and I'm like, 'Wow! It worked!' At that moment, I began to feel empowered again …'

Even though my initial thought is that it was random and reckless of Dad to ignore the rules, I pull back my judgement to recognise that the ways we seek to reclaim power aren't always logical. After he was so subjugated by the abuse of the law, I can now see that he needed to experience himself as above the law, irrespective of material realities and time. The recalling of the story of his youth represented his desire to feel untouchable; a way, perhaps, of mitigating fear while seeking reempowerment. I'm just grateful that he didn't get thwarted or in trouble; that he got to experience a sense of accomplishment and power.

However, the journey wasn't quite over: this officer gave Dad the paperwork for the *approval* of the exemption. Dad returned to court the next day. After a three-hour wait, he was called forwards by a soldier and given his certificate.

That was it. He had everything he needed to leave.

Bringing Him Home

2 April 2019

While it's already the morning of 2 April for us in Brisbane, the day of travel for Saja and Dad is yet to dawn. To ensure the pressure is on, we've got an early-morning interview lined up with Hamish McDonald on ABC.

I'm at the studio by 7 am. Jen joins from the ABC studio in Sydney.

At around 7.30 am, we're on. Jen kicks off the interview with a summary of Dad's case and the aforementioned issues at hand: the request for diplomatic protection and the urgency of getting Dad home. All we want is for Dad and Saja to be escorted through the airport by the Ambassador. In the interview, I make sure to mention Saja. While the case centres on Dad, I don't want people to forget that she's there too. If Dad is prevented from leaving again, she is too. If any more shit goes down, she's going to be the first affected after Dad.

Unbeknown to me, processes are already underway to extend diplomatic protection for Dad. Later that day, Saja forwards me an email from the Embassy: it confirms that she and Dad will be picked up by an Embassy car and driven to the airport, where access has been arranged for the Ambassador and two staffers to accompany them through the airport. Furthermore, the Ambassador will personally see them all the way to boarding.

4 April 2019

Dad and Saja's flight is due to land late tonight. There's a flurry of last-minute activity.

Holly prepares a press release announcing Dad's imminent return.

Jen has flown up from Sydney to Brisbane to be with us to welcome Dad home.

Duncan sets up a press conference at the Queensland State Parliament.

Peter is set to join us at the Queensland Parliament; for weeks he's been giving his public and private support.

As a family, we've been discussing whether or not to invite the press to the airport. It gets heated. I want to publicly celebrate Dad's return. I want to complete the showreel: we've got coverage of the case already, let's finish it off with triumphant footage of his first steps back into Brisbane. It would feel like a full circle: if there was already a public witnessing of our pain, then let our joy be witnessed too! My suggestion is that we invite a couple of journalists who've provided supportive coverage during Dad's imprisonment – in my mind, there's the producer and the cameraman from *The Project*, and one particular journalist from Channel 10 News who's always been nice to deal with. However, Mum, Amira and Harun all strongly oppose my suggestion, saying any media presence would be an invasion of our privacy during such a personal moment.

We phone Dad to solve our impasse. After all, he is at the centre of all this. Now he's no longer in prison, we can reach out and directly ask him what he wants us to do. He matter-of-factly states that he doesn't want the attention. So, that puts a quick end to our media debate.

I update Holly so that the press release goes out with a note to say that the Hamouda family request privacy at this time. To add another layer of protection, all media enquiries are to go to Holly, who will help ensure that no one shows up to the airport unannounced.

*

In the afternoon, I drive up to the Queensland State Parliament. It sits upon Turrbal land, overlooking the river Maiwar. It was only a few weeks ago that we were here during Duncan's first speech where he teared up, after which he took us on a personal tour of the building.

As I write, I have no memory of parking the car, walking up to the building or who greeted me at the entrance. I do remember sitting in a private room, with just Duncan, Jen and Peter, as we waited until the press conference was due to start. I remember my jiggling leg. I remember my nerves. I remember Jen being chatty and effervescent, Duncan beaming and Peter, reserved. I don't remember what we talked about. Then, we were outside.

There's a stand with a microphone. A crowd of journalists and cameras. It's silent. I step up to the microphone and unfold my piece of paper. I speak. The lump in my throat swells until my voice cracks. Jen approaches me, puts her hand on my back and whispers, 'You're doing great.' At that moment, I love her for her seeing how hard I'm trying to hold it all together and offering encouragement. I finish my speech. Jen, Peter and Duncan all speak too. Do I remember what they said? No. There's a recording somewhere. All I can think of is the airport and that Dad will be arriving tonight, around 9 pm. Jen is going to be the only person outside of our family accompanying us to the airport. If I were seventeen, I'd do a law degree just because of Jen. I'm not. I'm tired. I want a hug from my dad. I just want us all to go home, together.

Hazem

Here, Dad tells his story of coming home.

Hazem: Once I got the ID and the military exemption certificate, I spoke to Glenn and I said, 'Okay, we're going to book the ticket home, I need you to be there so we don't repeat the same thing that happened the first time, because these guys [the Egyptians] are unpredictable.' He then passed on instructions to [name redacted] to organise two cars, Australian Embassy cars: one to escort me, Saja and the Ambassador, and the other one for the rest of the staff. Two days later, [name redacted] came and picked us up from Zemalek and we went all together to the airport.

Lamisse: But how did you get him to agree?

Hazem: Based on what happened the first time.

Lamisse: Okay, so he was immediately agreeable?

Hazem: [...] Yes, he understood. Especially after we had pretty long conversations. And that solidified the fact that he understands what's going on, that I needed him to help me out as an Australian citizen.

Lamisse: All right, well I didn't experience DFAT like that, but I'm glad you did. So, you're in the convoy, you're way to the airport ...

Hazem: On the way to the airport, and when we get there, everybody is just, like, standing to attention as soon as they knew that he was the Australian Ambassador. That is, until we got to the passport control area. Even though Glenn was with me, again they would take my passport, along with my ID and the exemption certificate. And then they say, 'Can you please wait!' And then they take my documents and go away. Then a National Security officer comes in and says, 'Could you come with me?'

Lamisse: Ugh …

Hazem: But this time, I asked Glenn to come with me. It's like, no way am I walking by myself [...] I went upstairs and it was a nice office. The officer said, 'Please, sit down.' Glenn, the staffer and Saja were all there, but they sat outside. So I sat in the office by myself. After half an hour, I was like, 'What the hell is going on here? I got a plane to get!' So, I went to one of the people sitting down and asked him, 'What's going on?' and he said it was just routine checks. So, I step outside the office and say I'm not waiting anymore. Then I spoke to Glenn and told him what's going on. So he said, 'I'll make some calls.' So, I went back into the office to sit and wait. But time kept passing, so I came out and I saw Glenn was just walking up and down talking on the phone. But still, nothing is happening. So, I asked him what's going on again and he said I just have to wait a bit longer. I got frustrated, so I reiterated that there was no way I would be going back. I'm getting on that plane!

Lamisse: The waits are just excruciating.

Hazem: Yeah, I got frustrated. And I iterated again: there's no way I'm going back. I'm going to walk on this plane, I'm going to leave this airport. Period. I then check my phone to see if there's someone I could talk to, but I really didn't know who I could talk to ... Eventually, Glenn comes back with a big smile. He gives me a nudge, as though to say it's okay. So, I go back into the office and the guy has my passport, my ID and my exemption certificate, and he hands it over to me [...] So, then I went out of the office and said: 'Yeah, ready to go,' and we walk through the airport together. As we were talking, Glenn would give me assurances, saying that we're okay and that there was nothing to worry about. We got to the gate, waited, took pictures and then said goodbye

Lamisse: And then you boarded the plane?

Hazem: Yep [...] I'd say this is probably the happiest moment of my stay in Egypt. I was ecstatic. But I also was in a state of stress: I didn't just need to board the plane. I needed that plane door to be shut. I needed the plane to be in the air before I could actually breathe. I didn't trust these guys. What could stop them from coming on the plane to take me? So, when the plane was up in the air, I felt like everything inside of me just came crashing down. Like, I literally crashed: crashed with a sense of relief. It's really over and I'm really heading home ...

The flight went via Rome and London, where Dad and Saja spent a night in a hotel. Dad recalls a fond memory of the buffet breakfast, after the year of deprivation.

Hazem: It was the best thing ever that you booked me in the hotel for transit, seriously. For the first time in over a year, I see an open buffet. And I get to choose what I want to eat. I think it took maybe half an hour to just pick what I wanted. And I remember eating with a lot of pleasure, so much pleasure. But Saja, she just went for cereal. I was like, 'What are you doing?' I thought that maybe it's because she's never been deprived, that

> she just falls into routine. It felt like Ramadan, but like I had been fasting for months, so I remember eating really slowly ... Just enjoying eating with the knife and the fork, gently cutting and eating the fruits, sipping the coffee, the juice ... I think I had a sample of everything in front of me. It was amazing.

They flew from London to Perth, and then to Brisbane. The long route was due to all the aforementioned security concerns. During the immigration clearance process in Perth, the Australian Federal Police took Dad aside for questioning. Unfortunately, we weren't informed that anyone entering Australia who's served time in jail overseas is likely to be checked.

> **Hazem:** So, they take me to a back area, a back-office type thing, and Saja is with me. There [was] a conveyer belt, and there were a couple of customs officers there behind a table, and they asked me to empty my luggage for them to check. As they are searching my luggage, they keep asking me questions, like: 'How long have you been in Egypt for?' and 'Are you carrying anything illegal?' So, I explain to [the officer] what I've been through, even though I'm sure she knows who I am and why I am here. Then she finds my journals, the ones from prison. She flips through them and says, 'What's this?' And I said, 'Well, that's my diary; they're personal notes for me.' And she asks, 'Can I take them and show the boys at the back?' And I said no. She thought that she could get consent from me, that I wouldn't have an issue with her taking them. She would repeat that question a couple of times, saying, 'Oh, it's nothing. We're just going to check them out; they're just going to check them out.' But I said, 'No, it's my personal things, so put it back please.'

As far as Dad was concerned, he'd been through hell and wasn't about to give up his right to privacy just to be agreeable: let the AFP get a written order from a judge to read his diaries if it was important. Even so, he was more rattled than he let on.

Hazem: I thought they would be a bit more considerate to my situation, and a bit more considerate about what I had to go through, and not to put any further undue distress on me.
Lamisse: I agree with you, but I also think that is a reminder of Australia's own dark side ...
Hazem: Which exists, of course.

It hurts to hear Dad talk about the coldness and suspicion he encountered in Perth. It wasn't the welcome home I wanted for him; I wanted him to feel safe, not to be triggered into feeling fear and alienation. From Perth, it was onwards to Brisbane. To us, waiting for him at the airport.

Hazem: When I saw you guys, I felt like a part of me came back, a part that had been in hiding. It came back when I felt at home, when I was with those who loved me and those who I love. I felt the warmth, and it made me realise that for the past year, I hadn't felt that. It was surreal, in a way, to be back home and in the arms of those I love. Then I saw Jen, and I was so overwhelmed. She had done so much work for me, she'd done such an awesome job ... her and Caoilfhionn. Anyway, there were so many hugs and kisses. I got to see Amalia for the first time, and to see Aveline again. It was like, *Wow, I'm back home. I'm really home. The big nightmare is over.*

Epilogue

After we welcomed Dad and Saja at Brisbane Airport, we thanked Jen again, said goodbye, and then walked off to our car to drive home. I was squished with Harun in the back of Mum's 4WD, sitting on that extra seat that turns a five-seater car into a seven-seater sardine can.

It was wholly surreal: here's your dad, returned – no fanfare, no compensation and no further support. Just drive home and put the dishwasher on. Wake up in the morning and share a coffee with him. *Hello, Dad, it's been a while since we saw you at the dining table.*

To celebrate, Duncan invited us to dinner at the Queensland Parliament. He gave us a way to anchor Dad's return in a ritual – by sharing a meal together. It was a simple but touching gesture. Inspired, we then organised a luncheon at our family home and invited people over. I set up a little display of things from the prison: a display book of Dad's letters, his prison jacket, some mementos (including the paper flower), a framed copy of the speech Duncan gave in Parliament and printed photos. I wanted people to interact with something tangible, to have their own moment of contemplation as they touched, read or looked. The luncheon was another anchor. Home wasn't just a place; it was with people. But after that lunch, we shut ourselves away from the world for a while.

It can be hard to keep sight of loved ones amid the depression, sensitivity and anxiety of PTSD. Pain is self-absorbing because it's all-consuming. At home, we were all easily shaken lumps of jelly, prone to sudden outbursts, loud fights, panic attacks, withdrawal, apathy and so many tears. Finding our triggers was trial and error. Adjusting to them, and learning to manage them, involved more trial and error. Healing isn't linear: it would have been amazing to take a box breath and never be triggered when stepping into a government office again.

Facetiousness aside, I remain angered by the lack of support. There was so much to juggle: we had to rebuild ourselves, while rebuilding our futures, while trying to maintain our day-to-day lives. Bills still had to be paid, and relationships still needed watering. The toll of prison is so far-reaching, yet so viciously underestimated: instead, a person is blamed for not getting better fast enough, for not getting a job soon enough, for not being able to afford therapy. The trauma-based behaviours become a way to accuse a person of 'lack' rather than to recognise that a person is changed, that there is a need for additional support through the process of recovery. By blaming the individual, there's little recognition for the fact that the wider world isn't so kind to people who've been to prison, particuarly people of colour.

In moving through PTSD, my parents almost divorced from the pressure: it was all too much. Family breakdowns are a devastating and all too common outcome of prison-related traumas. This is what Martin had warned me about: families often come together during the crisis and fall apart once it's over. Despite the struggles, my parents held on. Sometimes holding tightly, sometimes loosely, sometimes in a way that was healthy, sometimes problematic.

Amid trauma, it is harder to decipher what behaviours can be empathised with, and what needs to be condemned as abuse. That angry outburst? The emotional unavailability of your partner? Their anxieties? A need for control? A lack of control? And what of all the insecurities compounded by trying to get back to a 'normal life' when you can't yet hold down a job? It's messy. It's confusing. Moving through PTSD is a huge process. Ten subsidised therapy sessions aren't enough. To commit $200 a week as a low-income family to private sessions is a luxury.

As siblings, we kept digging for empathy for our traumatised parents, all while we made the journey through our own pain too. To get through it all, Mum turned to her garden and pottery. Dad turned inward to his faith. I left for Germany to join Thomas, engaging in my own rollercoaster of trying to hold onto a relationship while psychologically compromised. Yet, most of that year in Cologne was spent depressed on the couch, much to Thomas's despair. I continued engaging with yoga, dancing and painting. The painting slowly fell away, as did the dance. The yoga stayed. Then it was pottery, theatre, more yoga, pilates and a brief return to painting. But always, there was writing. I swapped creative and somatics practices in and out of my life based on what I was seeking. I channelled what came up in my writing, processed what emerged in my body on the page.

I began to inverse how I'd been socialised. I'd been taught to lead with my head, to think before I do. Now, I lead with my body. I feel before I think, I do then I reflect.

In the publishing world, I have noticed there is this idea that these stories need to be written and released while they're 'hot' but they don't – in fact, I'd argue they need the opposite. Writing early is valuable to releasing memory while it is fresh and sharp. After the memories are released onto a page, they need time to simmer down, to cool into acceptance and understanding. The rawness of pathos needs balancing with critical reflection; our lives are rich soil for theorising, for connecting the dots between what we think is a single, individual experience into collective awareness and solidarity.

While I may have experienced the prison in another country, I live in Meanjin, on Jagera and Turrbal land, and I am committed to solidarity with all those who've experienced the injustice of displacement and incarceration. With this book, Dad and I sought to add our account to the records of those who came before us, those who are speaking now, and those who'll come after us. Whether speaking of Egypt, or the colony that is Australia, we stand with all those who have faced, or face, the violence of the State and the prison. My experiences have led me to seek ways to understand my relationship with complicity and resistance in the colony I call home, to move in recognition of the locations I hold as settler and migrant, as exiler and exiled. I want to disrupt: no tech, but the categories and structures that oppress us.

In the end, this book has been written across three cities and a pandemic: Cologne, Vienna and Meanjin. I'm so grateful to my family and friends across the world, to everyone who has held me through the years of rebuilding from the rubble of myself. On a wider level, I am so grateful to all the Black, Indigenous, Arab and Muslim feminist scholars, women, men and gender-diverse intellectuals, whose legacies shadow my thinking; a thinking and action to be nurtured for the rest of my living life.

There is no promised land free of pain and suffering (unless there's a heaven), and there is no such thing as being perfectly healed. I mean that for healing on all levels: from yourself to the Earth, from intimate relationships to the political and the intergenerational. The only truth about healing, while you are alive in this world, is that it is messy, imperfect, participatory and never-ending. It isn't on Instagram: it is the dirt of life.

And it is one of the most radical things you can ever commit to.

Arabic Glossary

My father and I have collaborated on transliterating the Arabic in this book. Since Egyptian Arabic is colloquial, I initially elected to use Franco-Arabic in the transliterations. Franco-Arabic uses numbers to replace the letters that have no English equivalent. It is a way of writing that emerged out of texting and online messaging. Furthermore, my own Arabic is broken, so transcribing how I fumble through the language already invited inaccuracies into the text. After a struggle over how to transliterate Egyptian Arabic, my father and I went for a style that more closely reflects MSA (Modern Standard Arabic) conventions. Thus, whatever inaccuracies you find, as an Arabic speaker, are ours.

The struggle to create uniformity out of a dialect, the demand that a book must reflect agreed upon grammar conventions, reminded us of the fluidities and resistances inherent in language. That we speak not to be accurate, but to be understood.

General

Aywaa – Yes (informal, Egyptian slang)

Al'hamdullilah – Thanks to be God.

Assalamu'alaykum – Peace be upon you; Response: Wa 'alaykumasalam wa rahmatullahi wa baraktu – And peace be upon you, and God's mercy and blessings.

Athaan – Call to Prayer

Basterma (Pastirma) – Seasoned, air-dried cured beef

Bintak Barah, warayah – Your daughter is outside, follow me.

Betingaan – Eggplant

Batatas – Potatoes

Ba'ad Izznik – Excuse me

Baba henak – Dad is there

Halawa – A crumbly sweet made from sesame paste

Hena Hena quwayis! – Here! Here is good!

Henaak – Over there!

Huwa – He

Hijab – A headscarf

Emshy – Literally 'walk' but also used to mean go/go away

Enta – You (masculine singular)

Enty – You (feminine singular)

Felucca – a sailboat

Fouul – A meal made from fava beans, usually eaten with bread

Jannaza – The Funeral Prayer

Jilbab – A long, loose-fitting coat

Jum'ah/Goma'a – Friday. Used in reference to Friday prayer. Egyptian Arabic shifts the J sound of Modern Standard Arabic sound to the hard G sound.

Leh – Why

Masha'allah – All blessings are from God

Mashy – Okay

Mamnoo'a – Forbidden

Masr – Egypt

Masri – Egyptian (masculine singular)

Masriyya – Egyptian (feminine singular)

Minfadlak – Please

Merayah – Mirror

Mobiyal – Mobile phone

Na'am – Yes (formal)

Qalam / 'Alam – Pen. Egyptian Arabic turns Q into a silent letter.

Oktob – Write (verb)

Om ta'aala! – Get up! Come here!

Roba bikya! – From the Italian *Roba Vecchia*, which translates to 'old clothes'. This phrase is yelled by people who make a living by buying and selling unwanted appliances, electronics and furniture.

Rooh – Go (verb)

Shukran – Thank you

Shtafa – A water hose used for cleansing yourself after defecating

Ta'aly/Ta'aly hena – Come/Come here

Tahajjud – A voluntary night prayer performed in the last third of the night

Ustraliya – Australia

Wu'du – The ritual washing before prayer

Wadi – A valley that is desert, except when it rains

Yalla – a versatile phrase that indicates urgency or encouragement, such as: come on, let's go and hurry up

Prison Terms

The following three sections of Tora are used for prisoners in remand detention:

Tora Tahqiq – Investigations Unit

Tora Istiqbal – Tora Reception

Tora Mazraa' – Tora Farms

Al-Aqrab 1 & 2 – Scorpion Prison, the maximum security sections of Tora

Nadarah – The barred and meshed window on the door of the prison cell

Nimrah – Refers to the two-handed width (40–60 cm) allocated for an prisoner to sleep and sit

Ziyarah – Visit

Prison Staff

Al-Amn Al-Watany – The National Security Services

Ma'moor – Prison warden

Mokhber – Formal informants who report to the Mabahiz

Morshid – Informal informants, secretly selected from among the prisoners to report back to Al-Amn Al-Watany. Also known as 'snitches'

Shaweesh – Uniformed guards who work for the warden

Zabit Amn Watany – refers to a National Security Officer

Phrases and Conversations

Page 147

'Mish fahma.' – I don't understand.

'Ana asfa, mish fahma.' – I'm sorry, I don't understand.

Page 154

'Shantitik feen?' – Where are your bags?

'Eh?' – What?

'Ah-heh.' – Those/There.

'Eh da?' – What's that?

'Akl.' – Food.

'Lazem tageebi akl li-babaki.' – You must bring food for your father.

'Ah … mish arfa … Momken murra gayya.' – Ah … I didn't know … Possibly next time.

'Ma'lesh.' – It's okay.

Page 159

'Enty bint Hazem?' – Are you Hazem's daughter?

'Na'am.' – Yes.

'Mashy. Estany hena.' – Okay, wait here.

Page 160

'Au'dy hena, abuki gay.' – Sit here, your father is coming.

Page 192

'Ezzayak ya, Hazem?' – How are you, Hazem?

'Kolo tamam.' – Everything is fine.

Page 215

'Temanya w'nous.' – Half-past eight.

Page 240

'Ya ustaza. Eiza tikalimi babaki? – Hey miss, do you want to talk to your dad?

'Eh?' – What?

'Babaki, henaak. Mish eiza tikalimi wla eh?' – Your Dad. You. Do you want to talk to him or what? He's over there.

'Akeed. Akeed! – Of course. Of course!

'Lah.' – No.

'Leh?' – Why?

'Floos!' – Money!

'Aah … mashy.' – Aah … okay.

Page 304

'Kolo fereekh?' – All chicken?

'Ayuwa.' – Yep.

Page 325

'Ma'lesh, kefeyya.' – It's okay, stop.

Page 326

'Mashy, il-baab maftooh.' – Okay, the door is open.

References

Quotes

Abdel Fattah, Alaa. *You Have Not Yet Been Defeated*: Selected Works 2011–2021. Fitzcarraldo Editions, 2021.

Abdel-Fattah, Randa. *Coming of Age in the War on Terror.* New South Publishing, 2021.

hooks, bell. *All About Love: New Visions.* William Morrow, 2000.

On Rabaa'

"All According to Plan: The Rab'a Massacre and Mass Killings of Protestors in Egypt." *Human Rights Watch,* 12 August 2014, https://www.hrw.org/report/2014/08/12/all-according-plan/raba-massacre-and-mass-killings-protesters-egypt

"Egypt: Verdicts expected for 739 defendants in grotesque mass death penalty trial." 29 June 2018, https://www.amnesty.org/en/latest/news/2018/06/egypt-verdicts-expected-for-739-defendants-in-grotesque-mass-death-penalty-trial

"Egypt: Twelve dissidents face execution while security forces enjoy impunity over Rabaa' massacre." *Amnesty International,* 13 August 2021, https://www.amnesty.org/en/latest/news/2021/08/egypt-twelve-dissidents-face-execution-while-security-forces-enjoy-impunity-over-rabaa-massacre

ElGendy, Abdelrahman. "From prison: Ammad: Encountering disability and friendship in Tora." *Mada Masr,* 14 July 2018, https://www.madamasr.com/en/2018/07/14/opinion/u/from-prison-ammad/

Walsh, Declan. "American Held in Egypt Prison Die After a Hunger Strike." *The New York Times*, 13 January 2020, https://www.nytimes.com/2020/01/13/world/middleeast/egyptprisoner-moustafa-kassem-dies.html

Youssef, Adham and Ruth Michaelson. "Egypt sentences 75 Muslim Brotherhood supporters to death." *The Guardian*, 8 September 2018, https://www.theguardian.com/world/2018/sep/08/egypt-sentences-75-to-death-in-rabaa-massacre-masstrial

On Extraditions from Malaysia

Ahmed, Kaamil. "'No one's safe': Fears grow for four Egyptians deported from Malaysia." *Middle East Eye*, 22 March 2019, https://www.middleeasteye.net/news/no-ones-safe-fears-grow-four-egyptians-deported-malaysia

Allawy, Samer. "Malaysia denounced over detention of Egyptian president's critics." *Al Jazeera*, 9 March 2019, https://www.aljazeera.com/news/2019/3/8/malaysia-denounced-over-detention-of-egyptian-presidents-critics

"Aussie wife, rights group condemn disappearances." *Kuwait Times*, 9 April 2019, https://www.kuwaittimes.com/aussie-wife-rights-group-condemn-disappearances/

"Fact Sheet: Extraordinary Rendition." *American Civil Liberties Union ('ACLU')*, 2023, https://www.aclu.org/other/fact-sheet-extraordinary-rendition

Legal Opinion

Joint Statement on Human Rights in Egypt, US Mission Geneva, 12 March 2021: https://geneva.usmission.gov/2021/03/12/joint-statement-on-human-rights-in-egypt

J. Robinson and C. Gallagher, *Opinion: Hazem Hamouda, Breaches of International Law and Australia's Right to Exercise Diplomatic*

Protection, Doughty Street Chambers. Attached to private email from Jen Robinson to author, dated 18 March 2019

On Death Penalty

"Death Penalty 2021: Facts and Figures." *Amnesty International*, 24 May 2022, https://www.amnesty.org/en/latest/news/2022/05/death-penalty-2021-facts-and-figures/

"Executions Around the World." *Death Penalty Information Center*, 2023, https://deathpenaltyinfo.org/policy-issues/international/executions-around-the-world

On National Strategy

"Egypt: A Year of Whitewashing Despite Dire Crisis." *Human Rights Watch*, 12 January 2023, https://www.hrw.org/news/2023/01/12/egypt-year-whitewashing-despite-dire-crisis.

"Egypt: Human rights crisis deepens one year after national human rights strategy launched." *Amnesty International*, 21 September 2022, https://www.amnesty.org/en/latest/news/2022/09/egypt-human-rights-crisis-deepens-one-year-after-national-human-rights-strategy-launched/

Salem, Aida and Rana Mamdouh. "Egypt's human rights strategy is finally out, but will bring few 'major developments' in criminal justice reform, says source." *Mada Masr*, 12 September 2021, https://www.madamasr.com/en/2021/09/12/feature/politics/egypts-human-rights-strategy-is-finally-out-but-will-bring-few-major-developments-in-criminal-justice-reform-says-source/

The Arab Republic of Egypt. "National Human Rights Strategy." *Supreme Standing Committee for Human Rights*, September 2021, https://sschr.gov.eg/media/gapb5bq4/national-human-rights-strategy.pdf

Further Reading/References

On Prison

https://egyptprisonatlas.org (Egypt Prison Atlas, founded by American-Egyptian ex-prisoner Aya Hijazi)

https://www.hrw.org/report/2016/09/28/we-are-tombs/abuses-egypts-scorpion-prison

https://www.egypttoday.com/Article/1/107888/Egypt%E2%80%99s-President-Sisi-Large-prison-complex-to-be-inaugurated-in

https://www.middleeasteye.net/news/egypt-sisi-open-biggest-american-style-prison

https://www.madamasr.com/en/2021/09/12/feature/politics/egypts-human-rights-strategy-is-finally-out-but-will-bring-few-major-developments-in-criminal-justice-reform-says-source

On Human Rights

https://www.hrw.org/news/2021/03/12/condemnation-egypts-abuses-un-rights-body

https://www.hrw.org/news/2022/01/28/human-rights-watch-submission-un-human-rights-committee-advance-its-review-egypt

https://youtu.be/_ENu_7KqnTA (Egypt's Human Right's Crisis – Europe's Responsibility?)

On Prisoners & Deaths in Custody (this is NOT an exhaustive list)

https://www.hrw.org/news/2023/03/08/egypt-harsh-sentences-against-rights-activists

https://hrf.org/remembering-shady-habash-a-victim-of-egypts-horrific-prison-conditions

https://www.ramyessam.com/post/photographer-director-shady-habash-dies-at-the-age-of-24-in-egyptian-prison

https://artistsatriskconnection.org/story/a-letter-from-tora-prison-galal-el-behairy

https://www.aljazeera.com/news/2022/5/29/egypt-court-jails-former-presidential-candidate-for-15-years

https://www.nytimes.com/2020/11/30/world/middleeast/Abdel-Razek-Egypt-rights.html

https://www.theguardian.com/global-development/2021/jun/14/giulio-regeni-last-messages-before-his-death-in-egypt-counter-spy-claims

https://www.dw.com/en/egypts-former-president-mohammed-morsi-dies-in-court/a-49238572

https://www.nytimes.com/2020/07/28/world/middleeast/egypt-women-tiktok-prison.html

https://www.ohchr.org/en/press-releases/2022/11/egypt-must-immediately-release-alaa-abdel-fattah-turk-says

https://www.theguardian.com/world/2022/oct/17/from-my-cell-i-could-see-people-being-tortured-sanaa-seif-on-fleeing-egypt-and-fighting-to-free-her-brother

On Hunger Strikes

https://www.madamasr.com/en/2022/02/15/news/u/3-activists-begin-hunger-strike-to-protest-remand-detention-rotation

https://www.madamasr.com/en/2014/10/02/panorama/u/hunger-strike

https://www.al-monitor.com/originals/2022/03/jailed-egyptian-activists-hunger-strike-protest-pretrial-detention

https://www.amnesty.org/en/latest/news/2019/07/egypt-mass-hunger-strike-at-al-aqrab-prison-over-denial-of-family-visits-and-dire-conditions

https://www.hrw.org/news/2022/02/25/egypt-hunger-strike-against-indefinite-detention

https://www.theguardian.com/world/2022/nov/15/alaa-abd-el-fattah-has-broken-hunger-strike-sister-says

Early Coverage of the 2011 Revolution

http://archive.nytimes.com/www.nytimes.com/interactive/2012/02/12/opinion/sunday/20120212-tahir-timeline.html

https://choice.npr.org/index.html?origin=https://www.npr.org/2012/02/09/146636605/wael-ghonim-creating-a-revolution-2-0-in-egypt

https://www.theatlantic.com/technology/archive/2011/09/so-was-facebook-responsible-for-the-arab-spring-after-all/244314

https://www.zdnet.com/article/wikileaks-how-the-diplomatic-cables-sparked-the-2011-arab-revolutions

https://foreignpolicy.com/2011/02/24/reflections-on-the-revolutions-in-tunisia-and-egypt

https://www.channel4.com/news/arab-revolt-social-media-and-the-peoples-revolution

https://www.aljazeera.com/opinions/2011/3/18/understanding-egypts-revolution

https://www.npr.org/2011/03/15/134538629/ramy-esam-the-singer-of-the-egyptian-revolution

https://www.aljazeera.com/opinions/2011/3/21/the-globalisation-of-revolution

https://www.nytimes.com/2011/02/21/business/media/21link.html

https://www.theatlantic.com/technology/archive/2011/02/preserving-the-online-legacy-of-the-egyptian-revolution/71675/

https://www.theatlantic.com/international/archive/2011/02/laugh-o-revolution-humor-in-the-egyptian-uprising/71530/

Books

Davis, Angela, *Are Prisons Obsolete?*. Seven Stories Press, 2003.

Frankl, Victor. *Man's Search for Meaning*. Beacon Press, 1992.

Kumar, Deepa. *Islamophobia and the Politcs of Empire: 20 Years after 9/11*. Verso, London & New York, 2021.

Kundnani, Arun. *Muslims are Coming!: Islamophobia, Extremism, and the Domestic War on Terror*. Verso, London & New York, 2014.

Manzoor-Khan, Suhaiymah. *Tangled in Terror: Uprooting Islamophobia*. Pluto Press, 2022.

Morsi, Yassir. *Radical Skin, Moderate Masks: De-radicalising the Muslim and Racism in Post-racial Societies*. Rowman & Littlefield, 2017.

Razack, Sherene H. *Nothing Has to Make Sense: Upholding White Supremacy through Anti-Muslim Racism*. University of Minnesota Press, 2022.

Salem, Sara. *Anticolonial Afterlives in Egypt: The Politics of Hegemony*. Cambridge University Press, 2020.

Vitale, Alex S. *The End of Policing*. Verso, London & New York, 2017.

Qureshi, Asim, editor. *I Refuse to Condemn: Resisting Racism in Time of National Security*. Manchester University Press, 2020.

Acknowledgements

First, I must thank the incredible team at Pantera Press. A special mention to Lex Hirst for believing in me and approaching me with the invitation to write. Thank you being such a wonderful person and publisher; for all the chats, check-ins, the questions and support throughout the years of bringing this book to life. Secondly, to my editor, Anne Reilly. Your empathy and critical eye helped shaped this book into something readable; I would have been lost without your detailed edits and generous feedback. To Alison Green, thank you for the support on pulling together the Australia Council of the Arts grant, from the feedback on the proposal to supporting my maths-illiterate brain to finish the budget. And of course, thank you to Australia Council of the Arts for the grant: that financial support proved invaluable, allowing me to take time to focus on writing.

To the #BringHazemHome team – Jen, thank you for your big heart, for staying in touch and reading a draft of this book then giving it such a stunning review. Thank you, Peter, for your friendship in the years since Dad's release. It's been valuable to have someone who understands this journey too. Martin, for the emotional support. Of course, Duncan Pegg. Duncan passed away in 2021, but a piece of his generous legacy lives within our family's memory; a politician who truly lived for his community.

Next, I must thank all my friends. Gosh, I am so lucky to have met, and connected with, such an incredible array of human beings. From Cairo to Cologne, Vienna to Dubai, Lisbon to London, to Meanjin, Naarm and Gadigal Land. If you are reading this, you know who you are, and I love you.

However, some of you need to be mentioned by name. Firstly, Drew and Salma. Thank you for everything you did during the year from hell. To my brothers from another mother, Frederico and Jonas. Thank you for loving and exploring Egypt with me before things turned terrible. A special thank you to Frederico's parents – Isabel and Paulo – for including us in your prayers and being my Portuguese family.

Thank you to my AUC partner-in-crime, Claire, for being there to reflect and reminisce with me over the years. To Professor Martina, thank you for trying to keep me enrolled, for all the support you offered to me as your student, and as a friend.

To my Egyptian friends that I'm too nervous to name: should you read this, you know who you are (especially 'Suleiman'). I'll never forget the solidarity and care. It meant so much to be part of your world, to share love and late nights, stories and dancefloors. Most of all, thank you for holding my hand in the dark. I miss you, and I hope we all meet again.

To the Brisbane Free University crew and the Institute for Critical Race Research: thank you for being the best thinking space to be part of. Thank you for the radical theory and rich discussions, and the soul-enriching motivation of simply being in a room with people who care and the space to write. An extra special thanks to the incredible Anna Carlson; the way you live your values is inspiring and your critical self-reflection has pushed my own. Traces of you are in the thinking of this book.

To Cara, to Azra. Two of my longest-serving friends, what a sentence it must have been as you rode with me through years of madness. The love and support I have from both of you is unsurpassed. To Reem, to Amna. Thank you for being there during the aftermath, for holding me through Cologne, the pandemic and Vienna. And to Nour, finding you in Vienna was such a blessing. Thank you for sharing your intellect, love and unwavering commitment to Palestine and revolution with me.

To Omar, thank you for all the advice about writing, touring and the author life. Shout-out to Sara Saleh, Hasib and Jeanine for SWF 2022, Whit for her gentle wisdom and all my theatre buddies in Side-Effect Physical Theatre, ZenZenZo and QSE.

Finally, to the love of my life, Thomas. Thank you for listening to me talk about 'the book' for the last four years, for reading drafts and letting me ramble through memories and theories, fears and hopes. Thank you for supporting my dream to write. Also, to Thomas's parents, Carla and Hermann. Thank you for unhesitatingly inviting me into your family from the start, and for support you've given to Thomas and I over the years.

To my extended family in Egypt: though a vast distance separates us, though our relationships have been damaged by migration and trauma, you are always in my heart. I hope that, one day, we can repair the severing and be reunited with love and healing.

To my beloved immediate family: Dad, Mum, Jasmine, Saja, Amira, Harun, Kareem, plus my nieces, Aveline, Amalia. It is a joy to have you as my family, to arrive at a place where we understand how much we love and care for each other, to survive hardship and reach this level of vulnerability and care. Being together with you all is the source of my deepest happiness. Thank you for letting Dad and I write this book.

To my grandmother, Zizi, who passed away in 2022. You left a legacy: one of women breaking norms, a legacy of strength and survival. However, what I remember you for is your softness, the kind, loving, sweet gentleness. It puts my heart at rest to know you got to spend time with Dad again before you died. Allah yerhama.

There's many more people I'd like to thank, yet to write to you all would be another chapter. Thank you all for teaching, holding, loving, thriving, surviving, dancing, laughing and learning with me. Our lives are enriched by connection, and my gosh, I feel so wealthy being able to love you all.

Lastly, to all those still in Tora prison. Though you may feel defeated, you are seen. You are alive. We've seen you. We remember you. We write of you, and we talk of you, bringing you out of the prison with our words.

One day, you will be free.

About the authors

Lamisse Hamouda (she/her) is an Egyptian-Australian writer, theatre-maker and youth worker who lives on the unceded lands of Meanjin (Brisbane). Her writings have been published in various publications in Europe and Australia, including Arts of the Working Class, Diversity Arts Australia, SBS and Jdeed Magazine, and her poetry was included in the anthology, *Arab, Australia, Other: Stories on Race and Identity.*

Hazem Hamouda is a Muslim, an Egyptian and an Australian. A former I.T. consultant, Hazem was arbitrarily arrested and imprisoned in Egypt in 2018. His plight was covered by various media outlets, including Channel 10's *The Project*, SBS and the ABC. Based in Meanjin (Brisbane), he teaches Arabic at a local community centre, and lives with his family and a couple of backyard chickens.